John Harper Sproule, Jr.

Air Force Engineer

Letters, College through 1963

J. Michael Sproule
9-1-2023

John Harper Sproule, Jr.

Air Force Engineer

Letters, College through 1963

All Rights Reserved

©2023 by J. Michael Sproule

No part of this book may be reproduced or transmitted in any form or by any means, electronic or mechanical, including photocopying, recording, or by any data storage and retrieval system, without the express written permission from the author.

ISBN: 9798852195098

Printed in the United States of America

Contents

Air Force Engineer 1

Editor's Biography and Notes 1

List of Photographs 3

Prologue: An Air Force Engineer 4

Chapter 1. Commencing College—January 1937 to March 1938 16

Chapter 2. Back to the Collegiate Grind—January 1940 to June 1940 19

Chapter 3. Boardinghouse Hasher—September 1940 to December 1940 . 31

Chapter 4. Classes, Commitments, Conscription, and Catholicism—January 1941 to June 1941 50

Chapter 5. Frustration, Friends, Films, War, and KVS Visits—September 1941 to December 1941 68

Chapter 6. An Urge to Finish Amid Hurdles—January 1942 to June 3, 1942 99

Chapter 7. Onto the Air Force: Leaving Laramie, Arriving Dayton—June 11, 1942 to August 31, 1942 131

Chapter 8. Dayton Days: A Bachelor in the Air Force—September 1, 1942 to December 29, 1942 149

Chapter 9. Eglin Field Testing—March and April 1944 199

Chapter 10. Morocco, Maxwell AFB, England and the Continent, Merchant Marine—1956, 1958, 1962, 1963 218

Epilogue 235

Appendix: Family of John Harper Sproule, Jr. 238

Air Force Engineer

Air Force Engineer takes form as a biographical compilation of letters informing the education and early career experiences of John Harper Sproule, Jr. (1918-1997). With just a few exceptions, the letters are addressed to Katherine Veronica [Glenn] Sproule, the sweetheart and eventual wife of JHS. The letters not only flesh out the vicissitudes of their long-term and long-distance relationship but also convey a portrait of middle-class life in the 1930s and 1940s, particularly those years when the two were living separately (1937-1942). Here we find a panoply of quotidian life—amusements, living quarters, mass media consumption, jobs, and people beginning with the Depression and extending through World War II and the Cold War.

Editor's Biography and Notes

J. Michael (Mike) Sproule is the son of John Harper Sproule, Jr. and Katherine Veronica [Glenn] Sproule and became heir to a trove of their letters, missives which remained from 1947 to 1997 in a package sturdily wrapped by John Sproule. My first experience with this bundle took place in 1960 when the family was moving from 406 Wilbur Avenue to 3713 Briar Place in Dayton, Ohio. I asked Dad what this vaguely labeled package might hold. He remarked that the contents were letters "which you will probably never see." And such was the case until it fell to me to clean out Mom and Dad's house in Reno, Nevada after Dad's death in 1997. Coming upon this package containing their letters from 1937 to 1944, I asked my Mom (whom we had relocated to our hometown of Palo Alto, California) whether she might enjoy my opening the bundle and reading the letters to her. Due to macular degeneration, Mom was legally blind by this time although she seemed to have retained a surprising degree of sight. At any rate, she consented, and so began my education in the character and environment of my parent's early relationship.

After my own retirement in 2001 as a faculty member in communication studies at San Jose State University, I undertook two subsequent administrative positions—(1) director of the School of Media and Communication at Bowling Green State University and (2) dean of the College of Arts and Sciences at Saint Louis University. Ending my academic career in 2008 from Saint Louis, I continued my scholarly writing in Pacific Grove, California with a number of projects extending through the publication of *Democratic Vernaculars* (Routledge) in 2020. From this time, I have devoted a portion of my efforts to organizing and chronicling family history. *Air Force Engineer* represents one book-length outcome of these endeavors.

To enhance the focus and readability of the letters, I have employed a number of conventions. To signal the excision of whole sections, readers will find a bracketed indication of the number of paragraphs omitted—e.g., **[2 PARAGRAPHS]**. Ellipses denote the redaction of parts of a paragraph. Where one paragraph segues directly into another, a notation of **[/]** will be deployed. From time to time, readers will observe explanatory remarks given in brackets. In editorial notes, John Harper Sproule, Jr. will be referred to, generally, as JHS or Dad; and Katherine Veronica [Glenn] Sproule will be referred to as KVS or Mom.

List of Photographs

Cover: John Harper Sproule, Jr., Wright Field 1942

Lowther Sproule on harvester ca. 1910

Lowther and Mary Sproule ca. 1920

Kiva and Harper Sproule 1917

John and Walter (Gene) Sproule ca. 1927

Sproule summer camp Central Wyoming ca. 1927

Sproule family group in Vista California 1928: Seated on the ground in front, left to right, are Malcolm Anspach and John Harper Sproule, Jr.; seated in chairs in the center, left to right, are Amy Sproule Wilkening, Mary Remsberg Sproule, and Lowther Sproule; standing left to right are Kiva Sproule, John Harper Sproule, Sr., Walter Eugene Sproule, Grace Sproule Wells, Rodney Anspach, [unidentified woman], Alice Sproule Anspach, Orland M. Anspach, Chester M. Wells, Charles Wilkening

Clyda Lakey [Martin] Burns on stage ca. 1910

Glenn family group ca. 1923: left to right, Agnes, Joe, Katherine, Bernard, Emma Pauline, Anna

Glenn siblings in Riverton 1940: left to right Agnes, Bernard, Anna, Joe, Katherine, Harold Bowe [stepbrother]

John Harper Sproule, Jr. and Katherine Veronica Glenn Sproule newlyweds 1943

Katherine Veronica Glenn Sproule 1946

Prologue: An Air Force Engineer

Commencing with John Harper Sproule, Jr.'s experiences as an engineering student at the University of Wyoming, this epistolary accounting extends through the first 21 years of his 38-year career as a civilian engineer for the U.S. Air Force who focused initially on bomber armaments and concluded his labors in electronic warfare. With the exception of a few missives to his son, J. Michael Sproule, the letters communicate sentiments penned for the benefit of Katherine Veronica [Glenn] Sproule in an array stretching from January 1937 to October 1963. I will hereafter refer to John Harper Sproule, Jr. chiefly as JHS or Dad.

John Harper Sproule, Jr. was born in Riverton, Wyoming to John Harper Sproule, Sr. (1887-1964)—universally known as Harper—and Kiva Leota [Seaman] Sproule (1889-1966) on November 10, 1918—the last day of World War I. Dad's nuclear family became complete upon the birth of his brother, Walter Eugene, in 1920. The Harper Sproule family's presence in Riverton owed to a fortuitous homestead drawing in 1906 in which Harper's brother (JHS's uncle), Luther Sproule, secured the desirable low number of 29 [initially that of 34 but reduced on the basis of dropouts]. As a consequence, as Dad explains in his "The Sproule/Glenn Family Chronicle" (which he began in March 1991), "Uncle Luther and grandfather [Lowther] were able to select a site on bottom land of the Wind River about 3 miles from the Riverton town site."

The entire Sproule family group which had migrated to Riverton from Delta, Colorado and Raton, New Mexico consisted of patriarch Lowther Sproule (1845-1931), his wife Mary Remsberg Sproule (1861-1936), their sons Luther (born 1885) and Harper (born 1887), and their three daughters Grace (born 1882), Mary Alice (born 1889), and Amy (born 1895). The progeny of Lowther and Mary eventually gained spouses: Elizabeth (wed Luther), Kiva (wed to Harper), Chester M. Wells (wed to Grace), Orland Anspach (wed to Mary Alice), and Charles Wilkening (wed to Amy). From 1906, the Sproules made ends meet chiefly through a combination of irrigated farming and gardening on the homestead, and one family photo of about 1910 shows Lowther atop a harvesting machine in a field. Anima husbandry also became a factor in family income as evidenced by a notice in *The Riverton Review* (December 24, 1915, p. 6) that "H. L. Givers, Wm Madden and L. Sproule [shipped] another carload [of hogs] to the Omaha market last Saturday. Harper Sproule and Pete Fuller accompanied the stock."

1917 was a pivotal year for the Sproule family of Riverton from the fact that Lowther and his sons sold the foundational homestead, with Lowther and Mary removing to Vista and Wilmar, California, where they lived until their deaths. The brothers Harper and Luther now established their own families, Luther marrying Elizabeth Boeke [Sproule] in Riverton on October 1, 1917, and Harper wedding Kiva Leota Seaman [Sproule] in Emmett, Idaho on November 20, 1917. Harper and Luther thereupon became engaged in ranching businesses, each apparently with an outside partner, although we find some co-mingling of resources as evidenced by a July 28, 1921 stock certificate titling over 372½ shares in the "Sproule Live-Stock Company" to Harper on the authority of company President Luther. Yet in Dad's telling the brothers largely struck out on their own—Luther focusing on raising steers and Harper raising sheep, each in separate locations. Dad describes this division in his "Sproule/Glenn Chronicle":

". . . Uncle Luther had a farm/ranch out of town, but his primary involvement was with cattle which were kept out on the range and managed (or 'run' as the usage then current would have it) by his partner who was named Harry Cohen as best I remember. My father was in the sheep business and, with the sheep out in the range, was away from home for extended periods in the fall through winter and into spring. In the summer the sheep were trailed [i. e., herded with sheep dogs] up to a summer range . . . [and] . . . our whole family were with the sheep."

Luther's place was about 6 to 8 miles out of Riverton whereas Dad recalls his own branch of the family residing in Riverton proper in two successive houses—albeit with his father absent for large parts of the year. The Harper Sproule family's first in-town residence amounted to a "log cabin" on Riverton's outskirts where they remained from at least the time of Dad's birth (1918) until around 1924 when Harper's family relocated to a closer-in residence on Riverton's Chatterton Lane.

Close by on Chatterton Lane were Dad's great-aunt Clyda Burns and her mother Permelia Lakey (Kiva's grandmother). Clyda, sister to Kiva's mother Mae Lakey Seaman, was unfailingly known as "Puss," this nickname a derivative of an early moniker of "Kitty." Clyda had pursued a career on the vaudeville stage and was notoriously vain about her appearance while also being especially sensitive as to her age. Oftentimes, in family lore, Clyda would remark to Kiva that an aunt might actually be younger than her niece. Dad long recognized the less than generational age spread between Clyda and Kiva—estimating the difference to have been about 12 years. And in fact, Clyda's burial records at Riverton's Mountain View Cemetery betray a secret never fully known to Dad, namely, that his great-aunt Clyda entered the world on March 18, 1877. This brutal revelation may be contrasted to Clyda's asserted age of 42 on her 1932 license to marry Charley Burns—this putatively positioning Clyda as but a single year older than niece Kiva as opposed to the actuality of a full dozen years difference in age.

Another in-town neighbor of consequence was the Glenn family which had moved to a Riverton city address in 1928 to become across-the-street neighbors of the Sproules. Previously, John Lawrence Glenn, his wife Emma Pauline Carrington Glenn, and their five children had made their home in a relatively remote ranch outside of Arapahoe, Wyoming, south of Riverton. Mom (KVS) recalled that her family arrived there when she was about age 5 (i.e., in 1920), before which time the Glenn group had successively lived in Onaka, South Dakota and North Platte, Nebraska. After supervising harvesting of the crop, newly widowed Emma brought her five children into town: Joseph Patrick (1913-1980), Katherine Veronica (1915-2000), Agnes Elizabeth (1917-2007), John Bernard (1918-1982), and Anna Belle (1922-1986). Another sibling, Harold Bowe (1901-1962), Emma's son by her deceased first husband, James Edward Bowe, had been raised from about age 10 by an aunt in Kansas owing to Harold's inability to get along with his querulous (in Mom's telling) stepfather John Glenn.

From what I understand of the relationship between my parents, John and Katherine (Kay) Sproule, their romance did not begin in earnest until around 1937, although Mom tells of a much earlier and unsuccessful attempt by Dad to place his arm around her in a movie theater. Romantic feelings still in abeyance, Dad certainly noticed from an early age Mom's unflinching determination and her practical originality as he reports in his "Sproule/Glenn Chronicle":

"One of the first things I learned from Katherine was a new way to kill a chicken. My way was to hold the chicken by the leg and wings with the left hand, lay the neck on the chopping block and then chop off the chicken's head with the ax in the right hand. In contrast Katherine's method was to hold a chicken with its neck on the ground, put a hoe handle or other rod across the neck, step on this rod to hold it down and then to quickly pull the chicken to separate it from the head."

Although Dad reports quickly becoming friends with the Glenn fivesome, he added that "I can remember scuffling with one of Glenns and having two or three others join in the fray."

As previously noted, the Harper Sproule family's routine annually took them from their home in town to a regular summer camp in the mountain pastures. Two photographs of this setting from about 1927 and 1928—and centering on the young John and Gene—give glimpses of a log-cabin's corner, a covered wagon with wooden wheels, a wood-fenced corral, and meandering sheep. These depictions are consistent with Dad's description given in his "Sproule/Glenn Chronicle":

"The destination for the sheep being trailed from winter to summer range was an area of several square miles in the foothills of the Bighorn Mountains in Central Wyoming. . . . Our summer cabin was located on a small creek. . . . The log cabin, which served as our summer home, . . . [was next to] . . . a log horse corral and a fenced in garden where my mother grew strawberries and summer vegetables. . . . Our summer encampment usually also included a sheep wagon and a ridge pole tent, which served as sleeping quarters for my brother and me."

JHS and Gene often would be tasked with fishing and occasionally hunting to supplement the fare available at the campsite. Again, from Dad's "Chronicle":

> "Mother would often tell my brother and me to go catch a mess of trout for supper. We would catch a tobacco can fall of grasshoppers, take our willow poles and go up or down the creek fishing for supper. Usually we could catch a dozen or so trout seven to nine inches long in an hour or so, and thus fill out the supper menu. There were also a lot of sage chickens in the area, though it usually fell to my father or another adult to take a shotgun and bring in some sage chicken to eat."

Dad once explained to me that as a result of his various summer camp chores he came to regard horseback riding, hunting, and camping more along the lines of work than recreation. And to my knowledge Dad never rode a horse, cast a fishing line, fired a gun, or pitched a tent during all the years I knew him—from 1949 (my own birth year) to Dad's death in 1997. The culinary results of fishing and hunting aside, the summer-camp menu featured "some form of mutton—that is sheep meat." As Dad relates in his "Chronicle":

> "Regardless of how well mother prepared various forms of sheep, I ate so much over the years that since college, and subsequent time, I don't think I've eaten lamb or mutton or other sheep meat over four or five times in fifty plus years."

By at least 1934 Harper's ranching operation was not going well as a consequence of problems with his business partner (as Dad obliquely notes in his uncompleted "Chronicle") and, it may be assumed, from the generally adverse business environment of the Depression. And for reasons not known to me, the marriage between Harper and Kiva was on the rocks. So that Harper's absence from the family became more complete as compared to his longstanding practice of frequently working remotely from wife and children excepting summers. It seems that Harper remained in the vicinity of Riverton at least through 1936 as indicated in a death notice published for his mother, Mary Sproule, in the *Alhambra*

[California] *Post Advocate* (August 18, 1936)—this placing both Harper and Luther in Riverton. But it is evident that Harper somewhat before 1940 had made his way to California, positioning him closer to his sisters Amy [Sproule] Wilkening and [Mary] Alice [Sproule] Anspach and Alice's young sons Malcolm and Rodney. He would remain there until his death

The story told me was that the original relocation of some family members to California came about at least partially in connection with Amy's treatable case of tuberculosis necessitating a climate more conducive than that of Wyoming. Some of the letters that JHS wrote from college at Laramie to Katherine Glenn [Sproule] report that Harper would on occasion visit his ex-wife, Kiva, in Riverton. And there was mention in 1942 of a recent second marriage by Harper. In this connection, the family archives document that John Harper Sproule, Sr. secured a Reno divorce from Kiva Sproule on January 15, 1942.

When their parents separated, JHS and Walter Eugene along with their mother moved to a location on the outskirts of Riverton, one pleasantly situated on a branch of the Wind River. This came about when, in 1935, Kiva purchased 120 or so acres of property "on a tax deed from the county"; and later in 1937 she sold an 80-acre portion of this property (Frank P. Hill, Atty., November 5, 1968 to JHS). My cousin Leon Sproule reports that our grandmother's success in securing the lot partially owed to the other participants having agreed not to bid the price up against a woman with children whose husband had in essence abandoned her. Dad used to tell the story that grandmother secured a workman to build a small cottage on the property with $15.00 worth of lumber that she purchased separately.

In "The Sproule/Glenn Family Chronicle" Dad describes the cottage structure as "a simple 3 room wood frame house with no bathroom or running water . . . a kitchen/dining room with a wood burning kitchen stove, a living room heated with a round coal burning stove and one bedroom . . . [and] . . . a two hole outhouse toilet." My first experience with this edifice came when my parents took me, age 5, to visit grandmother in Riverton in 1954. My juvenile remembrance was of a small flat-roofed building of about 20 feet by 20 feet in which a curtain stretche across one of the rooms, on the other side of which stood a (to me) giant iron wood-burning stove. This must have been what Dad described as the "kitchen/dining room" on one side of which was "the shed kitchen, a low ceiling room to the rear of the kitchen mostly used for storage."

By the time I first toured grandmother's ranchette, she was living in a mor serviceable house earlier built by Walter Eugene at a time when he lived o the property with his wife Alice and their children—[Kiva] Marie, Leon, Jocelyn, and Steven (this before a later South Dakota arrival, Rebecca). While grandmother's new W. E. Sproule-built house had running water, th outhouse remained, the use of which was explained to me by my Dad. I suppose it was the original one Dad described, for it sported two seats. Other of my impressions as a citified five-year-old taking in grandmother's ranchette included the property's pleasant location on the Wind River, the irrigation channels, and a small barn in front of which lay a cow patty recently bisected by a narrow Model-T type tire. Returning to Riverton fo a short visit in 2013 along with my son, Kevin, we found this former Sprou property chiefly occupied by a trailer park with gravel roads adjacent to which I believe the original house and barn still stood in modified form as part of a residential area. Castoff jagged concrete segments now adorned the riverbank. Riverton proper has now spread out to grandmother's old home which in the 1950s and early 1960s was still distinctly separated fro the town.

Somehow long before my time, a nomenclatural tradition had grown up among the Sproules of Riverton such that a family member might be calle by his or her middle name. Such was the case with John Harper, Sr. (know as Harper), Mary Alice (known as Alice), Walter Eugene (known as Gene), Kiva Marie (known as Marie) and myself (James Michael Sproule known a: Mike). On his part, JHS was referred to as "Junior Sproule" until 7th grade. Dad explained the eventual change of this (to him) stigmatizing appellatio in "The Sproule/Glenn Family Chronicle": "Grades 1 to 6 were in one building and 7 to 12 in the 'high school' building up the hill. When school started for the 7th grade, I did not respond when the teacher, in calling th roll said: Junior Sproule. When she finished the roster, she asked if there was anyone whose name had not been called. Thereupon I raised my hand and upon the teacher's inquiring, I said my name is John Sproule." And so it would be for the rest of Dad's life.

Because track and field required Dad to "hike 5 mi. home after sports" to his mother's Wind River ranchette southwest of Riverton, it clearly represented a priority for him in high school. Shot put was his specialty, and Dad retained his 16-pound shot (with chiseled-in initials JHS) until 1986 when, in the rush to pack up during the move from Tipp City, Ohio to Reno, Nevada, this item remained behind in the mix of goods left for the new owners, John and Rita Angel. Dad's treasures forsaken also included his weighty collection of *National Geographic* magazines extending back to the 1890s. The Angels did not object to inheriting some of the previous owners' old- timey stuff given that they, like Dad and Mom, operated an antiques business in Tipp City. Sometime later, when Dad and Mom visited Tipp, they stopped by the Angels' shop to find Dad's old 16-pounder offered for sale under the label of "Civil War cannon ball."

Track and field competitions brought about one of Dad's more notable high-school experiences which he summarizes as "district meet smallpox." It seems that, after a senior-year track and field competition, Dad began to feel under the weather during the ride back—this culminating in a diagnosis of smallpox. Dad describes his having been quarantined at home for "several weeks" and his having consequently "missed graduation" (according to notes for JHS's uncompleted "Sproule/Glenn Chronicle"). I recall Dad's remarking on numerous occasions that no one else in Riverton, nor anyone who had attended that particular track meet, ever came down with smallpox.

Leon Sproule, my cousin, relates what I believe might be a different version of Dad's smallpox story—or this information might pertain to another and separate family medical travail (in Leon Sproule's *The Spirit of Humanity* {Bloomington, IN: Balbola Press, 2022}, p. 32). In Leon's telling, grandmother Kiva, in 1922, was faced with both her sons suffering from smallpox, thereupon forced by Rivertonians to quarantine "in a sheep wagon up in the Rocky Mountains." If this account originates in Dad's vicissitudes of spring 1936, it may reflect the stigma of quarantining and Dad's possibly being relegated to the old sheep wagon retained from summer camping in the Bighorn Mountains. Dad several times remarked on how he and his best friend, Lewis Kelly, would sometimes for fun bunk in this old wagon.

Graduating from Riverton High School in 1936, JHS enrolled in the University of Wyoming, the sole public four-year university in the state. Dad recalled that the only support his mother could provide was the $5.00 proceeds from the sale of a cow. Dad's first college years at Laramie are not well known to me except that after a few academic quarters, Dad returned to Riverton in 1938 believing that he would be more successful in school if he could save up a surplus for tuition and board rather than holding jobs at the same time that he undertook studies in engineering.

Dad later remarked that his taking off time to pursue a fulltime job had not been successful because he found himself unable to save much. So, we observe him returning to college in 1940 in about the same dismal financial condition with which he began in September 1936. Fiscal negatives aside, it appears that in the interim between Dad's two periods of study at Laramie, he significantly deepened his relationship with Katherine Veronica Glenn who on February 15, 1943 would become his wife, thus commencing a marriage of 54 years duration. (They would have been married on February 14 Valentine's Day, but Mom didn't want to co-mingle two separate opportunities for romantic remembrance.)

In 1937, Dad commenced his practice of regularly writing from college in Laramie to Kay Glenn of Riverton. Also graduating from Riverton High in 1936, Mom had wished to attend college, and had exerted herself to this end such that she won membership in the National Honor Society of Secondary Schools. She may have contacted the University of Wyoming but, in any event, came to UW's attention given a letter of August 12, 1937 by W. P. Reed, Director of Personnel, to KVS as follows:

"The college ability test you took in the spring of 1936 indicated that prospects as a university student should be very good if you are willing to apply yourself. The score placed you in the top quarter of Wyoming high school graduates. Our records, however, do not show that you attended any college last year, and I am wondering if we can help you in any way." He then suggested some alternatives "if finances have been one of your problems," observing that she was one of six children with father deceased.

Unfortunately, obstacles greater than finances had, in fact, intervened. Owing to the onset of her mother Emma's breast cancer in 1937, KVS found it necessary to remain in town and, with the aid of her siblings, help their ailing mother (who died in November 1938). In addition, the older kids also were maintaining the household so that the youngest, Anna, might continue at Riverton High School until her graduation in 1940. At this point, the kids gradually began to gravitate from Riverton, with Joe working for the railroad, initially as a cook, Bernard joining the CCC [Civilian Conservation Corps] and later the Army, and Agnes (Ay) migrating to Cody for secretarial work at Husky Refining. Mom and Anna were the last to leave, finally heading out to Portland, Oregon in spring 1942. After Mom left Portland for Dayton, Ohio in early 1943 to join Dad in marriage, Agnes and Anna relocated to Los Angeles.

Because the older Glenn children had received a somewhat helter-skelter education during their early years living on a remote-from-town ranch, Emma Pauline made some adjustments to the reported ages of the kids when she enrolled them in Riverton schools. I don't know the particulars except in the case of KVS whose age was reduced by two years—from a 1915 nativity to one of 1917. One of Dad's letters references Mom's consternation when learning that her Nebraska birth certificate blatantly displayed the date of 1915. But except for Mom's applying for social security on the basis of a 1915 birth, she uniformly presented herself as a child who had entered the world in 1917. Her driver's license listed her birth date as 1917—presumably because her original one would have been based on self-report data in a simpler era. Even her long-term care insurance policy executed in the late 1980s listed a birth date of 1917, and this is the date cast into her bronze memorial plaque in a niche in Our Mother of Sorrows Cemetery in Reno, Nevada, alongside that of her husband JHS.

The letters of John Harper Sproule, Jr. commence January 1937, in Dad's second quarter at Wyoming, and they extend to his two-week session of study in 1963 at the Merchant Marine Academy in New York. The unifying element in these letters spanning 26 years is their focus on Dad's becoming a college-credentialed engineer and practicing his craft for the U.S. Air Force in armaments and electronic warfare. And Dad lived in interesting times which span the great Depression, World War II, and the Cold War. His life is an American story of humble beginnings and upward mobility in the mid-20th century.

While the letters chronicled in *Air Force Engineer* come to a close in 1963, JHS and KVS continued in Dayton, Ohio until 1978. At that point, they opened an antique store, "John's Artiques," on the first floor of their large Victorian home at 105 West Main in Tipp City, Ohio. In 1980, Dad retired from the Air Force and greatly expanded his hobbyist's interest in rural estate auctions, eventually attending some 3000 such sales in the southwestern area of Ohio. Mom and Dad relocated to Reno, Nevada in 1986 to be closer to their son (Mike), daughter-in-law (Betty), and two grandchildren (John and Kevin) then residing in Palo Alto, California. Dad died suddenly of a heart attack in summer 1997, and at this time Mom moved to an assisted living facility in Palo Alto about a mile from her son's family.

To enhance the focus and readability of the letters, the editor has employed a number of conventions. To signal the excision of whole sections, readers will find a bracketed indication of the number of paragraphs omitted—e.g., **[2 PARAGRAPHS]**. Ellipses denote the redaction of parts of a paragraph. Where one paragraph segues directly into another, a notation of **[/]** will be deployed. From time to time, readers will observe explanatory remarks given in brackets. In editorial notes, John

Harper Sproule, Jr. will be referred to, generally, as JHS or Dad; and Katherine Veronica [Glenn] Sproule will be referred to as KVS or Mom.

Chapter 1. Commencing College—January 1937 to March 1938

The earliest letters between JHS and KVS report Dad's experiences from h
second quarter of college through his decision to lay out for a time to ear
enough money such that he need not work while continuing his studies.

　　　**** To Miss Katherine Glenn, Riverton, Wyoming (1/10/1937, Postmarked 1/11/37 at 11:00 AM). Return address: J. H. Sproule, 406 S. 12th, Laramie, Wyo. [Typed letter] "Dear Kay—— Well, I am now back to the old grind. Math at 8:00, with a chaser of English or Chem. lecture; afternoons are filled with Drawing or Chem. labs. So on through the week Then up bright and early (8:00) to go work Saturday. Sunday is a day of re (sleep). Then Monday starts another verse of the same song." **[1 PARAGRAPH]**

"With that disposed of, I can ask now, how have you been? and say that I am well, how is the town?"　　**[/]** "Lewis [Kelly] and I went to see <u>Born t Dance</u> last night, at the owl sho [sic] (11:30) – (2:00). It is a show to see, songs dances, and all the rest. We saw the teasers for the <u>Stowaway</u>, (a Shirley Temple show, but with a Montgomery-Faye romance indicated) they looked good. Did you see the hell doll sho? I hated to miss it but it may come here so I can see it." **[4 PARAGRAPHS]** [handwritten] "With love John"

　　　**** To Miss Katherine Glenn, Riverton, Wyoming [handwritten letter] (2/10/1937, Postmarked 2/11/37 at 11:00 AM). Return address: J. H. Sproule, Laramie, Wyo. "Dear Kay— I suppose by this time you think that I have fallen off the sidewalks or something and have broken my pen However this is not the case. The case will be explained forthwith. Since received your last letter numerous things have transpired. Chief among the disturbances has been the mid quarter exams which I assure you are not in the least easy. . . ." **[1 PARAGRAPH]** "The typewriter I spoke of is use just now and so I have evolved the code of which various mention ha been made. What do you think eh? (of the code)" **[/]** ". . . I will have to quit because Lewis is here and we will probably do a little studying." **[/]** "(to be continued next week)" **[/]** "Love" **[/]** "John"

**** To Miss Katherine Glenn, Riverton, Wyo. (4/16/1937 [placed in envelope of 2/26/38]. Return address: 1309 Kearney, Laramie, Wyo. "Kay Dear" **[3 PARAGRAPHS]** "I really am sorry to hear of the cancer diagnosis [of Emma Pauline Carrington Glenn who died in November 1938]. It kind of seems that those close to me should be immune to such things. It seems hard to know just what would be best to do, doctors are generally right, but then we always wonder—. You know I hope for the best, dear." **[1 PARAGRAPH]**

"We had a military inspection Monday, by General Simmons, head of the ninth corps area. This was somewhat superficial, the real inspection that will determine our rating (you know we are rated as excellent) will be the 13-14 of next month. This will definitely not be superficial. Company G, the company I am in has been appointed to guard duty, a sort of sentry duty or something. I don't know all about it yet but I am sure I will before it is over. I don't know whether I will like it or not, but what is to be will be I guess in the military department especially." **[3 PARAGRAPHS]** "Love" **[/]** "John"

**** To Miss Katherine Glenn, Riverton, Wyo. (1/18/38, Postmarked 1/19/38 at 12:30 PM). Return address: 1309 Kearney, Laramie, Wyo. "Dear Kay—" **[2 PARAGRAPHS]** "I'm going out for track this quarter. We work out in the armory while it is cold. When it warms up this summer we will work outside. We are to have a triangular meet with Colorado Aggies and the School of Mines at Ft. Collins some time in February. We have some good prospects but our best bet seems to be in basketball. We've done pretty good so far." **[/]** "This is a terribly short letter but it is time I was up at the armory working out (my form—shot putting form—is terrible)." **[2 PARAGRAPHS]** "Love" **[/]** "John"

**** Letter to Katherine V. Glenn from John H. Sproule, 2/25/38 bundled with a letter from a Denver, Colorado friend of Kay's [Helen?] undated in an envelope with return address of 125 E. 18 Ave., Denver,

Colo., addressed to Miss Katherine Glenn, Riverton, Wyoming and postmarked 1/15/38 at 1:00 PM. JHS letter begins: "Dear Kay—" **[7 PARAGRAPHS]** "We have another meet the 5th at Boulder, Colo. The coach is going to take about 8 men and as I see it about 4 of them will be from Riverton. Great stuff—eh?" **[2 PARAGRAPHS]** "Yes, I have heard that I have some Irish blood in me. **[/]** "It is nearly time for supper so I will close for if you are not there when called you go hungry." **[/]** "Love" **[/]** "John"

  **** To Miss Katherine Glenn, Riverton, Wyoming (3/5/38, Postmarked 3/7/38 at 6:30 AM). Return address [none given]. ENTIRETY OF LETTER: "Dear Kay, I haven't communicated with you because I felt that on our last date you had some doubt as to your feeling toward me." **[/]** "I think that by now you have probably reached a decision one way or another." **[/]** "How about a show, the dance Sat. night (I suppose there will be one) bowling some night, the St. Patrick's dance or any thing you suggest—if you care? If so let me know." **[/]** "Or if you don't care—if you feel that you don't want to go with me anymore, just don't answer this note and I will know how you feel." **[/]** "As ever," **[/]** "John"

Chapter 2. Back to the Collegiate Grind— January 1940 to June 1940

After laying out of college for almost two years, JHS returns to Laramie with a disappointingly small nest egg and with an enhanced urge to maintain a long-distance relationship with Katherine Glenn. Here we find JHS's setting about to reorient himself to academic classes and sundries such as track and ROTC [Reserve Officers Training Corps], find employment, secure accommodations, and reassure his beloved that their much-deepened relationship remains a priority. None of these goals proves to be easy.

**** To Miss Katherine Glenn, Box 35, Riverton, Wyo. (1/3/40, Postmarked 1/4/40 with indication that letter was written from Laramie, Wyoming). Return address: [none given]. [Following is pretty much the entire letter, excepting only the full chart of classes.]

"Kay darling . . . " [/] "I miss you so much. It seems hard to realize that I won't be seeing you tonight—that I'm hundreds of miles away from you— that instead of driving up to your house or seeing you after work we'll be separated by nearly half a state." [/] "We (Lewis, Vernon [Kelly] & I) arrived safe & sound in Laramie about 7:30 Monday evening. We sent Vernon up with the suitcases in a taxi. When he came back we got something to eat. It was about 8:30 when we ate & we were getting hungry since we hadn't eaten since 11:00 & then only had a bowl of soup. After the show we went to see 'Every Thing Happens at Night' with Sonja Henie. It is a good show but the title has no bearing whatsoever." [/] "Got registered yesterday & started to classes today. Below is a chart of my classes. . . ." [lists classes in psychology, economics, French, track.] [/]

"We, Lewis & I, went out to the airport this morning so Lewis could see the pilot about his flying schedule. While we were out there, one of the fellows taking the flying course soloed—he was the first one to solo. It won't be long though until they have all taken their first flight alone. Lewis went out to take another lesson this afternoon, but I didn't go along. It sprinkled a little snow this morning until about 11:00 and then started to clear up. It looks rather nice out now." **[/]**

"When you write address the letters to 601 S. 15th Laramie, Wyo.—that's Bert Kelly's house where Lewis stays & I'm staying over there until I find a more permanent place. A place where we were going to batch was rented when we got back & we haven't found a place definitely yet. I'll let you know, in my next letter, of any change in address." **[/]** "I have a French class pretty soon so I must close. Write soon sweetheart." **[/]** "Remember, I love you." **[/]** "Johnny" **[/]** "P.S. Jan. 4—heard of a place that we could get & I saw about it this morning. It is close to where Lewis lives & not too far from the university so I rented it. My address therefore is 1319 Kearney, Laramie, Wyoming." **[/]** "All my love darling, Johnny."

**** To Miss Katherine Glenn, Box 35, Riverton, Wyo. (1/10/40, Postmarked 1/11/40, 6:30 PM). Return Address: 1319 Kearney, Laramie, Wyo. "Hello sweetheart—" **[/]** "I got both of your letters yesterday, one in the morning and one in the afternoon. If you could only know how glad my heart was to have your letters. Darling, I miss you terribly and getting your letters means a lot. Remember, I love you with all my heart." **[/]**

"Today was my busy day—I had five classes; really only four and then a track work out. Kelly was over and we sat around & talked. My roommate has an English theme to write so to help him a bit, I took his note cards and dictated a rough draft of a theme, to him. After I finished dictating that we walked to town. So by now it is getting late. It's my turn to get breakfast in the morning. (I get breakfast on Tue., Thur & Sat. and get lunch every day except Sun. Al—my roommate—gets supper every day except Sun. & breakfast on Mon, Wed & Fri. On Sun. we both get the meals. We both do dishes after every meal, taking turns washing & drying.) As I have to get up at 6:30 in the morning & it's now 2:00 AM I'll finish this in the morning." **[/]** "January 11.—I made my first attempt at making pancakes this morning. They didn't turn out as bad as I expected." **[1 PARAGRAPH]**

"Yes, darling I do hate to say good bye more especially to you than any other person in the whole world, because you mean so much to me. I guess under the circumstances, my coming down to this corner of the state, we couldn't avoid it.— But I do hate to say good bye to you." **[2 PARAGRAPHS]** "About a telephone here—yes there is one upstairs dial number 4025, but I'm afraid that it will be expensive for you to phone me. I'd love to talk to you though—you know that. If you could let me know when, I'd be sure to be here—we sometimes go up to the library at school—over to Kelly's etc. and I'd certainly hate to be gone when you called." **[1 PARAGRAPH]**

"Kelly went out this morning to take a flying lesson, I guess he's back by now, but I haven't seen him. He certainly likes flying. I'd like to take the course, but wearing glasses eliminates me. They have some nice planes to fly. I went out to the airport with Lewis a couple of times, but he didn't fly either time I went out with him so I have never seen him fly. I guess he'll get along just as well as if I were there all the time." **[/]** "Lewis keeps saying that he must write a letter to Sara Ann, but I don't think he has done so yet." **[1 PARAGRAPH]** "All my love" **[/]** "Johnny" **[/]** "I LOVE YOU"

**** To Miss Katherine Glenn, Box 35, Riverton, Wyo. (1/21/40, Postmarked 1/22/40, 3:00 AM). Return Address: 1319 Kearney, Laramie, Wyo. "Kay darling—" **[1 PARAGRAPH]** "It's still a little strange to be going to school. I haven't as yet arranged my time so as to have a definite time for study. As a result my studying suffers. This week end for example, I had a number of things which I intended to get done and didn't. I'll have to do them tomorrow night I guess." **[/]** ". . . This house work is easier than I thought it would be. Perhaps we don't sweep the floor quite as often as we should; but we can't spend all our time just keeping house, can we?" **[/]**

"This place we have is a basement room. We have cupboards, gas plate etc. for cooking, two tables, chest of drawers, closet, chairs & bed and that is how our place is furnished. This is a private house—the landlady has a couple of sleeping rooms upstairs and another batching apartment, in addition to ours, in the basement. About phoning—I agree that you wouldn't want to call and have to talk to the landlady." **[/]** ". . . Vernon [Kelly] got Al, my room mate, to go to church with him this evening and when they got back they looked cold as ice cubes." **[/]** "I think the reason Vernon goes to church is that he gets to meet some (that's the way it sounds) girls he knows by going to church." **[5 PARAGRAPHS]** "Remember that I love you with all my heart. Good night, darling." **[/]** "With all my love" **[/]** "Johnny"

    **** To Miss Katherine Glenn, Box 35, Riverton, Wyo. (1/29/40, Postmarked 1/30?/40, 11:00 AM [?]). Return Address: 1319 Kearney, Laramie, Wyo. "Kay darling," **[2 PARAGRAPHS]** "A pause now to put on a kettle of macaroni. It is nearly 11:30 and dinner or lunch or what ever it is is my job." **[/]** "We do have a cozy little place. Suppose that it is a bit small, but what do we need a lot of room for?" **[1 PARAGRAPH]** "Another short pause now to wash the dishes. We wash our dishes after every meal—because we have only two plates, two knives etc." **[2 PARAGRAPHS]** "I personally don't have any idea what Gene [Sproule] does or where he keeps himself. Mom said in her last letter that he had a new puppy so maybe he is training it or something." **[/]**

"Say, there is no danger of my misplacing any of your letters. So write just what you feel. I read your letters over and over and I think they are swell. **[3 PARAGRAPHS]** "I have a class in 12 minutes so will rush to school now. **[/]** "Economics is over now and I am over at the school library. I can't go home because I have a French class at 4:00 o'clock." **[1 PARAGRAPH]** "It been so cold that I haven't been working out for track. But I think I'll work out a little this evening. We may not have another warm day for a month **[/]** "It makes it work out fine when I go out for track because Al (his last name is Justus) gets supper and he generally has it all ready when I get home." **[2 PARAGRAPHS]** "Love and kisses to my sweetheart" **[/]** "Johnny" **[/]** "Post Scriptum I suggest that you have your hats bought before I come home. Then you will not be influenced by their appearance on me."

    **** To Miss Katherine Glenn, Box 35, Riverton, Wyoming (2/6/40 Postmarked 2/7/40, 11:00 AM). Return Address: 1319 Kearney, Laramie, Wyo. "Kay darling," **[2 PARAGRAPHS]** "I'm getting along fine. Perhaps I don't have all my subjects as well in hand as I might, but then I never in all my school days, had all my studies up to date. I have one economics course 'money & banking' which I thoroughly dislike. As a consequence I don't give it the attention and study that I should." **[/]**

"I've learned a little French, but am by no means expert yet. The pronunciation is a lot different from any thing I ever learned before, but I hope to get it some time. From your Spanish can you read this? [includes a romantic passage in French] If you don't understand this I will give you a translation, next letter." **[5 PARAGRAPHS]** "Sweetheart, about your letters. You know I treasure them. After I have read them I put them in my trunk. It's a metal trunk and I lock it. So this is the answer to the question of where I keep your letters—I lock them in my trunk. This should make you feel safe in writing what is in your heart, darling. I'll be the only person to see your letters." **[3 PARAGRAPHS]**

"About track—we work out in the Armory. The Armory is a wing of the gym—it has a dirt floor with about two or three inches of saw dust on it. It has a saw dust floor to make it easier on the feet of the R.O.T.C. cadets who drill in it. That is its principal use—ROTC drill that is. The Armory has a floor space, just to make an estimate, equal to nearly three times that of the R.H.S. gym. I may be wrong on that but I know that over 800 ROTC cadets come to order in it; that means a certain amount of space between each man and between different parts of the companies." **[4 PARAGRAPHS]** "Goodnight sweetheart, with all my love—" **[/]** "Johnny" **[/]** "X X X" [This letter also includes a sheet containing a coded message, the code of which uses the letters of the actual message with a variety of other letters surrounding them; the tone is romantic in nature.]

**** To Miss Katherine Glenn, Box 35, Riverton, Wyo. (2/14/40, Postmarked 2/15/40, 3:30 PM). Return Address: 1319 Kearney, Laramie, Wyo. "Kay, my darling—" **[2 PARAGRAPHS]** "A translation of that French in the last letter—" **[/]** [translation begins:] "Kay, my darling, I love you with all my heart my sweetheart. When I get back, I'll kiss you."

"(I was just writing this when your call came. It was sure swell to hear you. When I found for sure that the call was for me I was so excited I could hardly hold the telephone. I imagine that I sounded that way. That was the first long distance call I ever had and being from you makes it the most important. Sweetheart, I'll always remember it. Your call was the nicest Valentine that I can think of. Did you omit saying that you love me because it was over the telephone? I don't care if the whole world knows I love you. I really fell too, you know.)" **[/]** "To finish the translation of that French—when I get back, I'll kiss you again and again. I send you all my love." **[2 PARAGRAPHS]**

"I've been able to catch up on some sleep lately. I can sleep as long as I like on Sat. and Sun. And having only one class on Tue. and Thurs. makes it almost like having three weekends. If I could get a job which I hope I can, I wouldn't have so much leisure time, but I'd rather be working—I just waste my leisure time anyway." **[1 PARAGRAPH]** "I'm very sorry that the head broke off the Valentine I sent but even if it wasn't very big or very strong remember that it brought my love." **[2 PARAGRAPHS]** "X X With all my heart, love & kisses to my darling," **[/]** "Johnny" **[/]** "X X X"

**** To Miss Katherine Glenn, Box 35, Riverton, Wyo. (2/19/40, Postmarked 2/20/40, 12:30 PM). Return Address: 1319 Kearney, Laramie, Wyo. "My darling Kay," **[/]** "Your swell letter came tonight and it has brightened my whole evening. Sweetheart, you write the nicest letters. I love you & I also love to hear from you. Do you know that the one thing I don't like about Sunday is that there is no mail delivery and consequently your letters are held in the post office till they deliver the mail on Monday. This holding up of your letters is something that I don't like." **[1 PARAGRAPH]**

"I won't have quite so much leisure time now because I got a job today. It's a job in the bee laboratory and I suppose that there will also be some outside work. I have been after it for two or three weeks and when I went to see the fellow in charge today, I got the news. I even worked a couple of hours today. The work will be easy I think—I won't make much, but you would be surprised to see how economically I have been living. I guess you can't spend what you haven't earned." **[/]** "About some outside assistance—I think that I could probably get a loan through the Rebekah

Lodge since Mother is a member, but you have to sign too many things to suit me—anyway if I can get along without it I won't be so much in debt if and when I get out of school." **[/]**

"I went out to the airport with Lewis [Kelly] Saturday to watch him fly. He soloed Friday and he was rather pleased. He hadn't been able to fly for nearly two weeks because of the weather and he was getting rather disgusted since he was all ready to solo. He does seem to have a lot of misfortune. For another example—he was almost electrocuted today. He was in the electrical laboratory and was unhooking a motor which was switched on. He just got a good shock though, and is as well as ever." **[5 PARAGRAPHS]** "Remember that I love you with all my heart and that I'm yours forever." **[/]** "With all my love and kisses" **[/]** "Johnny"

**** To Miss Katherine Glenn, Box 35, Riverton, Wyo. (2/27/40, Postmarked 2/28/40, 12:30 PM). Return Address: 1319 Kearney, Laramie, Wyo. "Kay darling," **[/]** "This is the third morning that I have been up. I say morning because it is about a quarter till three. I had an economics paper that I had to hand in Monday and so to finish it I stayed up till about three o'clock Sunday night. Last night I was writing an English theme for a fellow and I stayed up till two thirty working on it. I finished his theme, did my French assignment, my psychology assignment (after a fashion) and a few other odds and ends tonight and so it is late again. I usually have lots of time during the day to do my studying, but since I got that job I don't seem to be able to find time to do anything. As a result my sleeping hours have been cut. Next week will be different though, I hope. Instead of finding something to occupy my leisure time, I seem to have no time for anything." **[/]**

"I'm glad that you like the compact. I didn't say 'happy birthday' or anything in my last letter because I thought that I would surprise you. I tried to send your present so that it would reach you on your birthday. Did it? . . . ." **[2 PARAGRAPHS]** "I think that school will be out the fourteenth of March. That is the last day of test week. And speaking of tests I think that I am going to have three of my final exams the first day of test week. I'll bet I won't get to bed at all the night before. I always have a certain amount of cramming to do before an exam and multiplying that by three will not give me much time for sleep." **[3 PARAGRAPHS]** "Good night darling" **[/]** "With all my love X X X X X X X X X X X" **[/]** "Johnny X X X X X"

   **** To Miss Katherine Glenn, Box 35, Riverton, Wyo. (2/29/40, Postmarked 3/1/40, 12:30 PM). Return Address: 1319 Kearney, Laramie, Wyo. Letter is entirely in code which is some kind of a letter-substitution cipher.

   **** To Miss Katherine Glenn, Box 35, Riverton, Wyo. Two letters are enclosed in one envelope. The first is by JHS (3/5/40, Postmarked 3/6/40, 12:30 PM) and the second is by Kay Glenn (3/9/40). Return address is 1319 Kearney, Laramie, Wyo.

   [1] JHS (3/5/40): "My darling Kay," **[8 PARAGRAPHS**—in which these points are made: JHS Says that he doesn't remember the fellow, Sanders, who died in an auto accident mentioned in previous letter by Kay Glenn. JHS explains a previous code used in an earlier letter involving letter-substitutions; also he includes a translation from the French used in a previous letter.]

"Spring vacation will start the 15th of March. I don't think that I will be home until the night of the 16th, for this reason—Kelly has to make an inspection trip to inspect some electrical mining machinery. He is going somewhere near Rock Springs. He will come back through Rawlins on the 16th. I plan to take the bus to Rawlins on the 16th and meet him there. His folks will bring us home from Rawlins and so it will be Saturday evening when I get home as things stand now." **[3 PARAGRAPHS]**

"I've been going out for track, but I don't think that I am doing any better than average. Possibly I will have a chance to eat and sleep more at the start of next quarter than I have this quarter. We will have our first meet about the sixth of April, I believe, so I have plenty of time at least to get a little better than I am now." **[/]**

"My days never seem long enough. I worked seven hours today, had a French class, went out for track, got supper, etc. I always do a certain amount of fooling around, which is why I never have enough time probably. I suppose I would have plenty of time if I didn't go over to Kelly's for a chat now and then—and other things should probably be eliminated, such as reading magazines and listening to the radio which would result in more time to put in on my school work." **[/]** "Kelly also has a lot of work piled up on him. Most of his work consists of experiments which he has to write up before the quarter ends. I don't have anything of that sort, my school work consists mostly of cramming for my final exams. It won't be long before finals are over and I can start in all over again." **[4 PARAGRAPHS]** "With all my love" **[/]** "Johnny" **[/]** "X X X"

[2] NOW THE LETTER OF Kay Glenn (3/9/40) enclosed in this envelope: "Dear Johnny," **[/]** "That was very sweet of you to translate that code. When I came to the French is when my worst trouble began, don't let it happen again—ahm, ahm!" **[2 PARAGRAPHS]** "Since you guys won't get here until Saturday evening (and not being sure of that), I won't plan anything special. Just in case you're in Rawlins at 9:00 or there about, you can call 193 Collect, and then I'd know you couldn't get here." **[4 PARAGRAPHS]** "Well, Johnny, since I don't seem to be able to keep my eyes open easily any more, I'll stop here and will write again sometime." **[/]** "Love," **[/]** "K."

**** To Miss Katherine Glenn, Box 35, Riverton, Wyo. (3/13/40, Postmarked 3/14/40, 12:30 PM). Return address: 1319 Kearney, Laramie, Wyo. "Kay Darling," **[/]** "I just finished my quarter's work today. I had my last final this afternoon. It is something of a relief to have all the final exams over. I have done quite a bit of worrying over them, but now that they are over they don't seem so bad. I did do a bit of studying and with my house work, going out for track etc, I just haven't been able to sit down and write you like I like to. I don't like to sit down and scribble a note. I would rather write you and try to convey what I'm feeling." **[1 PARAGRAPH]**

"Knowing how much we want to be together makes it rather hard to write what I must. I'm going to have to stay here until the twenty first. I have my exams finished, but I have some work to do that I have neglected to do because of studying for finals. Instead of going over to work I would go by and say that I had some studying to do and this has piled up so that I must work part of vacation to make up for it. I may be able, alas, to get in a little work which will apply for April. If I can do this I will have more time next quarter. Kelly wants to stay here for a while and get in some flying. The instructors seem to have wasted some time or something and he feels that it may be pretty close whether he gets a private license or not. And by staying and getting in some flying he will make more sure that he will get his license. If we both come home together it will save an additional trip over to Rawlins." **[2 PARAGRAPHS]**

"The picture 'Grapes of Wrath' was here last week, but I didn't go to see it for two big reasons—time and money. There seemed to be a confliction of opinion as to how good the show was, so I really don't know whether it was any good or not. 'Gone with the Wind' will be here this week end. This is a picture which has certainly caused a lot of talk. It must be good—they are going to charge $1.12 for tickets. Yes—one dollar and twelve cents per ticket—that is a lot of money to see a show. It is supposed to be four hours long. The seats would have to be pretty well padded for me to sit and watch a picture for four hours with out getting up and taking a walk around the block to stretch." **[1 PARAGRAPH]** ". . . Remember I love you with all my being." **[/]** "All my love and kisses to my darling." **[/]** "Johnny." [followed by 15 X's]

**** To Miss Katherine Glenn, Riverton, Wyo. (3/27/40, Postmarked Laramie, Wyoming 3/27/40, 6:30 PM). Envelope mark: Hotel Shirley-Savoy, Denver, Colorado. Addressed from Laramie Wyoming. "Ka darling—" **[/]** "I only have time to write a note, but I want to let you know that I got here safe & sound." **[/]** "I was busy all day yesterday registering and last night I tried to see if I could borrow a few of the text books that I will need this quarter." **[1 PARAGRAPH]** "I registered for 16 hours this quarter. Mostly just finishing up courses of which I have only taken a part—the first half or two thirds—and so I thought that it would be a good idea to finish them up." **[1 PARAGRAPH]** "Remember I love you sweetheart" **[/]** "With all my love" **[/]** "Johnny"

**** To Miss Katherine Glenn, Box 35, Riverton, Wyo. (4/1/40, Postmarked, Laramie, Wyoming 4/2/40, 12:00 PM). Envelope mark: Hotel Shirley-Savoy, Denver, Colorado. Return address: John Sproule 1319 Kearney, Laramie, Wyoming. "My Darling Kay-" **[2 PARAGRAPHS]** "I'm taking the same Psychology and French this quarter as I did last quarter. I'm taking an Economics course—I had the first part when I was in school before. I'm also finishing up a Physics course and I'm taking my last quarter of Basic Military." **[/]** "With this schedule and working I have only three hours during the week that I can call my own—that is I don't have any specific thing to do at those hours (Mon. & Wed. at 11:00 to 12:00 and Thur 8:00 to 9:00) . . . ." **[/]**

"Lewis and I built a ping pong table over at his place. We're rather proud of this table. Where we were inquiring about what the materials would cost us, the first place we went the salesman wanted to sell us a top for the table that would cost $7.68. He said that it would be the only thing that would be satisfactory. This in addition to the top we would have to buy material for braces legs etc, bolts to fasten the legs on, paint and that sort of thing—all in addition to the $7.68 top. We fooled them though. We went to another place and bought our material without telling them what we were going to use it for. We bought some bolts at a hardware store and screws paint and paint brushes at the dime store. In that way the whole table (material, that is) for only $5.40. We haven't painted it yet, but when we get it painted we'll have a good table and good looking too." **[2 PARAGRAPHS]**

"I pledged Lamda Tau Delta fraternity yesterday. It's the one that Lewis is a member of. You have to be a pledge for a quarter and then you can 'go active'—become a full fledged member. While I'm a pledge I'll eat one meal a week there and go to meetings Monday nights. Tonight was my first meeting although I have been invited up to the fraternity house to eat before." **[/]** "Did you ever see anybody get the 'hot foot.'? You know how it is supposed to work—you stick a match in between the shoe and the sole and light it with another match. The match will burn for quite awhile before the heat will soak through the shoe to the foot, but when it does it gets very hot all at once. . . ." **[3 PARAGRAPHS]** "To my darling with all my love and kisses" **[/]** "Johnny"

**** To Miss Katherine Glenn, Box 35, Riverton, Wyo. (4/8/40, Postmarked Laramie, Wyoming 4/9/40, 6:30 PM). Envelope mark: Hotel Shirley-Savoy, Denver, Colorado. Return address: John Sproule 1319 Kearney, Laramie, Wyoming: "My darling Kay," **[3 PARAGRAPHS]** "And speaking of professors reminds me of the turmoil that is going on down here. Have you heard anything about it? There seemed to be some discussion as to whether Pres. Crane would have his contract renewed and then Gov. Smith ordered the contract of about a dozen others here on the campus held in abeyance (I'm going to disregard that legal term and say) held up. I heard tonight that they were all fired—I don't know whether that is so or not. There were a large number of petitions circulating about the campus the last few days although I can't see where they would do much good. If these men are fired (some of them are very popular with the students), I wouldn't be surprised to hear of a student strike—what ever the case I'm getting a lot of laughs at how some of the people are getting stirred up." **[1 PARAGRAPH]**

"I have to work 8-12 1-4 tomorrow. It seems that I always have about three things that I must do and I find my self with hardly time enough to do one. You really hit the nail on the head when you said that it sounded as though I had my hands full. I must waste time, but even though I <u>try</u> to get my school work done on time I seem to fall behind. For instance, today all that I did this evening was attend a frat meeting, play a couple of games of ping pong and write to you." **[1 PARAGRAPH]** "All my love always" **[/]** "Johnny" **[/]** "X X X X"

**** To Miss Katherine Glenn, Box 35, Riverton, Wyo. (4/14/40, Postmarked Laramie, Wyoming 4/15/40, 12:30 PM). Envelope mark: Hilton Hotels [with eight locations listed, five of them in Texas]. Return address: 1319 Kearney, Laramie, Wyo. "Kay darling," **[2 PARAGRAPHS]** "We had a track meet here yesterday with the southern branch of Idaho College. Wyoming wasn't conceded a chance to win, but they came a lot closer to winning than I thought they would. I got third place in the shot put and javelin throw. I didn't think that I would do that good because when I awoke yesterday I didn't feel as though I even wanted to get up. I think we are going to Denver for a track meet next Saturday, I don't suppose that I will do any good, but it will be a nice trip." **[1 PARAGRAPH]**

"The radio is playing and the song is 'Smoke Gets in Your Eyes'. You know the lyrics—'They asked me how I knew my true love was true.' 'I of course replied—something here inside cannot be denied.' Do you know, sweetheart, that something inside me is always reminding me of how sweet and lovely you are—and of how I love you. I wish that we could be somewhere, tonight, together where earthly cares would not trouble us. But being apart will make reunion all the sweeter. This letter brings you all my love darling. I love you with all my being for for ever and ever. I must say goodnight now (I do study once in a while)." **[/]** "With all my love and kisses" **[/]** "Johnny" [3/4ths of this page taken up with an elaborate array of X's spelling out a giant "I LOVE YOU"]

[Enclosed in the envelope is a sheet of lined paper, blank except for what in Kay Glenn's writing is an address: "Riverton, Wyoming / April 18, 1940 / Dear Mr. Sproule,"; presumably a sheet she had started to write in response but didn't finish.]

**** To Miss Katherine Glenn, Box 35, Riverton, Wyo. (4/21/40, Postmarked Laramie, Wyoming 4/22/40, 12:30 PM). Return address: J. Sproule 1319 Kearney, Laramie, Wyo. "Hello darling—" **[1 PARAGRAPH]** "The trip to Denver was swell except for Wyo losing 63 to 77 and the fact that I didn't do any good. We were gone all day. We left at 8:30 and didn't get back to Laramie till about 10:00 PM. We had excellent weather at Denver and the trip was held up only once. We had a flat tire—the first that I ever saw on a bus. That held us up for 40 minutes in Ft. Collins. We just had tea and toast and salad before the meet, but we had a chicken dinner afterwards which made up for the short rations beforehand." **[3 PARAGRAPHS]**

"I always dread Sunday nights. They always are so lonesome—we used to go out to a show or a ride, at least we were together, and now it's months between times we see each other." **[1 PARAGRAPH]** "Do you ever hear these radio programs where they play a song and award some little prize to the ones sending in the correct title? I was listening to one a while ago and I think I'll send in the title to the song they were playing. I think it was 'Oh Believe of all those Endearing Young Charms'. The prize is an eversharp pencil. The station was in Bakersfield Calif. and I don't know whether my letter will get there in time or not. I'll let you know if I win anything." **[1 PARAGRAPH]**

"Kelly and I sent a picture in to Popular Aviation Magazine some time ago and they published it in the magazine issue. Kelly got a check for $3.00 for it the other day. It might be possible to get some more printed. At least there's a possibility." **[1 PARAGRAPH]** "Lewis is getting up at about four o'clock now so he can go out and fly an hour before he goes to school. He hopes to be able to finish his flying course in about three weeks." **[1 PARAGRAPH]** "With all my love to the sweetest person in the whole world" **[/]** "Johnny" **[1 PARAGRAPH]** "P.S. I put a kiss for you on the lower left hand corner of this page. J."

**** To Miss Katherine Glenn, Box 35, Riverton, Wyo. (4/26/40, Postmarked Laramie, Wyoming 4/27/40, 12:30 PM). Return address: J. Sproule 1319 Kearney, Laramie, Wyo. "Sweetheart," **[4 PARAGRAPHS]** "The Engineers had an Open House last night that they invited the public in to see the various things which they have in the laboratories. Students were operating the different machines and they would explain the operation of the machine and the kind of work that it would do. . . ." **[/]** "I think that Kelly still hears from Sara Ann, at least once in a while. I didn't know that she wasn't coming back. Did she find a job or is she just staying with some of her relatives?" **[/]**

"I hope that you like 'G.W.T.W.' I wish now that I had gone to see it. Most every one I talked to seemed to think that it was it was a fine show. I saw 'Road to Singapore' with Bing Crosby, Dorothy Lamour and Bob Hope. It was a good show I thought—some very good songs and a lot of laughs." **[2**

PARAGRAPHS] "Is Anna [Glenn] going to work for Spiker when you quit? I think you are perfectly right about quitting—one jobs enough for anyone to have to do." **[1 PARAGRAPH]**

"What's this about Anna and Cleo about wrecking A [Agnes Glenn] and you? You don't mean in Cleo's Ford by any chance do you?" **[2 PARAGRAPHS]** "Every week brings vacation that much nearer and and [sic] that will mean that we will be together again. Then we can go to Hudson to dance, to shows and picnics and maybe to Thermopolis for a swim. It won't matter much to me just what we do so long as we are together." **[3 PARAGRAPHS]** "With all my love." **[/]** "Johnny" **[/]** "P.S. The phone number is 9025"

**** To Miss Katherine Glenn, Box 35, Riverton, Wyo. (5/5/40, POSTMARKED Laramie, Wyoming 5/6/40, 6:30 PM). Envelope mark: Hotel Shirley-Savoy, Denver Colorado. Addressed from Laramie Wyoming Return address: 1319 Kearney, Laramie, Wyo. "Hellow [sic] Darling," **[/]** "I was very glad you called last night. It was swell to hear your voice and to hear you say that you love me. There was so much to say and it seemed as though we had just started talking when the operator said that time was up." **[3 PARAGRAPHS]**

"I got that pencil I told you about. I was very surprised because I had some doubt, as to whether the letter would get there in time. I really didn't win very much, but maybe next time I might have a chance at something better. I do wish that it had been a pen so I could have passed it on to you, however I have a fountain pen which you can have if you like." **[/]**

"Kelly is feeling a little more relieved now. He passed his flight test for his private ticket yesterday morning. . . ." **[/]** "We were about to buy an airplane last week. We had it figured so that by selling time to the CAA students who had finished their course and wanted to fly more, we would make the plane pay for itself. It would have been swell if we could have made it work. We could have flown home on weekends and even during the week since the trip would have only taken in about two hours. The thing that held us back was the fact that we didn't have the $2500 purchase price." **[1 PARAGRAPH]**

"How did you like 'Gone with the Wind'? I hope that you liked it. I wish now that I had gone to see it—most everyone that I know went to see it, but I thought that $1.12 was a large sum for one show (I was bent nearly double—almost broke—right at that time or I would probably have gone) **[2 PARAGRAPHS]** "Speaking of songs—there certainly are a lot of good new songs. I like the song 'One Cigarette for Two'—it reminds me of the times we have shared a cigarette sitting under the stars together." **[/]** "Sweetheart there are so many things I love about you. . . ." **[/]** "Johnny"

    **** To Miss Katherine Glenn, Box 35, Riverton, Wyo. (5/12/40, Postmarked Laramie, Wyoming 5/13/40, 12:30 PM). Return address: John Sproule 1319 Kearney, Laramie, Wyo. "Kay darling," **[1 PARAGRAPH]** "Military inspection will be held Tuesday and that will finish up military for the year. Of course that does not take into consideration the possibility that the U.S. may get into the battle across the puddle. . . ." **[/]**

"And speaking of driving—you should have seen me driving a golf ball this afternoon. Kellys folks came down for the week end and we went out to the golf course. Glenn, Bert and Thelma were playing and Lewis and I were walking around with them. I played four or five holes—I didn't do terribly bad after the first hole. I had a hard time hitting the ball the first few times but I got so that I could at least [hit] the ball. Maybe we might play some golf this summer? I think it would be a lot of fun. Glenn told me that they were building a golf course at Sand Draw." **[/]** "Lewis, Ray Berryman and I went to see 'It's a Date' with Deanna Durbin. It was a very good show— especially with Deanna Durbin singing, I think she's very good don't you?" **[/]** "No, I'm not smoking Kools anymore but I still have those coupons which I have saved. I guess [I] have to send for something one of these times." **[5 PARAGRAPHS]** "All my love always" **[/]** "Johnny"

    **** To Miss Katherine Glenn, Box 35, Riverton, Wyo. (5/19/40, POSTMARKED Laramie, Wyoming 5/20/40, 12:30 PM). Return Address:

John Sproule 1319 Kearney, Laramie, Wyo. [Enclosed, but not commented upon, are two charge slips from the Mountain States Tel & Tel. Co., one addressed to 'Katherine V Glenn, N 7th St., Riverton Wyoming, and the other, a note in shorthand with no other identifiers.] "Kay darling," **[1 PARAGRAPH]** "With the inspection held last Tue. military was finished up (except for the final exam which we will have this Thur). That gives me a couple more free hours a week. I applied for the advanced course (to get a reserve officers commission) but they turned me down because of my eyes." **[1 PARAGRAPH]**

"So you got in on the victorious side of the elections? And I imagine that if Roosevelt runs again there won't be much question of who will win." **[5 PARAGRAPHS]** "I wish with all my heart that you were going to the frat dance with me. I believe it will be good. I think that it will be the first formal dinner dance here with the dinner served at small tables on the dance floor." **[1 PARAGRAPH]**

"The varsity show was put on Thursday. It's a show written, directed, and put on by the students. It had some rough spots, but I thought that as a whole it was pretty good. They had some good singing and acting, but the part that I liked best was the satirization [sic] of some of the professors here at the university. As an example: the head of the English department is a man by the name of Coulter. He is generally disliked and mostly because of a book which he compiled (wrote would flatter him). He, as the head of the dept., can say what books are to be used as text books and so uses his book as a freshman English text. In this show they had a professor Colder who was an exact takeoff of Coulter. That act mostly brought down the roof—I'd like to know want Coulter thought—everyone really had a good laugh." **[5 PARAGRAPHS]** "All my love to the sweetest person in the world," **[/]** "Johnny."

**** To Miss Katherine Glenn, Box 35, Riverton, Wyo. (5/27/40, Postmarked Laramie, Wyoming 5/28/40, 12:30 PM). Return Address: John Sproule 1319 Kearney, Laramie, Wyo. "Kay darling," **[/]** "I should be home in about two weeks." **[1 PARAGRAPH]** "The dinner dance last Friday was very good I thought—if you had been with me it would have been perfect." **[2 PARAGRAPHS]** "I can hardly wait to be with you again, darling, 'cause I love you so much it hurts to be away from you." **[/]** "All my love and kisses," **[/]** "Johnny"

   **** To Miss Katherine Glenn, Box 35, Riverton, Wyo. (6/3/40, "Monday night June 3," POSTMARKED Laramie, Wyo. 6/4/40, 6:30 PM). Return Address: 1319 Kearney, Laramie, Wyo. "Hello darling," **[/]** "Only one more week till I will be with you. Kelly's folks are coming down and I expect that we will be home Mon (the 10th)—so in precisely one week I hope to be holding you in my arms." **[2 PARAGRAPHS]** "Avec tout mon cour, bonne amie," **[/]** "Johnny"

   **** To Miss Katherine Glenn, "Hotel Townsend, Casper, Wyo." (6/26/40, Postmarked 6/27/40, 6:30 AM) Return Address: Box 1765, Riverton, Wyo. "Kay darling," **[1 PARAGRAPH]** "I'm very happy that you are having a good time. Of course I miss you, but then you won't be gone nearly as long as I was." **[/]** "There hasn't been anything exciting going o in Riverton—same old town." **[2 PARAGRAPHS]** "Remember I love you sweetheart" **[/]** "Johnny"

Chapter 3. Boardinghouse Hasher— September 1940 to December 1940

JHS relocates to what will be his final residence at Laramie, namely, the boarding house operated by Mrs. Fred Buchholz [aka Mrs. Buck] where JHS undertakes a second job at this residence to pay for his meals. For breakfast and dinner, he sets the table along with doing dishes and general clean up—duties which he short-hands as "hashing." Finances remain uppermost as JHS continues to labor in the Bee Lab and finds it necessary to withdraw from pursuing a fraternity owing to the cost—and from track owing to the time. Apart from classwork, relationship maintenance looms large for JHS, and his few leisure-time pleasures represent a guilty diversion from the scholastic load. The military draft now also looms, with a sporadic attention to politics.

 **** To Miss Katherine Glenn, Riverton Wyo. (1:30 Friday, Postmarked Rawlins, 9/20/40, 3:00 PM). Stationary from "The Ferris Hotel, Rollins, Wyoming"; envelope from "Hotel Lassen, Wichita, Kansas"; "Hi Darling," **[/]** "I wonder what you are doing now—I'm sitting here in the hotel writing to you. I got packed last night (took me till about 4:45. I had breakfast and was waiting for my ride at 5:00 (the driver overslept!) and it was 6:30 or so before he came down—I met him at the bridge—we got into Rawlins about 11:15—I've had lunch, bought my bus ticket and am ready for the bus which will leave for Laramie in about 3 hours." **[5 PARAGRAPHS]** "Remember that I love you with all my heart, darling—I'm longing for the time when I will see you again." **[/]** "Your sweetheart" **[/]** "J."

 **** To Miss Katherine Glenn, Box 35, Riverton, Wyo. (9/24/40, stamp and postmark torn out). Return Address: 1309 Kearney, Laramie, Wyo. "Kay darling," **[1 PARAGRAPH]** "The night I got here (Friday) I stayed with Lewis because one of the fellows folks was here for the night and had the bed which I was to occupy. I called Mrs. Buck (short for Buchholz) that I wouldn't be down till Saturday (which I would rather have done—I'd really rather have stayed with you) so she wasn't expecting me.

So I left my things here and went over with Lewis and stayed that night. He was supposed to get up at 4:30 am and go out and fly, but he had a sore foot (a blister on his heel got infected—I think it's under control now) and so he woke me up (about 4:45) and I went over to the Engineering Building on the campus where he was supposed to catch a ride out to the airport and told them that he was unable to go out and fly. When I got back we both went back to bed and slept till about 3:00 that afternoon." **[1 PARAGRAPH]**

"I have been getting settled and I think I have things pretty well lined out now. I started right in to work for Mrs. Buck, I wait table and wash dishes for my board. I don't think the work is very hard and who knows I may become a very expert dish washer. Mrs. Buck is very easy to work for—she talks a mile a minute all the time, but if I am busy I don't pay much attention to what she is saying—I just say yes or no according to what I think she is talking about." **[/]** "I haven't got any other job yet, but I'm going to try very hard—I think I've got a prospect of one." **[/]**

"I've been working on my schedule and I have it worked out now to where I'll be taking about 15 hr.—10 hours of Engineering subjects, 3 hours of French and 2 hours of English. I don't know what my fees will be yet but as a guess I'd say between $30 and $35. However I don't think I'll have to buy many books . . . ." **[1 PARAGRAPH]** "I sure hope that you can come down for Homecoming—that would be the swellest thing, and say if Helen actually doesn't want Kelly to know about her wanting to come down I won't say a word. Anyway Lewis might not be here then—if he finishes this flying course and gets a chance to go farther ahead with his flying someplace else he would probably quit school and keep on with his flying." **[2 PARAGRAPHS]** "With all my heart" **[/]** "Johnny"

    **** To Miss Katherine Glenn, Box 35, Riverton, Wyo. (9/30/40, Postmarked 10/1/40, 5:30 PM). Return Address: J. Sproule, 1309 Kearney, Laramie, Wyo. "Sweetheart," **[6 PARAGRAPHS]** "I didn't tell you about the old fellow that I met on the bus when I came from Rawlins did I? He was a queer old guy, but he sure liked to talk. He got to talking about all the places he had been and then he showed me a bunch of old coins he had collected. In among these he had a bunch of Indian head pennies. Some one mentioned that Indian head pennies were worth two or three cents and so I offered him a dime for three and he sold them to me. So now I have three i. h. pennies. I'd have bought some more, but that's all he wanted to sell." **[2 PARAGRAPHS]**

"I'm thinking of dropping out of the fraternity at least for a while. I was up to a meeting this evening and I didn't enjoy it much and then there are the dues I would have to pay. I could probably join again later if I wanted to." **[/]** "I don't have anything definite on an additional job, but I think that I'll get one lined up though. I wouldn't mind having another job to handle and I think that I have plenty of time." **[/]** "Love and kisses to my darling Kay," **[/]** "Johnny"

   **** To Miss Katherine Glenn, Box 35, Riverton, Wyo. ("Wed. Night", Postmarked 10/3/40, 12:30 PM). Return Address: J. Sproule, 1309 Kearney, Laramie, Wyo. "Darling," **[2 PARAGRAPHS]** "I've been hearing the song 'Blue-Berry Hill' lately and I remember that you liked it. Hearing it brings me the memory of all the times I've met my thrill—no matter where or when I meet you, when I see you or hear your voice or feel the touch of your hand, the thrill is always there. It comes up welling up in my heart and—oh darling, I love you so terribly much; nothing else in the world matters to me except you." **[/]** ". . . Good night precious and here are the kisses (each cross represents 1,000,000 kisses)" [about 200 X's are given] **[/]** "Your loving sweetheart Johnny."

   **** To Miss Katherine Glenn, Box 35, Riverton, Wyo. (10/7/40, 11:45 AM, Postmarked 10/8/40, 12:30 PM). Return Address: John Sproule, 1309 Kearney, Laramie, Wyoming. "Darling," **[/]** ". . . Anyway it's great to hear from you even if the mail is held up a day. And thanks <u>heaps</u> and <u>heaps</u> for the carton of cigarettes—it's swell to have someone who is thinking of you." **[/]** "Well, sweetheart, it is 10 minutes till 12:00 now and so I'll have to go up and get busy—set the table, wait on the table, eat, and wash the dishes." **[3 PARAGRAPHS]** [JHS includes a matrix of his schedule: classes in the morning, calculus, engineering, French, "Forge Shop" on 1:00

to 4:00 Tuesday and "Machine Shop" on 1:00 to 3:00 Friday.] **[3 PARAGRAPHS]** "All my love and kisses" **[/]** "Johnny"

  **** To Miss Katherine Glenn, Box 35, Riverton, Wyo. (10/12/40, Postmarked 10/14/40, 5:00 PM). Return Address: J. Sproule, 1309 Kearney Laramie, Wyo. "Darling," **[3 PARAGRAPHS]** "I guess Lewis [Kelly] and Ray [Berryman] will be over this evening after a while. The fraternity initiation are being held tonight. Lewis and Ray want me to go active. Ray offered to lend me the initiation fee ($15.00) but I can't afford to join so I'll pass up their offer. As I said they will probably be over to give me another talk, but I'll refuse again." **[1 PARAGRAPH]**

"The songs you sent me are all so swell. The ones I like best are <u>Only Forever</u> and <u>Blueberry Hill</u>, but they are all good." **[/]** "I'm going to be looking for you right up to the last minute. And then if you can't come down to 'homecoming' I will be terribly disappointed, but I'll realize that if you can't come it was just impossible to get away. O and if you can't come and want to call me the phone number is 4443 [and on the envelope KVS has written "4443"]. Talking to you over the telephone would be the next best thing to seeing you. . . ." **[2 PARAGRAPHS]** "Remember my heart is yours" **[/]** "Johnny"

  **** To Miss Katherine Glenn, Box 35, Riverton, Wyo. (no time given, Postmarked 10/15/40, 12:30 PM). Return Address: J. Sproule, 1309 Kearney, Laramie, Wyo. [Within the primary envelope is another envelope marked "To be opened just before you go to bed."] This letter: "Precious sweetheart" [with "I LOVE YOU" written down the center of the page, one letter under another; there follows four lines of French with English translation underneath]. **[/]** "Johnny"

  **** To Miss Katherine Glenn, Box 35, Riverton, Wyo. (10/19/40, Postmarked 10/21/40, 12:30 PM). Return Address: J. Sproule, 1309 Kearney, Laramie, Wyo. "My precious sweetheart," **[/]** ". . . I haven't settled down to study before 11:30 any night this week—in fact I haven't been to bed before 2:00 all this week. I should get to bed earlier, but I haven't been getting up until 8:00 or a quarter till. It all boils down to the fact that I can't get along without you—its heaven to be with you and h- to be away from you." **[1 PARAGRAPH]** "Even if you're working nights you're probably asleep by now—its 2:15. I was over to Lewis's this evening. I came home about an hour ago and worked a little math and now I'm writing to my darling." **[/]**

"My days are all so much the same—I get up, eat, go to school, wait tables and eat, go to school or to work, then wash dishes, try to study and then go back to bed—sometimes I do some little extra thing, go over to see Lewis or go downtown or see a show. Generally speaking, though, my days are all much the same." **[/]**

"I signed up for a gun Wed. (I mean I registered as required by the draft law) I don't think that any one person has much chance of having his name drawn—right away, anyhow. I think probably that if I am 'drafted' I can get a postponement of my examination (physical, to see if I'm fit enough to march around) because of the fact that I'm going to college. I don't think that they will let me in anyway (because of my eyes) at least I couldn't get into the advanced military course last spring." **[/]**

"Well now as to specifying at least ten articles that I would like for my birthday—I'll see how many I can think of—necktie, socks, shirt, handkerchiefs, belt, suspenders, billfold, cigarettes—that's all I can think of. I really don't want anything in particular—you have always given me such nice things before that I really don't think you need any suggestions. I'm going to give you one suggestion though—the thing that I would like very very much—my notion of a perfect birthday—would be to have you come down to see me. What do you think of that? The thing I'm afraid of is that it will cost too much." **[2 PARAGRAPHS]** "With all my heart" **[/]** "Johnny"

**** To Miss Katherine Glenn, Box 35, Riverton, Wyo. (10/21/40, Postmarked 10/22/40, 12:30 PM). Return Address: J. Sproule, 1309 Kearney, Laramie, Wyo. "Hi darling," **[1 PARAGRAPH]** "No, I won't have to go to school during 'homecoming.' It falls on Saturday and Sunday. All I'll have to do during that time is wait table and wash a few dishes which won't take long and even if I were on school days—I don't have too many classes. It's about 15 blocks to the Connor Hotel, but the most important thing is whether or not you'll be able to come—you can better decide where you'd like to stay after you arrive." **[/]**

"Well at least the waiting and washing dishes seems easier than it was at first. Whether or not I'm becoming expert is a matter that is open to question. But then this experience might help me get some other job sometimes. You never know what things are going to help you the most." **[2 PARAGRAPHS]** "I don't think that a fraternity is as important as some other things and so it looked like a frat. was one of the things that I could get along without. (That sentence looks a little screwy)" **[/]** "Lewis passed his test for a restricted commercial pilot's license the other day. I guess he'll keep on going to school although some of the other guys who were taking the course are trying to get in the army air corps." **[2 PARAGRAPHS]** "All my love to my sweetheart" **[/]** "Johnny"

　　　**** To Miss Katherine Glenn, Box 35, Riverton, Wyo. (10/24/40, Postmarked 10/25/40, 4:30 PM). Return Address: J. Sproule, 1309 Kearney, Laramie, Wyo. "Darling" **[4 PARAGRAPHS]** "We're translating 'The Three Musketeers' in French class—of course it is a much reduced edition. I translated about 10 pages for tomorrow's assignment. I sure don't like to get behind because then we have write out the lesson instead of translating a paragraph or two in class. We always have to translate the whole assignment, but it is not as tedious as having to write the whole thing out to hand in." **[2 PARAGRAPHS]** "You have all my heart for ever and ever." **[/]** "Good night darling" **[/]** "Johnny" **[/]** "XXXXX"

　　　**** To Miss Katherine Glenn, Box 35, Riverton, Wyo. (10/28/40, Postmarked 10/29/40, 12:30 PM). Return Address: J. Sproule, 1309 Kearney, Laramie, Wyo. "My darling," **[1 PARAGRAPH]** "When I read that you were sure that you could come down it seemed about too good to be true. It will be perfect to see you. I miss you so very, very much that seeing you will be the greatest joy I can imagine. How are you going to come down? And about staying at the hotel—my landlady has an upstairs bedroom empty and you could stay there. Whatever you wish of course, will be what is done. I'll gladly walk down to the hotel if you prefer to stay there." **[2 PARAGRAPHS]**

"We have some great political arguments here at the house. We argue back and forth about everything political. I'll bet that Ruth sure hates to see anyone turn from Republican to Democrat." **[4 PARAGRAPHS]** "Forever yours," **[/]** "Johnny" [There follows a discussion of how many millions and millions of kisses he will be wanting to give—the number is 9 followed by 45 zeroes]

**** To Miss Katherine Glenn, Box 35, Riverton, Wyo. (10/30/40, Postmarked 11/1/40, 9:30 AM). Return Address: J. Sproule, 1309 Kearney, Laramie, Wyo. "Kay darling," **[2 PARAGRAPHS]** "In a few days now I'll probably be having to fill out the questionnaire which the conscription board will send to me—my number was drawn 139th & so I'd guess I'm no. 139 now instead of 128. It's hard to know just what number is the one that's important. How many eligible conscriptees registered at Riverton?" **[3 PARAGRAPHS]** "It does seem like most everyone up there is getting married. One sometimes wonders if the draft has had anything to do with it." **[3 PARAGRAPHS]** "Millions of kisses to the sweetest girl in all the world." **[3 PARAGRAPHS]** "yr. obt. svt." **[/]** "Johnny"

**** To Miss Katherine Glenn, Box 35, Riverton, Wyo. (11/3/40, Postmarked 11/4/40, 11:30 AM). Return Address: J. Sproule, 1309 Kearney, Laramie, Wyo. "Kay darling," **[/]** ". . . I have a hunch that Roosevelt may eke out a close victory—but then Wilkie might win by a narrow margin. You will be able to confirm this prediction by the radio or newspapers shortly after you get this letter. I haven't yet received an absentee ballot unless it comes tomorrow I guess I won't get to vote. Unless perhaps I could go down to the polls here and swear that I am a qualified voter—I don't know just how that works. . . Kelly and I went to a dance last night—it was a small affair. I had a good enough time I guess, but nothing that I do seems really fun, because you're not with me. . ." **[/]** "One of the fellows brought a guitar with him when he came and once in a while in the evening I pick it and try to pick out a tune. I haven't learned much about playing a guitar yet but I might be able to chord a few simple tunes if I keep at it long enough." **[1 PARAGRAPH]** "All my love and kisses forever" **[/]** "Johnny" [Following are some romantic PSs.]

 **** To Miss Katherine Glenn, Box 35, Riverton, Wyo. (Undated, Postmarked 11/4/40, 11:30 AM). Return Address: J. Sproule, 1309 Kearney, Laramie, Wyo. The whole letter is as follows, written in large cursive on one side: "Darling, I love you Johnny"

 **** To Miss Katherine Glenn, Box 35, Riverton, Wyo. (11/4/40, Postmarked 11/5/40, 4:30 PM). Return Address: J. Sproule, 1309 Kearney, Laramie, Wyo. "Hello darling," **[1 PARAGRAPH]** "This is the last letter I'll write before we find out who won the election and so this is my last chance to make a stab at predicting a winner—I'll pick Wilkie by a 10% margin. . . . Boy, I won't be able to open my mouth down here among my room mates if Wilkie doesn't win. We had it hot and thick over politics, atomic energy and a number of other subjects this evening. . . ." **[4 PARAGRAPHS]** "Your devoted Johnny"

 **** To Miss Katherine Glenn, Box 35, Riverton, Wyo. (11/11/40, Postmarked 11/12/40, 12:30 AM). Return Address: J. Sproule, 1309 Kearney, Laramie, Wyo. "Darling," **[/]** "I will always remember this weekend. It was such a swell weekend. Having you with me is always the nicest thing I can imagine. I couldn't possibly have had a nicer birthday present than a weekend with you" [i.e., KVS came down for Homecoming]. **[1 PARAGRAPH]** "But it won't be so long now till Thanksgiving or if I can't come home then it won't be as long as from September to October. Your letters will make that time seem shorter and so all in all we won't be apart as long as we were from Sept. till now." **[1 PARAGRAPH]** "Yours forever" **[/]** "Johnny"

 **** To Miss Katherine Glenn, Box 35, Riverton, Wyo. (11/12/40, Postmarked 11/13/40, 12:30 AM). Return Address: J. Sproule, 1309 Kearney, Laramie, Wyo. "Sweetheart," **[/]** "I was out waiting for the mail man to come when he brought your letter this noon. I came right down stairs and read it—I always feel swell when I have a letter from you. When I came home from forge shop this afternoon, I read it again and now just before starting to write to you this evening I read your letter again—I like to read all your letters over and over, they are always so swell." **[1 PARAGRAPH]**

"Do you remember that lighted W on top of the Engineering Building? Kelly and I and a couple of other fellows went up and took it down this afternoon. Boy was it cold up there! We had to take the light bulbs out and then lay the W part down on the roof. As I said, it was sure cold up there where the wind could really get at you." **[1 PARAGRAPH]** "I finished my French for tomorrow a while ago. I was over to Lewis' for a little while this evening. I took along a couple of books—I thought I might study over there but I didn't get much studying done so I came home and finished it (well most of it anyway). And so now it's two o'clock. **[1 PARAGRAPH]** "All my love and kisses" **[/]** "Johnny"

  **** To Miss Katherine Glenn, Box 35, Riverton, Wyo. ("Wednesday night"), Postmarked 11/15/40, 12:30 AM). Return Address: J. Sproule, 1309 Kearney, Laramie, Wyo. "Darling," **[/]** "It's nearly bed time, but I've been sitting here thinking of you so I'm writing to let you know it." **[3 PARAGRAPHS]** "All my love forever" **[/]** "Johnny"

  **** To Miss Katherine Glenn, Box 35, Riverton, Wyo. (11/18/40, Postmarked 11/19/40, 5:30 PM). Return Address: J. Sproule, 1309 Kearney, Laramie, Wyo. "Kay darling," **[1 PARAGRAPH]** "As things look now it looks like I'll not be able to come home for Thanksgiving. I would like very much to come home for Thanksgiving and Christmas. . . . Object: to see you, of course. . . . But I thought that since Christmas vacation is not too long after Thanksgiving vacation, and since we will have such a longer vacation at Christmas, it would be best to come home at Christmas since I cannot be there both times. . . ." **[9 PARAGRAPHS]** "Forever yours," **[/]** "Johnny"

  **** To Miss Katherine Glenn, Box 35, Riverton, Wyo. (11/22/40, Postmarked 11/25/40, 12:30 PM). Return Address: J. Sproule, 1309 Kearney, Laramie, Wyo. "Kay darling," **[3 PARAGRAPHS]** "Mrs. Buck left for Missouri yesterday afternoon. Her father died. I think she will be gone about a week. While she is gone I am taking care of the house—keeping it clean—seeing that things don't freeze up and that sort of thing. Also I am doing my own cooking—the other borders will have to eat somewhere else while she is gone." **[/]** "Kenny Baker of radio fame will give a concert here Monday night. I'd like to take you. . . ." **[/]** "Since I can't take you to the concert I probably won't go. . . ." **[4 PARAGRAPHS]** "Kisses for my sweetheart" [with drawing of a heart] **[/]** "Johnny"

 **** To Miss Katherine Glenn, Box 35, Riverton, Wyo. (11/24/40, Postmarked 11/25/40, 12:30 PM). Return Address: J. Sproule, 1309 Kearney, Laramie, Wyo. "Kay darling," **[5 PARAGRAPHS** of romantic sentiments] "All my love and kisses forever and ever" **[/]** "Johnny"

 **** To Miss Katherine Glenn, Box 35, Riverton, Wyo. (11/24/40, Postmarked 11/26/40, 10:30 AM). Return Address: J. Sproule, 1309 Kearney, Laramie, Wyo. "My darling," **[4 PARAGRAPHS]** "I worked this afternoon, cleaning up some supers up at the honey house. It was very cold on my feet—the cement floor was not in the least warm. And then the atmosphere was brisk too, so I was cold all over when I got home." **[2 PARAGRAPHS]** "All my love and kisses forever" **[/]** "Johnny"

 **** To Miss Katherine Glenn, Box 35, Riverton, Wyo. (11/29/40, Postmarked 11/30/40, 2:30 PM). Return Address: J. Sproule, 1309 Kearney Laramie, Wyo. "Kay darling," **[2 PARAGRAPHS]** ". . . The Engineer's Ball was tonight. I imagine that it was a very nice dance. I would like to have gone if you had been here to go with me." **[/]**

"This afternoon Kelly and I bought a couple of model airplane kits and so now we are working on one of them—that is we worked on one this afternoon for a while and then a little more this evening. We decided to break loose and see a show. On Friday nights they have what is called Student Night—the university students can get in to the show for 25¢ if they present their activity tickets. Two bits is more within my means than 45¢. We saw 'Seven Sinners' with Marlena Dietrich. I didn't care for her much. I guess the show wasn't worth any more than two-bits." **[3 PARAGRAPHS]** "With all love" **[/]** "Johnny"

**** To Miss Katherine Glenn, Box 35, Riverton, Wyo. (12/1/40, Postmarked 12/2/40, 4:30 PM). Return Address: J. Sproule, 1309 Kearney, Laramie, Wyo. "Hi darling," **[2 PARAGRAPHS]** "That job I was telling you about is what I had to fill out the blanks for. The job is under the Federal Dept. of Agriculture—even though I am doing the same kind of [bee keeping] work [in the UW Entomology and Agricultural Lab] as I do under [Harold] Gilbert—and so I have all these blanks to fill out. I don't know why but I filled out three sets, all the same. I had to recall where I have lived for the past five years, what schooling I have had, what jobs I have held (wages, kind of work, and length of job) and that sort of thing. My title for this job will be Jr. Scientific Aid." **[/]**

"If the telephone operators have a party I would gladly accept the invitation to accompany you. I guess if it wasn't any good we could leave early. I want to have most of my vacation to spend just with you. . . ." **[/]** "What measurements did you want? If you told me that perhaps I could guess what you are going to give me so I'll just put them all down, how's that? Shirt: neck 16, sleeve 35; sox: 11½; shoes: 8½ D; necktie: no bow ties; trousers: waist 33, inseam 35; coat 40 or 41: gloves: 8½ or 9. If I've left any out you can ask me. And how's about writing yours down? I'm thinking you take size 12, but I'm not sure just what all that applies to besides dresses. . . ." **[2 PARAGRAPHS]** [In this paragraph JHS draws an elongated X across the page occupying the space of about two lines to signify a long kiss] "All my love always" **[/]** "Johnny"

**** To Miss Katherine Glenn, Box 35, Riverton, Wyo. (12/5/40, Postmarked 12/6/40, 11:30 AM). Return Address: J. Sproule, 1309 Kearney, Laramie, Wyo. "Hi darling—" [**5 PARAGRAPHS** of generalized romantic expression] "All my love always" **[/]** "Johnny"

**** To Miss Katherine Glenn, Box 35, Riverton, Wyo. (12/8/40, Postmarked 12/9/40, 12:30 PM). Return Address: J. Sproule, 1309 Kearney, Laramie, Wyo. "Kay darling" **[/]** ". . . I'm unfortunate enough to have a test on the last day of test week—that is Friday the 20th. By that time most everyone else will have finished and be home so I don't know how I'll come home. I haven't talked to Gilbert to see if he is going to Sheridan (so I could ride to Shoshone), ..." **[6 PARAGRAPHS]** "With all my love" **[/]** "Johnny" [JHS includes PSSs with romantic expressions.]

**** To Miss Katherine Glenn, Box 35, Riverton, Wyo. (12/13/40, Postmarked 12/14/40, 11:30 AM). Return Address: J. Sproule, 1309 Kearney, Laramie, Wyo. "Hi darling—" **[3 PARAGRAPHS]** "If you would like [to go] to the Job's Daughter's dance, then it would please me to go so I'll leave it up to you—you know more about who will be there and that sort of thing." **[3 PARAGRAPHS]** "Yours forever," **[/]** "Johnny"

**** To Miss Katherine Glenn, Box 35, Riverton, Wyo. (12/16/40, Postmarked 12/17/40, 11:30 AM). Return Address: J. Sproule, 1309 Kearney, Laramie, Wyo. "Kay darling," **[5 PARAGRAPHS** of generalized romantic expression] "All my love, precious!" **[/]** "Johnny" [Following are xxxx's as expressions for kisses]

**** To Miss Katherine Glenn, Box 35, Riverton, Wyo. (12/27/40, Postmarked 12/27/40, 11:00 PM). Return Address: J. Sproule, 1309 Kearney, Laramie, Wyo. [The stationery and envelope are from the Ferris Hotel, Rawlins, Wyoming, which includes a photograph of the hotel.] "Darling," **[/]** "Already I'm missing you so terribly much—though, as you can tell by the stationery, I'm only about halfway to Laramie." **[/]** "We left about six twenty and of course got here much too early for the bus—about five hours too early (we had to come early so that Cliff could get back today) . . . ." **[/]** "Besides the usual unpleasant wind here, today it is snowing. Not a great deal, but it is still nasty. Last fall when I was here it was raining—now it's snow and always the wind. I hate this town. Perhaps if I hadn't just parted from you every thing would not seem so bleak." **[3 PARAGRAPHS]** "Remember precious, I love you." **[/]** "With all my heart forever," **[/]** "Johnny."

**** To Miss Katherine Glenn, Box 35, Riverton, Wyo. (12/29/40, Postmarked 12/30/40, 12:30 PM). Return Address: J. Sproule, 1309 Kearney, Laramie, Wyo. "Darling," **[1 PARAGRAPH]** "How can I tell you how much I miss you? Wherever I am or whatever I do I miss you—walking along, I miss your firm steps beside mine—seeing a show I miss the touch of your hand, and afterward getting a snack somewhere. I miss your eyes across the table—while I'm sitting here I feel incomplete because you're not in my lap. I'm so lonely without you, my precious." **[1 PARAGRAPH]**

"I got my grades when I got here—they were not as good as I thought they were going to be. They averaged 2.1 and I did get a 2 in French and a 1 in English. I am going to bear down a little harder next quarter and try to get a better set of grades." **[1 PARAGRAPH]** "Goodnight, sweetheart." **[/]** "All my love forever," **[/]** "Johnny"

Chapter 4. Classes, Commitments, Conscription, and Catholicism—January 1941 to June 1941

JHS describes classes and vicissitudes of military conscription, along with his commenting on popular pursuits including friends, flying, and film-critical reports. We find a continuing imperative to woo and reassure an absent sweetheart which segues into a new commitment to Catholicism—this a condition for marriage set by KVS.

**** To Miss Katherine Glenn, Box 35, Riverton, Wyo. (1/1/41, Postmarked 1/2/41, 2:00 PM). Return Address: J. Sproule, 1309 Kearney, Laramie, Wyo. "Happy New Year darling," **[/]** "... Berryman and I went to see 'The Thief of Bagdad' New Year's eve. It was a fairly nice show, but not nearly so nice as if you had been with me. ..." **[5 PARAGRAPHS]** "Goodnight precious." **[/]** "X X X X X X X" **[/]** "Johnny"

**** To Miss Katherine Glenn, Box 35, Riverton, Wyo. (1/9/40 [1941], Postmarked 1/8/41, 12:30 PM). Return Address: J. Sproule, 1309 Kearney, Laramie, Wyo. "Darling," **[1 PARAGRAPH]** "I have been busier this last week than I ever have I think. The 2, 3, 4, 5 and 6th I worked 12 to 15 hours per night and then all day yesterday. I had registration to do + starting to wash dishes etc and then today classes started right in and I had classes most of the day. Anyway I've been pretty busy. I had an idea that I wouldn't mind working nights, but I've changed my mind— ..." **[/]**

"I registered for 16 hours this quarter and then I'm going to take another 3 hours by correspondence. This schedule plus my jobs may keep me busy this quarter, but I hate to be taking such a few hours as I did last quarter." **[2 PARAGRAPHS]** "Remember my precious, you are everything in the world to me." **[/]** "All my love forever" **[/]** "Johnny"

**** To Miss Katherine Glenn, Box 35, Riverton, Wyo. (1/10/41, Postmarked 1/10/41, 3:30 PM). Return Address: J. Sproule, 1309 Kearney, Laramie, Wyo. "Hi darling" **[1 PARAGRAPH]** "I got my conscription questionnaire the other day to fill out and return in five days. I have till Monday to get it in but I am going to get it in today and have it over with. I believe that they just use the questionnaire to classify you according to when you will be called (if you are). It was full of questions as to what you are earning; if you are going to school or not; have you any dependents; are you a conscientious objector and things like that." **[/]** "I've got to go down town and have those papers witnessed and I want to get some socks and things . . . ." **[/]**

"Lewis and I might fly over to Cheyenne in the morning. He wants to fly a little while and since it is only 50 miles to Cheyenne he might fly over there and back and take me along. I sure wish we were flying up to home instead." **[1 PARAGRAPH]** "Love and kisses to my darling" **[/]** "Johnny"

    **** To Miss Katherine Glenn, Box 35, Riverton, Wyo. (1/11/41, Postmarked 1/12/41, ? PM). Return Address: J. Sproule, 1309 Kearney, Laramie, Wyo. "Kay darling," **[/]** "The first week of the quarter is over now and things don't look as bad as they did. After one can get into a new routine the new quarter is always much like the next one." **[/]** ". . . Kelly and I flew over to Cheyenne this morning. We flew around over Laramie for a little while and then flew over to Cheyenne and back. It was the first time I had been in a plane for a year or so. I flew for a while on the way back and it was very clear that I hadn't flown for quite a while—after a few minutes though, it was much better." **[/]** "I think that perhaps I might go skating tomorrow afternoon; if all this good weather we have been enjoying hasn't ruined the ice, that is." **[2 PARAGRAPHS]** "Yours forever and ever," **[/]** "Johnny"

    **** To Miss Katherine Glenn, Box 35, Riverton, Wyo. (1/15/41, Postmarked 1/15/41, 3:30 PM). Return Address: J. Sproule, 1309 Kearney, Laramie, Wyo. "Darling," **[1 PARAGRAPH]** "I had classes this morning and then a lab this afternoon and then this evening I have tried to study and haven't gotten much done. Kelly and Berryman went to the 'Ballet Russe De Monte Carlo' up at the auditorium this evening—I didn't think it would be worth $1.00 so I stayed home. I think perhaps I'll start going skating a couple of times a week—it is a lot of fun." **[1 PARAGRAPH]** "I think that perhaps I'd better get an English lesson done and then go to bed. I don't think I ever get to bed before 12:30 or 1:00 o'clock—seems like I just can' get around to it before that." **[1 PARAGRAPH]** "All my love always" **[/]** "Johnny"

**** To Miss Katherine Glenn, Box 35, Riverton, Wyo. (1/19/41, Postmarked 1/20/41, 12:30 PM). Return Address: J. Sproule, 1309 Kearne Laramie, Wyo. "Kay darling," **[5 PARAGRAPHS]** "You know, the pictures that come here are pretty poor most of the time. Whenever I feel like going to see a show it's usually one I wouldn't go to see if I could get in fo nothing. I saw 'Boomtown', but we had to pay extra. I saw 'The Thief of Bagdad' new year's eve—it wasn't so bad but it wasn't too good either. Well, like I said we don't get good pictures here very often." **[2 PARAGRAPHS]** "All my love, sweetheart—" **[/]** "Johnny"

**** To Miss Katherine Glenn, Box 35, Riverton, Wyo. (1/22/41, Postmarked 1/22/41, 12:30 PM). Return Address: J. Sproule, 1309 Kearne Laramie, Wyo. "Kay darling," **[1 PARAGRAPH]** "Yesterday the school played host to a group of legislators (state). They swarmed all over the place. I was in the soils lab yesterday afternoon and every once in a while group would come in and look around. Some senator (I didn't catch his name) came up to me and I explained a bunch of equipment and experiments to him (some of stuff I had never used before, but I made hir think I knew all about it)." **[5 PARAGRAPHS]** "All my love forever," **[/]** "Johnny"

**** To Miss Katherine Glenn, Box 35, Riverton, Wyo. (1/28/41, Postmarked 1/28/41, 12:30 PM). Return Address: J. Sproule, 1309 Kearne Laramie, Wyo. "Kay darling," **[2 PARAGRAPHS]** "I did drop things for a while and go to see 'Comrad X' with Clark Gable and Hedy Lamarr. It was real good show—a lot of 'laffs'." **[2 PARAGRAPHS]** "All my love and kisse always," **[/]** "Johnny"

**** To Miss Katherine Glenn, Box 35, Riverton, Wyo. (1/31/41, Postmarked 2/1/41, 12:30 PM). Return Address: J. Sproule, 1309 Kearney Laramie, Wyo. "Kay darling," **[/]** "I've read your last letter over and ove

again. I know that you used to have doubts, but I thought that they were all settled now. Don't you know that I agree with you on the question of becoming a Catholic?" **[/]** "You say 'I don't really know exactly where we are'. Have you forgotten that we love each other? Becoming a Catholic is just a question of when I'll do it; just as it's a question of time until I'll have a decent job. As I see it, time is all that stands between us." **[/]** "What ever made you feel that I didn't want to go to mass with you? I wanted to go with you and I stayed home only because I really didn't feel very well."
[1 PARAGRAPH]

"I know that it is very unpleasant to be separated. I am always wishing that all our separations were over and that we would never be apart again. The only reason that I'm away so much is that I'm trying to get the qualifications necessary to hold a decent job—you understand that don't you?" **[2 PARAGRAPHS]** "All my love always," **[/]** "Johnny."

**** To Miss Katherine Glenn, Box 35, Riverton, Wyo. (2/3/41, Postmarked 2/4/41, 12:30 PM). Return Address: J. Sproule, 1309 Kearney, Laramie, Wyo. "My precious darling," **[/]** "I hope that all your fears are settled now. You know, when I got your last letter it had been nine days since I had heard from you. That's the longest time I have been without a letter from you for a long long time." **[/]** "And then sweetheart, when I read your letter my heart nearly stopped. You sounded as though—how shall I say it?—almost as though you wished we hadn't fallen in love with each other. I hope my letter was able to explain clearly that there was really no reason for you to have any fear." **[1 PARAGRAPH]**

"I've been working on one of my notebooks and on a speech (for a public speaking class at three in the morning) this evening. The notebook is due Wednesday and so I'll probably finish it tomorrow night. From the look of things I'll probably be fully occupied all week." **[/]** "Darling, I hope I get a letter from you tomorrow, saying that all your doubts have vanished and vanished for good." **[/]** "You know, my precious, that I've loved you with all my heart all this time—that I'm completely and entirely in love with you now—and that I always will be in love with you!" **[/]** "With all my love and kisses" **[/]** "Johnny"

**** To Miss Katherine Glenn, Box 35, Riverton, Wyo. (2/6/41, Postmarked 2/7/41, 12:30 PM). Return Address: J. Sproule, 1309 Kearney, Laramie, Wyo. "My darling Kay," [/] "I feel swell since you wrote that all your worries are over. I know that sometimes a person does want reassurances, and, precious, you will always get them from me. I love you so very much sweetheart!" [/] "If I could be with you all the time—be able to talk to you and hold you in my arms—these doubts would never arise. That's the trouble with being separated. Even though we are apart just now you are to remember that I love you and nothing will ever change that. Whenever you feel blue, darling just say to yourself—'Johnny loves me.' Because if I were able to be with you I would be whispering to you 'I love you Kay.'" **[2 PARAGRAPHS]**

"It's too bad about Sam Chopping getting killed—from the sound of things they weren't being too careful and it isn't very safe to crash into something." **[1 PARAGRAPH]** "Lewis is going to quit school here and go to Boeing Air School at Oakland, Calif. He will train there for five months and then start in as a copilot working for United Airlines. He is going to be able to get a degree by changing from Electrical Engineering to General Engineering—he has enough hours and the credits that he now has will qualify him for a General Engineering degree. He will be going to California about the first of March." **[4 PARAGRAPHS]** "Kisses for my sweetheart," [/] "Johnny" [Enclosed in the envelope with this letter is one in KVS's handwriting dated February 9, 1941 which is not completed and which evidently wasn't sent. It's very romantic, saying how much she loves JHS.]

**** To Miss Katherine Glenn, Box 35, Riverton, Wyo. (2/12/41, Postmarked 2/12/41, 12:30 PM). Return Address: J. Sproule, 1309 Kearney, Laramie, Wyo. "Kay darling," [/] "I have felt so very swell the last few days—you know why? Because I've had letters from you and that makes all the difference in the world. You write such swell letters, my darling." [/] "I had the last of my mid term tests today (or rather yesterday since it's 2 am. now; I remembered that when I wrote the date at the top) and so I felt like relaxing this evening. I didn't do a bit of studying—just fooling around with Kelly and another fellow. I don't often go through an evening without doing at least a little studying, but tonight I did relax for a while." **[2 PARAGRAPHS]** "I got a note from the track coach (and then I saw him today) asking me about coming out for track. I told him that I was carrying a full schedule and working so much that I wouldn't have the time to come out. Perhaps next quarter I will have more time. I sure intend to arrange it if possible. My grades are not going to be so good—I can tell that right now." **[1 PARAGRAPH]** "All my love and kisses" **[/]** "Johnny"

 **** To Miss Katherine Glenn, Box 35, Riverton, Wyo. (2/16/41, Postmarked 2/17/41, 5:30 PM). Return Address: J. Sproule, 1309 Kearney, Laramie, Wyo. "Kay darling," **[2 PARAGRAPHS]** "Kelly is going to go home for a couple of weeks before he goes to California. He is going home in the morning and so I went over to see him this evening." **[1 PARAGRAPH]** ". . . I know that I 'bit off' too much this time but I'm going to do as good as I can and chalk it up to experience." **[1 PARAGRAPH]** "Speaking of memories— you know, every once in a while I'll think of something that we did together or someplace we went together or a song that we liked or a show we saw and I can remember it so clearly. Darling, no one could even possibly take your place." **[2 PARAGRAPHS]** "All my love and kisses always," **[/]** "Johnny"

 **** To Miss Katherine Glenn, Box 35, Riverton, Wyo. (2/18/41, Postmarked 2/19/41, 5:30 PM). Return Address: J. Sproule, 1309 Kearney, Laramie, Wyo. "Kay darling," **[3 PARAGRAPHS]** ". . . I haven't been staying up as late as last week or so. I'll bet I have some long evenings of work before the quarter is over though." **[1 PARAGRAPH]** "Did I tell you that I've taken to doing my own ironing? You should see me flourish an iron over a shirt. It isn't so bad though. Mrs. Buck washes my things when she washes and then all I have to do is dampen and iron them. I have about all my shirts in the ironing and I guess I'll have to do them tomorrow night." **[/]**

"The show 'Kitty Foyle' was here this week end. I was going to see it, but I didn't get around to it. Some one said that 'Gone with the Wind' was coming back. Maybe I can go this time." **[/]** "Being apart hasn't changed my love any—not the least particle! I'm yours always and forever!

Remember that my precious darling to whom I send all my love and kisses—Johnny."

**** To Miss Katherine Glenn, Box 35, Riverton, Wyo. (2/19/41 "Just after you called", Postmarked 2/20/41, 12:30 PM) [stamp torn off]. Return Address: J. Sproule, 1309 Kearney, Laramie, Wyo. "Darling," **[/]** "I am so glad you called. It was wonderful to hear your voice again. I wished so much that we weren't so far apart—...." **[6 PARAGRAPHS]** "With all my love and kisses" **[/]** "Johnny"

**** To Miss Katherine Glenn, Box 35, Riverton, Wyo. (2/21/41, Postmarked 2/24/41, 12:30 PM). Return Address: J. Sproule, 1309 Kearney, Laramie, Wyo. "Hi darling," **[2 PARAGRAPHS]** "I hope that Bernard [Glenn] will like the National Guard and that he will get along o.k. Tell him I wish him the best of everything." **[/]** "Tonight Berryman and I went to the show. I don't remember the name but it was a Kay Kyser show—it was good, lots of laughs and good music." **[2 PARAGRAPHS]**

"Remember my precious darling that I love you for always and always." **[/]** [a heart-shaped drawing and an X] **[/]** "Johnny" [On the back of the first page of this letter are seven lines in shorthand that KVS would have written, perhaps for practice. And included in the envelope is a smaller envelope with a card the caption of which is "wishing you real happiness always!" followed by a handwritten note, "from your Johnny."]

**** To Miss Katherine Glenn, Box 35, Riverton, Wyo. (2/26/41, Postmarked 2/27/41, 10:30 AM). Return Address: J. Sproule, 1309 Kearney, Laramie, Wyo. "Hi darling," **[/]** "Do you know it sometimes seems to take an awful long time for the post office to deliver your letter. For instance the last one—it was mailed on the 22nd (that's the post mark) and it wasn't delivered till the afternoon of the 24th. I suppose though that the holiday for Washington's birthday had something to do with it." **[/]**

"Yesterday afternoon we pounded a lot of castings. In making these castings, we take the molds which we have made so far this quarter and pour them full of molten iron. Well yesterday we did that—we fired up the furnace and melted up the iron, and made these castings. I was tireder than I have been for a long time when that was over, but then we only have to do this once." **[/]** "This afternoon I spent in the testing lab, testing a number of metal specimens. They are placed in a large machine which has some metal jaws to hold the specimen so it won't slip. A load is put on the specimen, using a motor and a series of gears, and the load is increased until the specimen is pulled apart—just like one might pull apart a string only on a much larger scale. By a number of readings it is possible to tell how strong the material is, how elastic etc." **[4 PARAGRAPHS]** "Forever yours Johnny" [In the envelope is inserted what appears to be a Christmas-present tag captioned "Merry Christmas" and written by JHS in print: "To My Sweetheart."]

**** To Miss Katherine Glenn, Box 35, Riverton, Wyo. (3/2/41, Postmarked 3/3/41, 12:30 PM). Return Address: J. Sproule, 1309 Kearney, Laramie, Wyo. [On the envelope we find a 3¢ postage-due stamp with a cancellation marking of "Mar 4 1941"—probably because this letter consists of five sheets of thickish paper instead of the usual 1-3.] "Kay darling," **[1 PARAGRAPH]** "I have been working on some notebooks—a Soil Mechanics notebook to be exact—this evening. You know it seems as though I hardly ever get much school work done on weekends. On Friday night I am always so glad that another week of school is over that I just feel like resting—I'm usually sort of tired by the end of a week of school too and so that and the fact that I usually work all day Saturday are other factors which influence me to just sit and read on Friday nights. Then on Saturday night, since I have been on the go from 7 to 7, I don't have much ambition. So, you see, I do the greatest amount of work on Sunday from about 8 till bed time sometimes pretty late if I have something due Monday." **[2 PARAGRAPHS]**

"No, I haven't read "Quietly My Captain Waits' that you mentioned—about all I get time to read are the Collier's and the Saturday Evening Post. Mrs. Buck gets the Collier's and one of the fellows gets the Post and when I have read them each week that's about all the spare time I have." **[2 PARAGRAPHS]** "I'll bet you that when you get to bed at 4 o'clock you aren't troubled a bit by insomnia—or could I be mistaken about that? My experience has been that when I stay up late I always go to sleep right away. It's when I go to bed earlier that I have trouble sleeping." **[/]**

". . . I wish so very much that I could have been with you as you were finishing your letter or that you could be here as I am finishing this one. I love the touch of your tender lips and your sweet, soft hands as you hold me and kiss me. Nothing in the world is more wonderful than holding and kissing you and having you hold me tight and kiss me! I love you so terrib[ly] much, my darling!" **[2 PARAGRAPHS]** "Yours forever," **[/]** "Johnny"

**** To Miss Katherine Glenn, Box 35, Riverton, Wyo. (3/4/41, Postmarked 3/5/41, 2:00 PM). Return Address: J. Sproule, 1309 Kearney, Laramie, Wyo. "Kay darling," **[1 PARAGRAPH]** "I think that's a swell idea—training for chief operator. It's always good to be able to work up, be promoted to a position with more responsibility and of course more pay. . . ." [JHS inserts a marginal notation of "2 AM"] ". . . There wasn't time to finish this letter this morning. As I sat here thinking of you and writing the lines above the time rushed by until it was time for me to go upstairs and set the table. When I had finished busing and washing dishe[s I] had only time enough to change my trousers and get to school (only 3 mi[n] late). I had a lab all afternoon (that's why I changed to an old pair of pant[s) and I just got back to the house in time to set the table and go through th[e] evening routine of dishes etc. As soon as that was over I went up to the Men's Dormitory to work with another fellow on a notebook that is due next week. I just got home (at 2 minutes till 2) and I am writing this befor[e] I tumble into bed." **[4 PARAGRAPHS]** "All my love always," **[/]** "Johnny"

**** To Miss Katherine Glenn, Box 35, Riverton, Wyo. (3/12/41, Postmarked 3/13/41, 10:30 AM). Return Address: J. Sproule, 1309 Kearney, Laramie, Wyo. "Kay darling" **[1 PARAGRAPH]** ". . . Well, as ofte[n] happens to schedules of this sort, it was thrown out by the fact that I had to do a bunch of extra work—the temperature dropped and it was necessary to take a bunch of readings on those experimental colonies. Spending 12 or 13 hours a day taking readings coupled with my hashing jo[b] and schoolwork, didn't leave much time for getting my extra school work done. As a result I have been really pouring it on the past week." **[/]** "I pretty well caught up now, all I have to do is an English report and a couple or three daily assignments in English that I let slip." **[3 PARAGRAPHS]** "All my love always," **[/]** "Johnny" **[/]** "P. S. On looking this over I find that the sleep I have missed the past week hasn't improved my penmanship a bit. But I love you even though I am sleepy." **[/]** "XXX" **[/]** "J."

    **** To Miss Katherine Glenn, Box 35, Riverton, Wyo. (3/25/41, Postmarked 3/25/41, 5:00 PM). Return Address: J. Sproule, 1309 Kearney, Laramie, Wyo. "My darling Kay," **[3 PARAGRAPHS]** "I am going up to school this afternoon and see about making up my exams. I will probably just have to arrange a time with the instructor—. . ." **[2 PARAGRAPHS]** "Remember sweetheart, I'm yours forever!" **[/]** "X's for my darling—" **[/]** "Johnny"

    **** To Miss Katherine Glenn, Box 35, Riverton, Wyo. (3/27/41, Postmarked 3/28/41, 5:30 PM). Return Address: J. Sproule, 1309 Kearney, Laramie, Wyo. "Hello darling," **[1 PARAGRAPH]** "I've thought sometimes that it would be nicer if I had a room by myself. Then if I felt studious I could shut the door and shut out the noise or if I wanted company I could ask some of the others in or go visiting. Sometimes I stay up till the others have gone to bed just so I can study or write in quiet." **[/]**

"Yesterday I was busy getting registered (and standing in line and that sort of thing). Registration day is usually sort of confused—mostly because of the inefficient system that they have. My idea to get around all this confusion and waste of time is to have everyone register for the next quarter during the last part of the preceding one. . . ." **[/]** "I am taking only twelve hours this quarter—about a 25% reduction. I'm taking Math, two English courses, Surveying and Machine Shop. The below sketch will give you an idea as to when I have classes and when I have free time or time to work." **[/]**

[The grid shows the following courses: Calculus, Surveying Lab, English 41c, English 37c, Machine Shop—Calculus begins the day at 9:00 except Thursday, Machine Shop ends the day, 3-5 on Tuesday and Wednesday.

Completely free afternoons on Monday, Wednesday, Saturday.] **[1 PARAGRAPH]**

"I went around to see the various professors about making up my exams and they were all pretty nice about it. I imagine that I'll have them all done in a week or so." **[4 PARAGRAPHS]**

"It was a terribly short vacation and then the circumstances made it seem altogether unlike a vacation." **[1 PARAGRAPH]** "All my love and kisses always" **[/]** "Johnny"

[The referenced to "circumstances" pertains to the recent death of JHS's boyhood best friend, Lewis Kelly, in an airplane accident on March 16, 1941. Kelly had been recently commissioned as a 2nd Lieutenant and was c 23 reserve officers ordered to report for duty at Fort Wolters, Texas on 3/24/41. He was also scheduled to attend Boeing Air School in Oakland, California. The funeral would have been held during Dad's Wyoming quarter break. The incident was so painful, that Dad evidently is unable to write about it in this letter or in any other letter.]

**** To Miss Katherine Glenn, Box 35, Riverton, Wyo. (3/30/41, Postmarked 3/31/41, 12:30 PM). Return Address: J. Sproule, 1309 Kearney Laramie, Wyo. "Kay darling," **[2 PARAGRAPHS]** "One of the fellows here has a car and three of us drove up to Snowy Range this afternoon. It's about 35 miles west of Laramie. We were gone for a couple of hours and i was a nice drive." **[3 PARAGRAPHS]** "Goodnight sweetheart." **[/]** "All m love and kisses" **[/]** "Johnny"

**** To Miss Katherine Glenn, Box 190, Riverton, Wyo. (4/1/41, Postmarked 4/2/41, 12:30 PM). Return Address: J. Sproule, 1309 Kearney, Laramie, Wyo. "Kay darling," **[6 PARAGRAPHS]** "This is a sort of short letter but I've been plugging away here since about 7:30 or 8:00 (its 1:30 now) and my eyes are closing in spite of myself. I'm going to try to get to bed every night before 2 o'clock for a while and see how that goes." **[/]** "Goodnight precious." **[/]** "Lots of kisses" **[/]** "Johnny" [Note: the pos boxes in Riverton had recently been renumbered.]

To Miss Katherine Glenn, Box 190, Riverton, Wyo. (4/3/41, Postmarked 4/4/41, 12:30 PM). Return Address: J. Sproule, 1309 Kearney, Laramie, Wyo. "Kay darling," **[3 PARAGRAPHS]** "My fees were due today and when I paid them I was $31.50 poorer—one thing though, the payment comes only about every three months." **[2 PARAGRAPHS]** [Also, heart and X drawings.] "Johnny" **[/]** [JHS includes especially romantic PSs.; and in the next letter, he waxes poetic about his love for KVS.]

**** To Miss Katherine Glenn, Box 190, Riverton, Wyo. (4/7/41, Postmarked 4/8/41, 12:30 PM). Return Address: J. Sproule, 1309 Kearney, Laramie, Wyo. "Kay darling," **[/]** "I'm sitting here looking out my window. I can see the bright rays of the moon casting their glow over everything. Perhaps the moon is smiling over Riverton too—guarding my darling in her sleep—it's quite late now and I will be going to bed soon." **[1 PARAGRAPH]** "The shining moon occasionally darkened by fleecy clouds and the empty feeling of my arms remind me of the times we spent together. My memories of you are so very dear to me—and sweetheart, they are so very strengthening when I'm away from you." **[2 PARAGRAPHS]** "Yours forever" **[/]** "Johnny"

**** To Miss Katherine Glenn, Box 190, Riverton, Wyo. (4/8/41, Postmarked 4/9/41, 12:30 PM). Return Address: J. Sproule, 1309 Kearney, Laramie, Wyo. "Kay darling," **[3 PARAGRAPHS]** "I've been doing some painting too—painting some equipment over at the bee house. The secret as I've found it is to transfer the paint, via the brush, from the can to the object being painted then you don't get any paint on the surroundings (and yourself). Easy isn't it? But you must remember not to let any paint drop or splash!" **[/]**

"I haven't taken all my make-up exams yet, but I'm still plugging along." **[/]** "I saw the show 'Tobacco Road'. There isn't much of a story but the acting is very good. That's the first show I've seen for a long time. 'The Road to Zanzibar' with Bob Hope, Bing Crosby and Dorothy Lamour will be here Fri. + Sat. That might be a pretty good show." **[1 PARAGRAPH]** "Goodnight my darling." **[/]** "All my love always," **[/]** "Johnny"

**** To Miss Katherine Glenn, Box 190, Riverton, Wyo. (Undated card "An Easter Wish", Postmarked 4/12/41, 12:30 PM). Return Address: J. Sproule, 1309 Kearney, Laramie, Wyo. "Kay my darling," [This greeting is hand written; next comes a printed poem expressing glory, happiness, hope, faith; printed illustration on the front is of a church window with flowers and candles.] Signed: "Johnny"

**** To Miss Katherine Glenn, Box 190, Riverton, Wyo. (4/14/41, Postmarked 4/15/41, 11:30 AM). Return Address: J. Sproule, 1309 Kearney, Laramie, Wyo. "Kay darling," **[2 PARAGRAPHS]** "Hey! I'm glad you wrote to me. Your swell letter made me completely forget the forgotten feeling I'd had the past couple of days. Your darling letter which I received at 11:05 am. today drove all the clouds away—the sun came out and it was warm and sunny all day." **[1 PARAGRAPH]**

"I've been lucky so far in this surveying course I'm taking. Since the lab periods must necessarily be held outdoors where we can survey, warm weather is always something desired. So far it has been nice—when it snows it always snows in the early part of the week and we have surveying on Friday afternoons and Saturday mornings." **[3 PARAGRAPHS]** "Loads of kisses for my darling" **[/]** "Johnny" **[/]** [2 romantic PSs]

**** To Miss Katherine Glenn, Box 190, Riverton, Wyo. (4/16/41, Postmarked 4/17/41, 5:30 PM). Return Address: J. Sproule, 1309 Kearney, Laramie, Wyo. "Kay darling," **[1 PARAGRAPH]** "That idea I had to get away from having any morning classes sort of folded up. I thought that I could drop my morning classes and get the work done by taking the course by correspondence. That way I would do the same amount of school work but I wouldn't have to attend any classes in the mornings. It fell through because I found that I couldn't get any refunds on my fees—I was going to pay for the correspondence course with the refund I thought I could get." **[3 PARAGRAPHS]** "All my love and kisses" **[/]** "Johnny"

**** To Miss Katherine Glenn, Box 190, Riverton, Wyo. (4/20/41, Postmarked 4/21/41, 5:30 PM). Return Address: J. Sproule, 1309 Kearney, Laramie, Wyo. "Kay darling," **[2 PARAGRAPHS]** "And speaking of pictures, the snapshots that I was going to send you didn't turn out so good. When I was developing them I apparently used water that was too hot—when I was washing them all the emulsion came off and there was nothing but a clear strip of celluloid. This will serve as a reminder to be more careful when I develop the next roll." **[1 PARAGRAPH]**

"I haven't heard anything more from the draft board here since I got my classification card and number. I don't know when I'll have to take the physical exam etc. Not knowing just what's going to happen about this makes it hard for me to plan what I can do this summer." **[2 PARAGRAPHS]** "Goodnight darling," **[/]** "Johnny"

    **** To Miss Katherine Glenn, Box 190, Riverton, Wyo. (4/29/41, Postmarked 4/30/41, 10:30 AM). Return Address: J. Sproule, 1309 Kearney, Laramie, Wyo. [a postage-due stamp for 3¢, canceled with date of 5/5/1941] "Kay darling," **[/]** ". . . I always have a lot of things planned that take forever to get around to. Last week I built myself some shelves for books—I'd wanted to do it for a long time and finally got them made." **[/]**

"We have had two bunches of packaged bees come in and I think that there will be some come in tomorrow. They will be the last though. It makes quite a bit of work putting them out. We have to assemble hives for them and then see that they have feed and that they are getting along o.k. I have been doing some painting of equipment the last week. I'll be glad when that is over. I went out and worked a yard of bees Sunday morning to see how they came through the winter so we would know how many we would have to feed, how many didn't have queens and things like that. A week ago Bill Gilbert and I spent an afternoon tearing up a couple of old washing machines looking for some bevel gears. We want to make a feed mixer." **[/]**

"I went through with that maneuver I was telling you about—dropping calculus and taking it by correspondence. It cost me extra to do it, but I thought that it would be better to do that than to coast along as I was and not understand the course very good and consequently not get a very good grade. Besides it gives me my mornings free which will be an increasing advantage as spring gets here and I will have a certain amount of work to cram into the last few weeks." **[/]** "I took another final of last quarters last week. It was in a two hour course and I got an 88 on the final and a I in the course." **[2 PARAGRAPHS]**

"I don't know much more about the draft. They say that all these student who were classified as 1D will have to be classified again and that some students (I imagine engineering students) will be deferred because of occupational activity—going to school. It's hard to say just what they will or won't do. And there's the possibility that I can't get in because of my eyes. They are still the same." **[2 PARAGRAPHS]** "Yes sweetheart I remember very well how I used to come down to the office evenings whe you were working and being there with you would make it seem like a ve cheerful place. . . ." **[3 PARAGRAPHS]** "Goodnight my darling" **[/]** "Johnny"

[JHS's eyesight had always required major correction. In addition, he suffered a detached retina in one eye from an accident in the UW gymnasium such that he progressively lost the sight in that eye.]

**** To Miss Katherine Glenn, Box 190, Riverton, Wyo. (5/6/41, Postmarked 5/6/41, 5:30 PM). Return Address: J. Sproule, 1309 Kearney, Laramie, Wyo. "Kay darling," **[1 PARAGRAPH]** "We had an Engineering Open House this weekend—that is putting up displays and giving demonstrations to the public. I helped in the foundry where we poured some cast iron." **[5 PARAGRAPHS]** "I bought me a hat the other day. It brown—very dashing! Think you'll like me in a hat? **[/]**

"Have you heard the song 'Keep an eye on your heart'? If you haven't, I want you to listen for it 'cause that's what I want you to do—'keep an ey on your heart and save your love for me'. That's what I'm doing—saving my love for you!" **[/]** ". . . In an English class I'll have to write a preliminary report on a book I've been reading. After I've read two more books I'll write up the complete report. One redeeming factor—it will ta the place of the final exam." **[2 PARAGRAPHS]** [JHS includes a drawing two joined hearts, one marked "J" the other "K" and "Tons of Xs"] **[/]** "Johnny"

    **** To Miss Katherine Glenn, Box 190, Riverton, Wyo. (5/9/41, Postmarked 5/10/41, 10:30 AM). Return Address: J. Sproule, 1309 Kearney, Laramie, Wyo. "Darling," **[3 PARAGRAPHS]** "What, may I ask gave you the impression that I was cutting classes? I've just missed a few." **[6 PARAGRAPHS]** "Goodnight my sweet" **[/]** "All my love and kisses" **[/]** "Johnny"

    **** To Miss Katherine Glenn, Box 190, Riverton, Wyo. (5/13/41, Postmarked 5/14/41, 12:30 PM). Return Address: J. Sproule, 1309 Kearney, Laramie, Wyo. "Kay darling," **[1 PARAGRAPH]** "School by itself isn't so bad, but when it and my jobs are combined they do keep me pretty busy. I worked bees all day yesterday and then did some school work till about two o'clock. I took it easy today though, to make up for it." **[/]** "Sunday morning I got up at 5:30—just imagine—to see Berryman off to Colorado. He will be gone for about a week on a geology trip." **[/]** "Sunday afternoon was about the nicest weather we have had so far. It was real warm and no wind blowing. I did a little school work Sunday morning and then knocked a golf ball around for a while in the afternoon." **[4 PARAGRAPHS]** "All my love always," **[/]** "Johnny" **[/]** [Following is a postscript on the back of the page thanking KVS for sending his knife.]

    **** To Miss Katherine Glenn, Box 190, Riverton, Wyo. (5/16/41, Postmarked 5/17/41). Return Address: J. Sproule, 1309 Kearney, Laramie, Wyo. "Kay darling," **[2 PARAGRAPHS]** "I'd like to have all my school work under control by the first. . . ." **[3 PARAGRAPHS]** "Goodnight sweetheart. Remember!" **[/]** "All my love as ever" **[/]** "Johnny"

    **** To Miss Katherine Glenn, Box 190, Riverton, Wyo. (5/20/41, Postmarked 5/21/41, 10:30 AM). Return Address: J. Sproule, 1309 Kearney, Laramie, Wyo. "Kay darling," **[3 PARAGRAPHS]** "For the last two or three weeks I've been going to the show on Friday nights. That's college night—a small reduction in prices, down to 20¢—and a double feature. The shows aren't bad but then they're nothing extra. Charlie Chaplin's 'The

Great Dictator' was here this week-end, but I don't like Charlie Chaplin. I heard some say the show wasn't anything extra." **[1 PARAGRAPH]** "Back to pictures—I didn't see 'Kitty Foyle' but I'd guess that it was a pretty good show. I don't think that the shows here are any thing extra. On the average I don't imagine that they are any better than the ones in Riverton—the only thing they might get here sooner. Did I tell you I saw 'Gone with the Wind' when it was here on second run? I sure liked it except for having to sit so long." **[/]**

"A fellow I used to know who is working at Wright Field at Daton [sic], Ohio was here over the weekend on a vacation. I had a good visit with him but didn't get much else done." **[2 PARAGRAPHS]** "Good night darling. All my love is yours alone as always." **[/]** "X X X X X X" **[/]** "Johnny"

**** To Miss Katherine Glenn, Box 190, Riverton, Wyo. (5/23/41, Postmarked 5/23/41). Return Address: J. Sproule, 1309 Kearney, Laramie, Wyo. "Kay darling," **[2 PARAGRAPHS]** "You don't have to decide about what you'll do on your vacation right away do you sweetheart? How about waiting a while so we can see how things turn out? It would be swell to be together when you didn't have to work." **[2 PARAGRAPHS]** "All my love always" **[/]** "Johnny"

**** To Miss Katherine Glenn, Box 190, Riverton, Wyo. (5/27/41, Postmarked 5/28/41, 11:30 AM). Return Address: J. Sproule, 1309 Kearney, Laramie, Wyo. "Kay darling," **[2 PARAGRAPHS]** "I did take time off to see a show last night. 'Zeigfield Girl' or something like that. James Stewart, Hedy Lamarr, Lana Turner etc. It could have been better and it could have been worse." **[4 PARAGRAPHS]** "All my love and kisses" **[/]** "Johnny"

**** To Miss Katherine Glenn, Box 190, Riverton, Wyo. (6/1/41, Postmarked 6/2/41, 12:30 PM). Return Address: J. Sproule, 1309 Kearney Laramie, Wyo. "Kay darling," **[/]** "When I got home yesterday afternoon was tired and feeling sort of low, but when I got your pictures it made me feel swell—grand and glorious—happy—and all together on top of the world. I sure like your picture—it's tops." **[3 PARAGRAPHS]** "Darling it was swell to hear your voice Fri. afternoon even though we didn't get to talk very long. I was downstairs studying at that time and getting a little discouraged. But when I talked to you for a little while everything was rosy! And then the next day your pictures came—two extra special things in a row!" **[/]** "Goodnight my precious. Remember I love you." **[/]** "Yours forever and ever" **[/]** "X X X X X X X" **[/]** "Johnny" **[/]** [Following is a P.S along with more enthusing about the picture.]

    **** To Miss Katherine Glenn, Box 190, Riverton, Wyo. (6/5/41, Postmarked 6/6/41, 12:30 PM). Return Address: J. Sproule, 1309 Kearney, Laramie, Wyo. "Kay darling," **[1 PARAGRAPH]** "I understand that the Kellys will be down here this weekend and I should be able to come back home with them. I don't know when they will go back, but it should be Mon. or Tues. I thing [sic]. Just think—I'll see you next week." **[4 PARAGRAPHS]**

"Yes, I heard Roosevelt the other night—sounded a little warlike to me." **[1 PARAGRAPH]** "Yours forever" **[/]** "Johnny"

    **** To Miss Katherine Glenn, Box 190, Riverton, Wyo. (6/8/41, Postmarked 6/9/41, 12:30 PM). Return Address: J. Sproule, 1309 Kearney, Laramie, Wyo. "Kay Darling," **[/]** "I wish I wern't writing this letter—I wish that I were with you tonight! Kelly's had to go home today and I couldn't get that physical exam for the draft before Tuesday. It seemed to me that it would be better to stay here and take the exam than to have to come down here in the middle of the summer to do it whenever my number came up. This way I at least know how I come out on the physical." **[4 PARAGRAPHS]** "All my love and kisses always" **[/]** "Johnny"

Chapter 5. Frustration, Friends, Films, War, and KVS Visits—September 1941 to December 1941

We find increasing references by JHS to his frustration with both the slow pace of his college studies and the interminable separation from KVS. Further discussions include classes, the rooming house, friends, popular-cultural experiences, photography, and the ever-present draft. Notable incidents include the U.S. entry into World War II, a visit to Riverton by JHS Senior, and an impromptu trip by KVS to Laramie.

**** To Miss Katherine Glenn, Box 190, Riverton, Wyo. (9/22/41, Postmarked 9/23/41, 4:30 PM). Return Address: J. Sproule, 1309 Kearney, Laramie, Wyo. "Kay darling," [/] "I miss you like hell and I'll be missing you more and more each day until I see you again. I tried to imagine as I walked from the car that I was just leaving for a moment but it didn't work. I was tired and cold and unhappy." [/] "I have your picture here on my desk and I keep looking at it—thinking of all the swell times we've had—thinking of how much we love each other." [/]

"I feel so depressed at being away from you! All I can think is I love you I love you I love you. Remember that my darling. Goodnight with all my love and kisses." [/] "Johnny"

**** To Miss Katherine Glenn, Box 190, Riverton, Wyo. (9/23/41, Postmarked 9/24/41, 4:30 PM). Return Address: J. Sproule, 1309 Kearney, Laramie, Wyo. "Kay darling," **[1 PARAGRAPH]** "I went to town and did some shopping for Mrs. Buck—I saw Gilbert and I believe I have that $7.50 job again—tonight I tried to work out a schedule but it's all such a mass—I'll have to see the dean tomorrow and see what he has to suggest." [/] "My new room-mate is a young fellow from Denver who works for Western Public Service. He seems to be a nice kid—he's tall (6' 5") and good looking, plays the saxophone and is a pretty good artist—Bill Alexander by name. He and I have a room together—the apartment that I was in last year is being occupied by four football players." [/]

"I started right in hashing when I got here—we've been having 12 and 13 and that makes for quite a few dishes." **[3 PARAGRAPHS]** "Good night precious darling" **[/]** "With all my love and kisses" **[/]** "Johnny"

**** To Miss Katherine Glenn, Box 190, Riverton, Wyo. (9/24/41, Postmarked 9/25/41, 12:30 PM). Return Address: J. Sproule, 1309 Kearney, Laramie, Wyo. "Hi darling," **[1 PARAGRAPH]** "I got registered today and I worked out a schedule something like this:" [lists classes in the form of a weekly grid by day and by hour; classes include geology, chemistry, physics, mechanical engineering] **[/]** "The geology is a simple or basic course in geology designed to give a comprehensive introduction to dynamical, structured and historical geology." **[/]** "CE 29a is the first quarter of applied mechanics presenting the principles of mechanics designed to give a working knowledge of the fundamental concepts of static forces, friction centroids, kinematics, and kinetics including force, mass, acceleration, work, energy etc." **[/]** "ME26a is a study of the principles of industrial organization, factory plans, wage systems, personnel relations, safety engineering and factory control." **[/]** "ME11a is a lab in which we will test various instruments and apparatus, test power transmission machinery—valve setting—clearance determination of steam engine, etc." **[/]** "Physics 5x is a course in electrical measurements. Well that will give you some idea of what I will be doing—plus working here at the house etc." **[1 PARAGRAPH]**

"Ray and I walked down town this evening—didn't do much just had a coke and walked back. . . ." **[3 PARAGRAPHS]** "All my love and kisses" **[/]** "Johnny"

**** To Miss Katherine Glenn, Box 190, Riverton, Wyo. (9/25/41, Postmarked 9/26/41, 12:30 PM). Return Address: J. Sproule, 1309 Kearney, Laramie, Wyo. "Hello sweetheart," **[2 PARAGRAPHS]** "This afternoon I was supposed to have physics lab from 1-4, but it didn't meet so I checked on that $7.50 job and found for sure that I have it again—it isn't much but it will pay my room rent." **[/]** "I started to build some shelves when I came home this afternoon and then I worked on them a little while after I finished the dishes this evening." **[2 PARAGRAPHS]** [JHS draws a heart " X's" **[/]** "Johnny"

**** To Miss Katherine Glenn, Box 190, Riverton, Wyo. (9/26/41, 11:30 Pm, Postmarked 9/27/41, 10:30 AM). Return Address: J. Sproule, 1309 Kearney, Laramie, Wyo. "Kay darling," [This is an almost illegible two-page letter written lightly in pencil relating the basics of going to class getting the room setup, et cetera.] It ends: "With all of my love and every one of my kisses" **[/]** "Johnny"

**** To Miss Katherine Glenn, Box 190, Riverton, Wyo. (9/27/41, Postmarked 9/29/41, 12 M). Return Address: J. Sproule, 1309 Kearney, Laramie, Wyo. "Hello darling," **[1 PARAGRAPH]** "Here it is Saturday night and we always are together then—but this week we're not and I feel so lost. . . ." **[1 PARAGRAPH]** "Goodnight precious darling—dream sweet dreams!" **[/]** "All my love and kisses always" **[/]** "Johnny"

**** To Miss Katherine Glenn, Box 190, Riverton, Wyo. (9/28/41, Postmarked 9/29/41, 12 M). Return Address: J. Sproule, 1309 Kearney, Laramie, Wyo. "Hi sweetheart," **[/]** ". . . I haven't done my mechanics problems for tomorrow. I think I may arise early enough to do them in the morning. I went to the cinema this evening—saw 'Dive Bomber.' It isn't a bad show—action—technicolor—etc.—what more could one ask? . . . ." **PARAGRAPHS]** "Johnny"

**** To Miss Katherine Glenn, Box 190, Riverton, Wyo. (9/29/41, Postmarked 9/30/41, 4:30 PM). Return Address: J. Sproule, 1309 Kearney, Laramie, Wyo. "Kay darling," **[/]** ". . . I wondered what the 'something interesting' you mentioned might be—I never dreamed it could be anything as swell as you coming down." **[1 PARAGRAPH]**

"Jimmy Jenson, a fellow who lives up stairs came down—we drove out of town and listened to the fight over the radio in his car." **[1 PARAGRAPH]** "Good night darling" **[/]** "All my love and kisses always" **[/]** "Johnny"

**** To Miss Katherine Glenn, Box 190, Riverton, Wyo. (9/30/41, Postmarked 10/1/41, 11:30 AM). Return Address: J. Sproule, 1309

Kearney, Laramie, Wyo. "Hi darling," **[/]** "How's everything tonight? Swell I hope! I'm feeling much better at the prospect of your coming down Sat. or Sun. By much better I mean a whole lot of a lot better! Even the fact that my school work is killing me doesn't bother me." **[1 PARAGRAPH]** "Berryman was over for a while and we sat and talked and then Jimmy Jenson from upstairs came down for a while—he had been bowling. By the time he and Berryman left it was 1130. I worked on some mechanics and then I started to write to you. . . . ." **[1 PARAGRAPH]** "Good night Kay darling" **[/]** "All my love and kisses always" **[/]** "Johnny"

**** To Miss Katherine Glenn, Box 190, Riverton, Wyo. (10/1/41, Postmarked 10/2/41, 11:30 AM). Return Address: J. Sproule, 1309 Kearney, Laramie, Wyo. "Hello darling," **[4 PARAGRAPHS]** "We got up a pool on the world series game for tomorrow here at the house this evening. We put numbers from 1 through 10 in a hat and then draw. The total score of the game is the winning number. For instance the score today was 3 to 2 and so the number 5 would have won. We put in a quarter each so the winner will get $2.50." **[1 PARAGRAPH]** "All my love and kisses" **[/]** "Johnny"

**** To Miss Katherine Glenn, Box 190, Riverton, Wyo. (10/2/41, Postmarked 10/3/41, 11:30 AM). Return Address: J. Sproule, 1309 Kearney, Laramie, Wyo. "Kay darling," **[1 PARAGRAPH]** "Today I had an 8 o'clock and a 9 o'clock class and then at 10 there was an assembly at which the new president of the university was introduced. This afternoon I listened to the world series and then worked on some problems. Incidentally I didn't win that pool—I had 8 and 5 won." **[1 PARAGRAPH]** "I've been reading quite a bit but mostly just short stories in magazines. As a rule they are just trivial stories and I forget them as fast as I read them— they're just a means of taking my mind away from the ever-present fact that we are apart." **[3 PARAGRAPHS]** "I love you too darling, with all my being for always and always" **[/]** "X X X X X X X X" **[/]** "Johnny"

**** To Miss Katherine Glenn, Box 190, Riverton, Wyo. (10/3/41, Postmarked 10/4/41, 11:30 AM). Return Address: J. Sproule, 1309 Kearney, Laramie, Wyo. "Kay darling," **[/]** "Such wonderful news! I'm going to see you Sunday! Talk about happy days, that will really be one!" **[4 PARAGRAPHS]** "All my love and kisses" **[/]** "Johnny"

**** To Miss Katherine Glenn, Box 190, Riverton, Wyo. (10/6/41, Postmarked 10/7/41, 10:30 AM). Return Address: J. Sproule, 1309 Kearney, Laramie, Wyo. "Kay darling," **[1 PARAGRAPH]** "I took a nap till time for supper and then this evening I worked on my mechanics—sat and talked with my roommate and one of the fellows from the other room—and now it's bed time." **[1 PARAGRAPH]** "Goodnight now darling. I send you all my love and kisses" **[/]** "Forever" **[/]** "Johnny"

**** To Miss Katherine Glenn, Box 190, Riverton, Wyo. (10/7/41, Postmarked 10/8/41, 11:30 AM). Return Address: J. Sproule, 1309 Kearney, Laramie, Wyo. "Kay darling," **[/]** "Although it was only yesterday afternoon that you left it seems like an age we kissed and held each other close— . . . ." **[2 PARAGRAPHS]** "Goodnight sweetheart" **[/]** "All my love and kisses forever" **[/]** "Johnny"

**** To Miss Katherine Glenn, Box 190, Riverton, Wyo. (10/9/41, Postmarked 10/9/41, 3:30 PM). Return Address: J. Sproule, 1309 Kearney, Laramie, Wyo. "Kay darling," **[/]** "It was so late last night when I finished my mechanics problems that I'm writing this afternoon." **[1 PARAGRAPH]** "Bill told me that he's going to move up to where a fellow he works with rooms and so I'll have the room to myself. I think I'll like that. The past couple of weeks he's been working nights and I stayed away from the room in the daytime so he could sleep." **[3 PARAGRAPHS]** "Yours always + forever" **[/]** "Johnny"

**** To Miss Katherine Glenn, Box 190, Riverton, Wyo. (10/10/41, Postmarked 10/11/41, 11:30 AM). Return Address: J. Sproule, 1309 Kearney, Laramie, Wyo. "Kay darling," [There follow miscellaneous comments about movies seen, magazines read, people talked to.] **[/]** "Forever and ever" **[/]** "Johnny"

**** To Miss Katherine Glenn, Box 190, Riverton, Wyo. (10/12/41, Postmarked 10/13/41, 4:00 PM). Return Address: J. Sproule, 1309 Kearney, Laramie, Wyo. "Hello Honey," **[2 PARAGRAPHS]** "Bill took his things this evening and so I have the room to my self now. Now I can fix things up great to suit my self." **[/]**

"A good illustration of one of the disadvantages of the hashing job occurred this weekend—I mean having to be here every day and every day at a certain time. Ray got a part time job as Assistant State Geologist which he is doing along with his school work, and this weekend he went up to someplace around Shoshoni to look over an alum deposit and if I hadn't been tied here I could have come to see you. Disgusting isn't it?" **[2 PARAGRAPHS]** "Goodnight precious" **[/]** "All my love and kisses always" **[/]** "Johnny"

**** To Miss Katherine Glenn, Box 190, Riverton, Wyo. (10/13/41, Postmarked 10/14/41, 10:00 AM). Return Address: J. Sproule, 1309 Kearney, Laramie, Wyo. "Hi darling," **[2 PARAGRAPHS]** "It is about 12:30 now—I went over to Berryman's tonight—worked mechanics problems and sat around and talked." **[2 PARAGRAPHS]** "Goodnight dearest" **[/]** "All my love and kisses" **[/]** "Johnny"

**** To Miss Katherine Glenn, Box 190, Riverton, Wyo. (10/15/41, 12:15 midnight, Postmarked 10/16/41, 10:30 AM). Return Address: J. Sproule, 1309 Kearney, Laramie, Wyo. "Kay darling," **[1 PARAGRAPH]** "Then I studied a chapter in a book called Factory Management which I had to go to the library and get—that I had to do to get some material for a problem concerning a Machine-Hour Analysis." **[1 PARAGRAPH]** "Goodnight sweetheart. Remember!!!" **[/]** "All my love and kisses" **[/]** "Johnny"

**** To Miss Katherine Glenn, Box 190, Riverton, Wyo. (10/15/41, Postmarked 10/15/41, 10:30 AM). Return Address: J. Sproule, 1309 Kearney, Laramie, Wyo. "Darling," **[1 PARAGRAPH]** "I'd like it very much if you did come down again when Kenny goes after Helen—but I realize that it might give you an unpleasant schedule afterward and then it does cost you. . . ." **[/]** "About football—Wyo. just hasn't any team—I don't know when or if they ever will have. . . ." **[/]** "There was a piece in the paper the other night about an explosion in the Riverton bowling alley, but it didn't say much other than no one was killed." **[1 PARAGRAPH]**

"A road show of 'Hellzapopin' sp? is showing at the university auditorium tonight but I'm going to stay home for two reasons. 1. It would cost me a dollar and a half for a decent seat and 2. I have a lot of mechanics and EE problems to do. Both good sound reasons don't you think?" **[3 PARAGRAPHS]** "I'll write you again tomorrow sweet so bye now." **[/]** "All my love always" **[/]** "Johnny"

    **** To Miss Katherine Glenn, Box 190, Riverton, Wyo. (10/17/41, 10:45 PM, Postmarked 10/20/41, 12:30 PM). Return Address: J. Sproule, 1309 Kearney, Laramie, Wyo. "Hello darling," **[3 PARAGRAPHS** starting out as a standard letter, then a segue to something written later.] "Sunday night—Darling you did come down! It was perfectly wonderful to see you again!! Every time we're apart I find how well I've remembered everything about you when we are together again. And every time we are together my treasure of memories increases. . . ." **[/]** "All my love and kisses" **[/]** "Johnny"

    **** To Miss Katherine Glenn, Box 190, Riverton, Wyo. (10/21/41, Postmarked 10/22/41, 10:30 AM). Return Address: J. Sproule, 1309 Kearney, Laramie, Wyo. "Hello darling," **[/]** "I hope you're rested up from your trip down here and you are looking back at it with as much fond remembrances as I am. . . ." **[/]** "The two times you've come down have been so wonderful. The days are not quite so unendurable when I've been with you recently—I'm already joyously anticipating Homecoming." **[1 PARAGRAPH]** "So good night sweetheart. I love you." **[/]** [JHS inserts a heart drawing and an X] **[/]** "Johnny"

    **** To Miss Katherine Glenn, Box 190, Riverton, Wyo. (10/23/41, Postmarked 10/24/41, 9:30 AM). Return Address: J. Sproule, 1309 Kearney, Laramie, Wyo. "Hello darling," **[3 PARAGRAPHS]** "The gala Engineer's Ball is tomorrow night. I wish you were here so we could go—as it is, I think I'll stay home and do some Steam Lab experiments or study Mechanics." **[1 PARAGRAPH]** "All my love always" **[/]** "Johnny"

**** To Miss Katherine Glenn, Box 190, Riverton, Wyo. (10/25/41, 1:45 PM, Postmarked 10/25/41, 5:30 PM). Return Address: J. Sproule, 1309 Kearney, Laramie, Wyo. "Kay darling," **[3 PARAGRAPHS]** "I couldn't study last night and so I went to the show with Ray and Jimmy Jenson who lives upstairs. We saw 'Belle Starr' and some other show. I think it was called 'Moon Over Her Shoulder.' Lynn Bari was in it—it was just a light comedy. I liked it better than 'Belle Starr' which I thought was too mushy." **[4 PARAGRAPHS]** "All my love always" **[/]** "Johnny"

**** To Miss Katherine Glenn, Box 190, Riverton, Wyo. (10/27/41, Postmarked 10/28/41, 11:30 AM). Return Address: J. Sproule, 1309 Kearney, Laramie, Wyo. "Kay Darling," **[/]** ". . . The only course I'm worrying about is AC. + DC. power and I'm not alone in that. . . ." **[/]** "I think it will be nice if you do get some of the fiesta ware and especially since we both like it—you think? I do! I like the things you like. I only wish that I could be getting some things too dearest, but right at the moment my income has a hard time keeping up with expenses." **[2 PARAGRAPHS]** "Whats this business of needing a baptismal certificate? What do you need it for etc.? It's a new one on me. If you can't locate it will you have to be baptized again or what will happen." **[3 PARAGRAPHS]** "Goodnight now, Remember I love you!" **[/]** "Forever" **[/]** "Johnny"

**** To Miss Katherine Glenn, Box 190, Riverton, Wyo. (10/30/41, 8:40 PM, Postmarked 10/30/41, TR27, OMAHA & OGDEN R.P.O.). Return Address: J. Sproule, 1309 Kearney, Laramie, Wyo. "Darling," **[/]** "I got your grand letter this afternoon. It's swell to hear from you, your letter charged me up immediately." **[7 PARAGRAPHS]** "Forever" **[/]** "Johnny" **[/]** "P.S. XXXXX" **[/]** "P.S.[2] When I write to Mom and Eugene I'm going to see what he is planning about Homecoming—it's next week and have you seen him?" **[1 PARAGRAPH]** "I love you sweetheart" **[/]** "J." [Enclosed in the same envelope is a letter to "My Dear Kay" dated October 24, 1941 from Fort Lewis W. written by a soldier friend named Pfc. Vic Stout who describes his transit from Riverton to Fort Lewis and his having encountered Bernard Glenn there.]

**** To Miss Katherine Glenn, Box 190, Riverton, Wyo. (10/31/41 Postmarked 11/1/41, 12:30 PM). Return Address: J. Sproule, 1309 Kearne Laramie, Wyo. "Kay darling" **[/]** ". . . though I'm sorrier than I can say that you aren't coming down Homecoming. Sweetheart, I realize the circumstances which make your decision. . . ." **[1 PARAGRAPH]** "I developed a few more pictures tonight; and a couple of the one's which I did that lastnight [sic] are dry so I'm enclosing them. They aren't well bordered because I haven't as yet had time to make a mask to hold the printing paper but when I get that done the prints will have a little better appearance. As yet I'm just getting used to using the enlarger." **[/]** "Sweetheart, I send you all my love and kisses and remember I love you always!" **[/]** "X X X X" **[/]** "Johnny"

**** To Miss Katherine Glenn, Box 190, Riverton, Wyo. (11/3/41, Postmarked 11/4/41, 3:30 PM). Return Address: J. Sproule, 1309 Kearney Laramie, Wyo. "Darling," **[1 PARAGRAPH]** "But I'm sort of stymied by, 'I'm ignoring the third paragraphs of your letter until later—much later.' can't quite remember just what the third paragraph you refer to contained—now if I knew exactly what you were ignoring perhaps I might formulate some clue as to why etc. (or could I?)." **[/]**

"No, I don't have a birth certificate. I've often thought that I would see about getting one (if I can, I don't know whether I was registered or not— I'll have to ask) if I was ever in Cheyenne, but up to yet I haven't." **[1 PARAGRAPH]** "I spent Halloween developing some more pictures. I suppose you have the ones I sent by now—any way I'll send you some more—the ones I did Halloween night. No I didn't wax a window or upset thing Halloween so you see I was a very good boy." **[3 PARAGRAPHS]** "A my love always" **[/]** "Johnny"

**** To Miss Katherine Glenn, Box 190, Riverton, Wyo. (11/4/41, Postmarked 11/5/41, 11:30 AM). Return Address: J. Sproule, 1309 Kearney, Laramie, Wyo. "Darling," **[/]** "I'll have to admit that it gave me quite a start to see 'Dear Bob' when I opened your last letter. I realized instantly though that it wasn't your writing and I soon had an explanation **[/]** "The last couple of nights I've been up till about 2 or 2:30 so tonight

I'm going to bed a bit earlier I think. . . . As a matter of fact I slept through a couple of classes this morning—that is I didn't hear my alarm or it didn't ring or something and consequently I didn't get up in time. It's nothing serious though." **[/]** "I know that if A. [Agnes Glenn] goes to Cody to work you will miss her a lot. . . ." **[/]**

"I haven't been going to many shows—'A Yank the RAF.' was here this weekend, but I didn't go—as I remember I was home working Mechanics problems or something equally uninteresting. I always seem to have a lot of work to do on weekends—and since I worked for Gilbert Saturday, it meant that I had a lot to do Sunday night." **[1 PARAGRAPH]** "I think I could do better in printing pictures if I had a better method of adjusting the focus of the lens in my enlarger. . . ." **[2 PARAGRAPHS]** "'Night now" **[/]** "All my love and kisses always" **[/]** "Johnny"

    **** To Miss Katherine Glenn, Box 190, Riverton, Wyo. (11/10/41, Postmarked 11/12/41, 11:30 AM). Return Address: J. Sproule, 1309 Kearney, Laramie, Wyo. "Darling," **[/]** "It was wonderful to talk to you again! I've just come downstairs from talking to you and I'm still excited and perhaps not writing to lucidly—. . . ." **[/]** "My birthday has been swell—a letter and a telephone call from you have made it a very wonderful day." **[1 PARAGRAPH]** "Homecoming didn't amount to much this year—I think it seemed lifeless to me because you were not here. . . ." **[4 PARAGRAPHS]** "All my love + kisses" **[/]** "Johnny"

    **** To Miss Katherine Glenn, Box 190, Riverton, Wyo. (11/12/41, Postmarked 11/13/41, 11:30 AM). Return Address: J. Sproule, 1309 Kearney, Laramie, Wyo. "Hi darling" **[2 PARAGRAPHS]** "I went to the Engineers Smoker tonight. It's just a sort of get-together of students and professors and cigars + cigarettes are passed + we also had some apples. A few short talks were given and introductions of the profs made for the benefit of freshmen who might not know them. Lee Donley was master of ceremonies—he made the introductions and told some stories. His favorite about the bald headed man in the barber shop got a big hand. Another proff told a story purporting to explain why Donley got bald headed and he turned red clear to the top of his head." **[/]**

"Mom wrote me that Dad was at Riverton for a short visit. Last time he was out he stayed for a couple of weeks or so but I guess he was only there for a few days this time." **[/]** "Mom also wrote—I guess Dad was telling her—that my oldest cousin [Rodney C. Anspach, b. 1920] in Calif—he's almost as old as I am I guess—got married to a woman with a 13 year old daughter—that's getting a family in a hurry isn't it?" **[2 PARAGRAPHS]** "All my love + kisses" **[/]** "Johnny"

**** To Miss Katherine Glenn, Box 190, Riverton, Wyo. (11/13/41, 3:30 p.m., Postmarked 11/14/41, 12:30 PM). Return Address: J. Sproule, 1309 Kearney, Laramie, Wyo. "Darling" **[1 PARAGRAPH]** "Sweetheart there is absolutely no cause for you to be worried – if you didn't understand me when you called, if I sounded strange it was just because I was so excited. It's very distracting to hear your lovely voice and not be able to hold you in my arms and kiss you." **[5 PARAGRAPHS]** "Yours forever" **[/]** "Johnny"

**** To Miss Katherine Glenn, Box 190, Riverton, Wyo. (11/16/41, Postmarked 11/17/41, 3:30 PM). Return Address: J. Sproule, 1309 Kearney, Laramie, Wyo. "Darling" **[1 PARAGRAPH]** "Well Wyoming finally won a game! . . . Anyway they should do a lot better in basketball and people will forget the lack of glory in football." **[/]** "Jimmy and I went to the show tonight. It was 'Seargent York.' It was pretty good but I much prefer a lighter type of show. There was quite a crowd and we had to wait until the second show. We just got home a little while ago and I did my Mechanics problems and so it's about time for bed." **[/]** "I sure did get some sleep last night. Jimmy and I and two of the other borders played bridge last night until about 10:00 and then Jimmy and I sat in his room and talked for a while. . . ." **[2 PARAGRAPHS]** "All my love and kisses" **[/]** "Johnny"

**** To Miss Katherine Glenn, Box 190, Riverton, Wyo. (11/17/41, Postmarked 11/18/41, 10:30 AM). Return Address: J. Sproule, 1309 Kearney, Laramie, Wyo. "Darling" **[1 PARAGRAPH]** "Dearest I know how you feel about Riverton because I feel the same way about Laramie. The only thing is that I'm just stuck here 'cause the college is here. It would be swell if you did get a civil service job—I know how you dislike telephone operating. Well we can talk it all over when I get home." **[/]**

"I wish to God I could come up Thanksgiving—but there is the item of expense and also if I remain here I can get caught up in my school work and do away with this having to stay up till 2:00 or so. . . ." **[1 PARAGRAPH]** "I'm glad A [Agnes Glenn] likes her work etc. in Cody. . . ." **[4 PARAGRAPHS]** "Forever" **[/]** "Johnny"

  **** To Miss Katherine Glenn, Box 190, Riverton, Wyo. (11/21/41, Postmarked 11/21/41, 5:30 PM). Return Address: J. Sproule, 1309 Kearney, Laramie, Wyo. [Envelope stamped "Postage-due 3 cents."] "Kay darling" **[1 PARAGRAPH]** ". . . Wyoming played Colorado Mines here yesterday. Score 0-0. It was cold and windy and consequently Ray and I stayed here and listened to the game via the radio. He stayed with me Wednesday night and we didn't get up very early. We went to a midnight show Wednesday—it was 'Lady Be Good' with Ann Sothern, Robert Young + Eleanor Powell. Comment: average show." **[/]**

"Yesterday then after the game we [omission] over to the union + sat around talking + reading the papers until we got hungry and then Ray + I went down town and ate. We had a 75¢ turkey dinner. It was quite novel to be eating and a have some one else waiting table. We didn't serve meals yesterday at the boarding house so I had the full day off. First time I've had a whole day off since I came down here." **[/]** "Last night after we had eaten Ray + I went over to his house. I spent some time developing pictures and then we sat around and talked for a while. When I get this letter written I'll go over and see if those pictures are dry. I made those for Helen + Kenny and experimented with some others." [And enclosed in the envelope is a picture of a young man and a young woman embracing—presumably Kenny and Helen.] **[3 PARAGRAPHS]**

"The time goes so slowly that I wonder if it is not moving backward. It seems like a year since you were down—and looking ahead, Christmas seems such a long time away. But darling, if we write real often time will pass much faster I know." **[1 PARAGRAPH]** "It would be very nice if

Bernard [Glenn] came home Christmas but if he waits till February and then takes his furlough his year would be up—leaving Riverton March 8 and not taking any furlough would make his year up in February." **[1 PARAGRAPH]** "Yours always" **[/]** "Johnny"

**** To Miss Katherine Glenn, Box 190, Riverton, Wyo. (11/22/41, Postmarked 11/22/41, TR27, OMAHA & OGDEN R.P.O.). Return Address: J. Sproule, 1309 Kearney, Laramie, Wyo. "Darling" **[/]** "There hasn't been anything going on here at all. With no school I just lay around here in my room studying a while reading a while, working some, studying again in a seemingly endless monotonous progression." **[/]** "I miss you so very much darling. I hope the days till Christmas pass like the wind and so I can be with you again." **[2 PARAGRAPHS]** "All my love and kisses forever" **[/]** "Johnny" [Written on the back of the envelope is a list of 13 items given in shorthand with a corresponding number varying from 1.00 to 4.00, presumably a list of expenses prepared by KVS.]

**** To Miss Katherine Glenn, Box 190, Riverton, Wyo. (11/24/41, Postmarked 11/25/41, 12:30 PM). Return Address: J. Sproule, 1309 Kearney, Laramie, Wyo. "Kay darling," **[2 PARAGRAPHS]** "Darling I hope you had a nice Thanksgiving even if you did have to work some. . . ." **[3 PARAGRAPHS]** "All my love + kisses" **[/]** "Johnny"

**** To Miss Katherine Glenn, Box 190, Riverton, Wyo. (11/26/41, 11:55 pm, Postmarked 11/27/41, 11:00 AM). Return Address: J. Sproule, 1309 Kearney, Laramie, Wyo. "Hi darling" **[/]** ". . . We usually have about 5 or 6 problems for each assignment + we have 4 assignments per week, so it usually keeps me busy." **[2 PARAGRAPHS]** "This has been a very dull week—not a thing going on. Friday night though, Jessica Dragonette (who used to sing on the Firestone program) is giving a performance. I may go because my activity book is good for that—otherwise the admission would be $1.00." **[2 PARAGRAPHS]** "Yours always" **[/]** "Johnny"

**** To Miss Katherine Glenn, Box 190, Riverton, Wyo. (11/28/41, 10:50 AM, Postmarked 11/28/41). Return Address: J. Sproule, 1309

Kearney, Laramie, Wyo. "Hi sweetheart" **[3 PARAGRAPHS]** "You know it is funny the way songs come and go so soon. Right now 'Chattanooga Cho Cho' seems to be the most popular one around here." **[1 PARAGRAPH]** ". . . Writing helps bridge the endless time between vacations don't you think?" **[1 PARAGRAPH]** "Always yours" **[/]** "Johnny"

  **** To Miss Katherine Glenn, Box 190, Riverton, Wyo. (11/27/41, 1:15 PM, Postmarked 11/28/41, 5:30 PM). Return Address: J. Sproule, 1309 Kearney, Laramie, Wyo. "Darling," **[/]** ". . . I got your letter so I feel swell now. Dearest, my feelings go up or down in direct ratio to the frequency of your letters. . . ." **[2 PARAGRAPHS]** "It's swell that A [Agnes Glenn] likes Cody. And if there are a lot of boys there maybe she'll find one she really likes—I think everyone ought to be in love—I'm so happy being in love with you and knowing you love me that I wish everyone well." **[1 PARAGRAPH]** "All my love always" **[/]** "Johnny"

  **** To Miss Katherine Glenn, Box 190, Riverton, Wyo. (11/27/41, 10:05, Postmarked 11/29/41, TR27, OMAHA & OGDEN R.P.O.). Return Address: J. Sproule, 1309 Kearney, Laramie, Wyo. "Darling," **[2 PARAGRAPHS]** "Tonight Jessica Dragonette sang at the University auditorium. I was going but I decided I'd stay home and study. Then too, Mrs. Buck is ill, she has a pretty bad cold and being as everyone else here was going out this evening I thought it might be a good idea to stick around in case she should need anything. She went to bed right after supper and I did all the dishes + pots and pans etc. by myself (we only had 11 tonight for supper)." **[/]** "I think Ray + Mary were going to hear Jessica Dragonette but I haven't seen him today so I really don't know. . . ." **[1 PARAGRAPH]** ". . . It's almost incredible the way time speeds by when I'm with you. All whole day seems like just an hour. . . ." **[1 PARAGRAPH]** "Good night now darling." **[/]** "All my love and kisses" **[/]** "Johnny"

  **** To Miss Katherine Glenn, Box 190, Riverton, Wyo. (12/2/41, 11:40 PM, Postmarked 12/3/41, 10:30 AM). Return Address: J. Sproule, 1309 Kearney, Laramie, Wyo. [enclosed is some kind of postal receipt for $1.11] "Hi darling," **[1 PARAGRAPH]** "I've been sitting here at my desk working some Mechanics problems but mostly thinking of you and how I'd like to be with you. . . ." **[1 PARAGRAPH]** "And I am keeping in good health—guarding against taking cold staying home and working on my books a little—and trying to keep up on my sleep." **[2 PARAGRAPHS]** "All my love always" **[/]** "Johnny"

**** To Miss Katherine Glenn, Box 190, Riverton, Wyo. (12/3/41, 11:15 PM, Postmarked 12/4/41, 10:30 AM). Return Address: J. Sproule, 1309 Kearney, Laramie, Wyo. "Hi darling," **[2 PARAGRAPHS]** "Did you ever read Hemingway's 'For Whom the Bell Tolls'? I just finished it the other day. It seems like reading is the only thing I have time for outside of the work I have to do. And of course a little sleep now and then—but I'm really doing pretty good this year about getting plenty of sleep—I haven't stayed up all night studying once this quarter." **[1 PARAGRAPH]** "I think we can manage to get through the evening even if the telephone party is Jaenson's home. We won't have to tell a soul what we think." **[/]** "Darling good night now. I love you with all my heart now and forever." **[/]** [One drawn heart and an "X" for kisses.] **[/]** "Johnny"

**** To Miss Katherine Glenn, Box 190, Riverton, Wyo. (12/5/41, 11:58 PM, Postmarked 12/6/41, 4:30 PM). Return Address: J. Sproule, 1309 Kearney, Laramie, Wyo. "Darling," **[/]** "I don't hardly know what you mean by 'What happened to you?'. It seems to me like I've written more this week than for quite a while." **[/]** "Everything here is about the same—I just read over that about 'Everything' . . . and though it seems like a very trite thing to say it expresses the situation very well. . . ." **[/]** "The only pleasant thing about these days are the darling letters which you write me!!" **[/]** ". . . Only two more weeks now!!! As this time grows shorter I get happier!!! Darling I'll be the happiest person alive when I see you—no less!!!!" **[1 PARAGRAPH]**

"I think Ray and I are going down to visit Thelma + view the new addition the Kelly family tomorrow afternoon. It's a girl—7 lbs.—born this morning." **[3 PARAGRAPHS]** "Yesterday afternoon I had a bit of extra time so I went down to the machine shop and turned a lens cap for my camera out of a piece of brass. With this cap to slip over the lens I can carry the camera around without getting the lens dusty or fearing getting it scratched." **[/]** "I think tomorrow I may have to wash windows. Mrs. Buck has been talking about that for some time now so I suppose it's just as well to get it over with. . . ." **[2 PARAGRAPHS]** "Night sweetheart." **[/]** "Always and forever yours" **[/]** "Johnny"

 **** To Miss Katherine Glenn, Box 190, Riverton, Wyo. (12/8/41, 1:05 PM, Postmarked 12/8/41, 5:30 PM). Return Address: J. Sproule, 1309 Kearney, Laramie, Wyo. "Kay darling," **[/]** "I just got through with the dishes and I have to go to work so I'm sending you this note now. . . ." **[1 PARAGRAPH]** "All my love + kisses always" **[/]** "Johnny"

 **** To Miss Katherine Glenn, Box 190, Riverton, Wyo. (12/8/41, 7:40 PM, Postmarked 12/9/41, 12:00 PM). Return Address: J. Sproule, 1309 Kearney, Laramie, Wyo. "Hello darling," **[/]** "I just finished with the supper dishes so my time is my own for the rest of the day. And that means I'm writing to you 'cause I love you and cause I got 3 letters from you today. I think it's a record. They're ones you wrote the 4th, 5th, and 6th. Shall I answer in chronological order? O.k.!" **[5 PARAGRAPHS]** "It will be swell if A [Agnes Glenn] can come down for Christmas. I know you miss her a lot. And it always seems nicer to be able to get together during holidays—especially during such a festive season as Christmas." **[/]**

"But now that the long talked about war is actually here—unbelievable as it is—no doubt there will be a feeling of tension and uncertainty for some time—at least months. It will be a time for sacrifices—personal and social—and everyone will have to share responsibility for concentrating the resources and manpower of our nation. Wyoming will be in much less danger of attack and bombing than the coast areas but it will feel the war no less keenly and make no fewer sacrifices of its materiel and physical wealth." **[/]** "Dearest darling the uncertainty of the time and of general world conditions shows me over and over again how wonderful it is that you and I love each other. You are the only person in the world for me sweetheart. . . ." **[/]** "All my love always" **[/]** "Johnny"

 **** To Miss Katherine Glenn, Box 190, Riverton, Wyo. (12/9/41, 11:30 PM, Postmarked 12/10/41, 5:30 PM). Return Address: J. Sproule,

1309 Kearney, Laramie, Wyo. "Hello darling," **[1 PARAGRAPH]** "Honey I really don't think I'll be called—I am sure they are past my number here now and my classification as of July 5 is I-B. And when I took the physical exam here last summer before I came home the doctor said my eyes wouldn't let me in any branch of the service—that's what the doctor said when I tried to get in the officers training course here too. I think my best capacity for service would come from being able to fill some engineering job. This wouldn't be a conflict because I'd have to finish school." **[/]**

"Tonight Jimmy and I went down to a drawing at the theater for $2.00. It's called 'Hospitality Days' and you get tickets with each 25¢ purchase at various stores. We went down right after supper and were going to the show but it was jammed full so we came back and listened to the President's speech and then went back and stood outside during the drawing. I didn't win anything—as usual. I never did feel very lucky about that sort of thing. After the drawing we had a cup of coffee. . . ." **[/]** "I haven't found a ride home yet but I'll get there never fear—Even if I have to hitchhike. . . ." **[4 PARAGRAPHS]** "All my love and kisses" **[/]** "Johnny"

  **** To Miss Katherine Glenn, Box 190, Riverton, Wyo. (12/11/41, 1:09 PM, Postmarked 12/11/41, 5:30 PM). Return Address: J. Sproule, 1309 Kearney, Laramie, Wyo. "Hi darling," **[4 PARAGRAPHS]** "I haven't been thinking of much else besides how perfectly wonderful it would be to be with you again darling. Remember I love you for all time with all my heart." **[/]** "Yours always with all my love" **[/]** "Johnny"

  **** To Miss Katherine Glenn, Box 190, Riverton, Wyo. (12/12/41, 1:10 PM, Postmarked 12/12/41, 4:30 PM). Return Address: J. Sproule, 1309 Kearney, Laramie, Wyo. "Darling," **[/]** "I was so sleepy last night after staying up the night before that I fell asleep here at my desk. After I dozed off about 9:30 I decided I'd better go to bed and write to you today so it would be more legible if not more coherent." **[1 PARAGRAPH]**

"All the news is still of the war. They give the latest bulletins before every program. I suppose they will be doing that for some time now. If labor wi just quit squabbling over strikes etc.—they ought to settle all of that sort of thing by arbitration now—and keep working meanwhile." **[/]** "Ray was planning on going out to Los Angeles during Christmas vacation—His folks are out there now—. . . If he does go he should be able to find out something about the black-outs etc. that they're having." **[2 PARAGRAPHS]** "All my love always" **[/]** "Johnny"

   **** To Miss Katherine Glenn, Box 190, Riverton, Wyo. (12/14/41, 9:30 PM, Postmarked 12/15/41, 2:30 PM). Return Address: J. Sproule, 1309 Kearney, Laramie, Wyo. "Hi darling," **[2 PARAGRAPHS]** "Yesterday (Saturday) I spent all day working here at the house. I started washing the walls and ceiling of the kitchen right after I ate breakfast. I worked on that till 12:00 then waited table and washed the dishes and started in on the ceiling again. I finished the kitchen about 2:30 and then did the bathroom. I've never seen anything as greasy as the kitchen ceiling, esp. above the stove. I just got through with the bathroom in time to shower + shave + set the table for supper. To top it all off I had to do all the supper dishes by myself." **[2 PARAGRAPHS]**

"The war news has been a little more encouraging the last day or so—if you could ever speak of it as encouraging. As near as it is possible to ascertain, the advantage Japan gained by its back-stabbing tactics has been nearly nullified—the Russians are shoving the Germans away from Moscow and the Chinese are coming in to attack the Japs from the rear." **[2 PARAGRAPHS]** "And I'll be very glad to help you with your moving—it's always pleasure to do things for you my precious." **[/]** "Forever and always yours" **[/]** "Johnny"

   **** To Miss Katherine Glenn, Box 190, Riverton, Wyo. (12/16/41, Postmarked 12/17/41, 1:30 PM). Return Address: J. Sproule, 1309 Kearney, Laramie, Wyo. "Hi darling," **[/]** "I haven't been doing anything except studying for finals and working this week but it has been keeping me busy. . . . I haven't been able to find a ride yet, but I'm writing to the folks to see if they could come to Rawlins after me. The only thing about that is that I'm afraid they couldn't come Friday because Mom would probably be working. That would mean that I would possibly come to Rawlins Sat. as that would be as soon as they could come over. I may get a letter from them tomorrow so I'll know more definitely what is going on. I guess if we can't make arrangements by letter I could phone." **[3 PARAGRAPHS]** "All my love and kisses always" **[/]** "Johnny"

Cover: John Harper Sproule, Jr., Wright Field 1942

Lowther Sproule on harvester ca. 1910

Lowther and Mary Sproule ca. 1920

Kiva and Harper Sproule 1917

John and Walter (Gene) Sproule ca. 1927

Sproule summer camp Central Wyoming ca. 1927

Sproule family group in Vista California 1928: Seated on the ground in front, left to right, are Malcolm Anspach and John Harper Sproule, Jr.; seated in chairs in the center, left to right, are Amy Sproule Wilkening, Mary Remsberg Sproule, and Lowther Sproule; standing left to right are Kiva Sproule, John Harper Sproule, Sr., Walter Eugene Sproule, Grace Sproule Wells, Rodney Anspach, [unidentified woman], Alice Sproule Anspach, Orland M. Anspach, Chester M. Wells, Charles Wilkening

Clyda Lakey [Martin] Burns on stage ca. 1910

Glenn family group ca. 1923: left to right, Agnes, Joe, Katherine, Bernard, Emma Pauline, Anna

Glenn siblings in Riverton 1940: left to right Agnes, Bernard, Anna, Joe, Katherine, Harold Bowe [stepbrother]

John Harper Sproule, Jr. and Katherine Veronica Glenn Sproule newlyweds 1943

Katherine Veronica Glenn Sproule 1946

Chapter 6. An Urge to Finish Amid Hurdles—January 1942 to June 3, 1942

Frustration at the nonstop pace, dishes galore, continuing with Catholicism, the impact of war, and friends scattering. JHS tallies the letters and variously muses on roommates, photography, donating blood, and the makings of a good marriage. He affirms his sweety's hope-chest—her fiesta ware and silver salt shakers. JHS plans to borrow money to finance room, board, and tuition in a final push to graduate in summer.

 **** To Miss Katherine Glenn, Box 190, Riverton, Wyo. (1/4/42, 8:45 PM, Postmarked 1/5/42, 1:30 PM). Return Address: J. Sproule, 1309 Kearney, Laramie, Wyo. "Kay darling," **[1 PARAGRAPH]** "The trip back was uneventful. We got to Rawlins in time to meet the bus and left there nearly on schedule (I mean on time almost) and the bus was really jammed. The road was not too bad and we made good time." **[/]** "After having to wait for some time for a taxi I got here to the house about 8:15. I unpacked and I think I'll turn in and rest up for the scramble tomorrow." **[/]** "Goodnight sweetheart." **[/]** "All my love + kisses always" **[/]** "Johnny"

 **** To Miss Katherine Glenn, Box 190, Riverton, Wyo. (1/5/42, 10:45 PM, Postmarked 1/6/42, 1:30 PM). Return Address: J. Sproule, 1309 Kearney, Laramie, Wyo. "Hi darling," **[/]** "About all I got done, today was registering. I wasn't able to do much this morning but I finished it all up this afternoon. I finally compromised between the 17 + 22 hours options by registering for 19 hours. I did this by not taking Portuguese and taking that Curves + Earthwork course. I don't have too bad a schedule; as you can see I have quite a bit of time to get caught up on extra work on Tuesdays and Thursdays." **[/]** [JHS includes a matrix of his classes with Curves + Earthwork at 8:00 AM every day, Mechanics at 9:00 AM every day, Factory Management at 10:00 three days a week, Hydraulics at 11:00 three days a week, Steam Lab 1-3 on Monday, E. E. Lab 1-3 on Wednesday, E. E. Lab 1-3 on Friday.] **[1 PARAGRAPH]** "I started in in full swing on washing dishes today. Boy when there's just the dishes for you and I, I can help you and it won't take any time at all to do them." **[2 PARAGRAPHS]**

"Darling in the rush of things I didn't get those books which you were going to let me have to study. Could you send them to me? If it's in between paychecks why just send them collect. I can read and study them a little at a time and then when I get to taking instructions I won't be so ignorant about it all." **[/]** "School will start in full blast tomorrow and as I'll be having 8 o'clocks every day I'm going to try to get to bed early." **[1 PARAGRAPH]** "Forever yours and love and kisses" **[/]** "Johnny"

**** To Miss Katherine Glenn, Box 190, Riverton, Wyo. (1/6/42, 11:45 PM, Postmarked 1/7/42, 11:30 AM). Return Address: J. Sproule, 1309 Kearney, Laramie, Wyo. "Hello darling," **[3 PARAGRAPHS]** ". . . I feel restless and incomplete. But knowing that you love me makes any endeavor worthwhile sweetheart. And it is a very comforting thought to know that things will be much better for us even though we have to be apart just now." **[/]** "Remember I love you!!!" **[/]** "Night now darling" **[/]** "All my love always" **[/]** "Johnny"

**** To Miss Katherine Glenn, Box 190, Riverton, Wyo. (1/7/42, 7:15 PM, Postmarked 1/8/42, 11:30 AM). Return Address: J. Sproule, 1309 Kearney, Laramie, Wyo. "Darling," **[1 PARAGRAPH]** "Today was a pretty busy day for me because I had classes from 8 to 12 and from 1 to 4. And then I had my hashing to do at noon and tonight. I managed to get down town between 4 when I got out of class and 5:30 when I had to be back to set the table. I had to go to the dime store to get a picture taken for my activity ticket, and then I bought some razor blades and tobacco and came back past the Union book store and bought a couple of books I had to have for that Curves + Earthworks class and one for Hydraulics." **[/]**

"I just got the dishes done a little while ago and after I've written this I have some problems which will keep me busy for 3 or 4 hours. Tomorrow won't be so bad though because I only have two classes." **[/]** "I'm going to be able to work another month or so on that job I had with Gilbert. And so for now at least I won't be able to look for any other work 'cause I've about got my time occupied. I'll probably go over to the lab and work tomorrow afternoon, but it isn't very hard—yesterday afternoon I was over there and worked but Gilbert + I sat and talked over the war etc about half that time. I didn't mind though cause I'll get paid for the whole afternoon even if we didn't get a great deal done." **[3 PARAGRAPHS]** "All my love always" **[/]** "Johnny"

  **** To Miss Katherine Glenn, Box 190, Riverton, Wyo. (1/8/42, 11:15 PM, Postmarked 1/9/42, 11:30 AM). Return Address: J. Sproule, 1309 Kearney, Laramie, Wyo. "Hello darling," **[1 PARAGRAPH]** ". . . I have evolved this plan: to keep up with my work from day to day as much as I can and then do up on weekends the things I haven't been able to do during the week. That way I should be able to get to bed at a reasonable hour (so I can make my 8 o'clocks) and still keep my work up. This plan seems to be working so far at least. . . ." **[3 PARAGRAPHS]** "All my love for ever" **[/]** "Johnny"

  **** To Miss Katherine Glenn, Box 190, Riverton, Wyo. (1/9/42, 11:00 PM, Postmarked 1/10/42, 1:30 PM). Return Address: J. Sproule, 1309 Kearney, Laramie, Wyo. "Hello darling," **[2 PARAGRAPHS]** "By working Tue. and Thursday afternoon and Saturdays this week and next I can make up for not working in December and get in 15 hours for January and then I shouldn't have to go over there and work for a couple weeks. I'll be able to use that extra time for loafing or getting some school work done or—anyhow I can use it some way." **[1 PARAGRAPH]** "All my love and kisses always" **[/]** "Johnny"

  **** To Miss Katherine Glenn, Box 190, Riverton, Wyo. (1/11/42, 12:15 AM, Postmarked 1/11/42, Wed., TR 27, OMAHA AND OGDEN R.P.O.). Return Address: J. Sproule, 1309 Kearney, Laramie, Wyo. "Hi darling," **[2 PARAGRAPHS]** "Well tonight I went to the basketball game—Wyo beat Utah 64-50—which was a nice comfortable margin. It was a good game though and it looks like Wyoming will win quite a few games this season." **[/]** "After the game I went over to the Union to see who was around and got in a bridge game with some fellows. After playing a while part of us decided to go to the midnight show. One of the guys had a car so we didn't have to walk. The show was 'Birth of the Blues' with B. Crosby & Mary Martin. It was a pretty good show—light comedy and music and nothing very serious." **[/]**

"They're raising haircuts to 65¢ + shows to 35¢ effective Monday—so I decided I needed a haircut this afternoon—I had to wait for quite a while—they were really busy." **[2 PARAGRAPHS]** "Remember I love you darling." **[/]** "All my love always" **[/]** "Johnny"

**** To Miss Katherine Glenn, Box 190, Riverton, Wyo. (1/11/42, 11:10 PM, Postmarked 1/12/42, 9:30 AM). Return Address: J. Sproule, 1309 Kearney, Laramie, Wyo. "Hello darling," **[1 PARAGRAPH]** "There are a lot of things I'd like to do and I may be able to find time if I get accustomed to studying on a schedule so I can get it over with. I seem to spend at least a part of my time reading or doing some other unproductive thing." **[/]**

"For one thing, I haven't had time to develop or print any pictures for quite a while. . . ." **[/]** "Ray must be doing more work on his thesis than usual for I haven't seen him for 3 or 4 days. And I haven't had time to go over and see him." **[2 PARAGRAPHS]** "All my love always" **[/]** "Johnny"

**** To Miss Katherine Glenn, Box 190, Riverton, Wyo. (1/12/42, 10:50 PM, Postmarked 1/13/42, 10:30 AM). Return Address: J. Sproule, 1309 Kearney, Laramie, Wyo. "Darling," **[2 PARAGRAPHS]** "Ray was over for a while—he left just a little while ago—I'd just finished my Mechanics problems so we sat around + talked of this + that. Of course we didn't accomplish much but it is very restful I find." **[/]** ". . . I'm usually occupied till 11 o'clock or so but I've been fairly successful in getting to bed by twelve at least." **[4 PARAGRAPHS]** "All my love" **[/]** "Johnny"

**** To Miss Katherine Glenn, Box 190, Riverton, Wyo. (1/13/42, 11:48 PM, Postmarked 1/14/42, 10:30 AM). Return Address: J. Sproule, 1309 Kearney, Laramie, Wyo. "Hi darling," **[1 PARAGRAPH]** "But then the days all seem a lot alike—classes, studying or working problems and that sort of thing makes them all seem about the same." **[/]**

"For a while now (I guess for most of this quarter) there will be basketball games to go to on Friday or Saturday nights. That will be a diversion from the boredom of staying home doing school work. I won't mind staying home weeknights studying if I can keep up so I won't have to work Sundays. Then I can sleep late, and just generally loaf." **[/]** "I found that going to bed at a somewhat regular hour has made it easier to get up in the mornings to make my 8 o'clocks." **[2 PARAGRAPHS]** "Goodnight sweetheart" **[/]** "Johnny"

**** To Miss Katherine Glenn, Box 190, Riverton, Wyo. (1/14/42, 11:56 PM, Postmarked 1/15/42, 11:30 AM). Return Address: J. Sproule, 1309 Kearney, Laramie, Wyo. "Darling," **[6 PARAGRAPHS]** "All my love always" **[/]** "Johnny" **[/]** "P. S. I'm not missing you a damn bit less as the days go by."

**** To Miss Katherine Glenn, Box 190, Riverton, Wyo. (1/15/42, 11:50 PM, Postmarked 1/16/42, 8 AM). Return Address: J. Sproule, 1309 Kearney, Laramie, Wyo. "Hello darling," **[/]** "I'm sort of running out of stationery—had you noticed? And I haven't been able to get down town yet. Saturday afternoons are about the only time I have to get to town except perhaps on Sunday but then the stores are closed. Come Saturday then I should be able to get some." **[4 PARAGRAPHS]** "XXXXXX" **[/]** "Goodnight my love" **[/]** "Johnny"

**** To Miss Katherine Glenn, Box 190, Riverton, Wyo. (1/16/42, 11:35 PM, Postmarked 1/17/42, 11:30 AM). Return Address: J. Sproule, 1309 Kearney, Laramie, Wyo. "Hello darling," **[1 PARAGRAPH]** "I changed my brand of cigarettes too—I changed when I started to school again—from Luckies to Half + Half which I manufacture myself buying the tobacco by the pound + papers by the package." **[/]**

"I thought I'd get quite a bit done tonight, but I just sort of relaxed when I got through with the dishes. Ray + Mary Jane stopped in for a little while and that passed away part of the evening. I guess they had been listening to the broadcast of the game. . . ." **[5 PARAGRAPHS]** "Love and kisses" **[/]** "Johnny"

**** To Miss Katherine Glenn, Box 190, Riverton, Wyo. (1/17/42, 11:39 PM, Postmarked 1/19/42, TR 5, OMAHA & OGDEN R.P.O.). Return Address: J. Sproule, 1309 Kearney, Laramie, Wyo. "Hello darling," **[4 PARAGRAPHS]** "I've seen 'Keys of the Kingdom' advertised in book club advertisements but I've never read it—it's supposed to be good though. If you like it I'll try to get it at the library and read it." **[5 PARAGRAPHS]** "All my love and kisses" **[/]** "Johnny"

**** To Miss Katherine Glenn, Box 190, Riverton, Wyo. (1/18/42, 11:58 PM, Postmarked 1/19/42, 8:30 AM). Return Address: J. Sproule, 1309 Kearney, Laramie, Wyo. "Hello darling," **[/]** ". . . The two weeks I've been down here have seemed ten times as long as the two weeks I was home." **[2 PARAGRAPHS]** "Jimmy Jenson went home over the weekend—he is from Wheatland. I like for him to go home on weekends cause then I go up and borrow his radio and bring it down to my room. He doesn't mind so I might as well use it don't you think? But I think he is getting married in Feb. or March sometime so that will end my using his radio." **[/]**

"After Bradley moved out last quarter there were only three others staying here in the basement beside myself and of the three one was drafted, one joined the Air Corps and the other is moving up to the Cowboy Dorm. If or when Jimmy moves out there will be a whole new bunch here—or else it will be sort of empty—but I don't mind cause it's quieter then and I can get my work done with less disturbance. I don't have any kick about the guys who were studying here though because they were pretty quiet—around studying time anyhow." **[/]**

"Ray was over and wanted me to go to the show with him and Mary Jane but I didn't think I had time to go to the show when I would have had to come home and do my evenings work afterward. The show was 'How Green Was My Valley'. Something about some Welsh coal miners—I don't know how it would have been but it's been advertised quite a bit." **[2 PARAGRAPHS]** "All my love and kisses" **[/]** "Johnny"

**** To Miss Katherine Glenn, Box 190, Riverton, Wyo. (1/19/42, 11:58 PM, Postmarked 1/20/42, 10 AM). Return Address: J. Sproule, 1309

Kearney, Laramie, Wyo. "Hi darling," **[2 PARAGRAPHS]** ". . . When I got up a thick fog was covering everything. I followed the familiar route to school so I wasn't lost a minute. When the fog lifted though it left the trees and bushes about the campus covered with frost which was very nice looking in the sunlight—if you like winter scenes. I wished then (when the fog lifted) that I had thought to carry my camera along—the frosted trees might have made a nice picture." **[2 PARAGRAPHS]** "All my love always" **[/]** "Johnny"

   **** To Miss Katherine Glenn, Box 190, Riverton, Wyo. (1/20/42, 11:51 PM, Postmarked 1/21/42, 10:30 AM). Return Address: J. Sproule, 1309 Kearney, Laramie, Wyo. "Hello darling," **[1 PARAGRAPH]** "That's a pretty smart way to buy your Fiesta Ware—a piece at a time I mean— 'cause then you have it. It seems like whenever I try to save up enough money to pay cash for something I can never save quite enough—there's always something else coming up, but I did finally get my watch fixed." **[/]** "Yes darling I think those little silver salt + pepper shakers are nice." **[/]** "Well now, I believe you could quit smoking during Lent if you put your mind to it. And if you have a dollar bet besides, why it's practically a cinch." **[/]** "' For Whom the Bell Tolls' is a good example of Hemingways style and manner of writing so if you've ever read any of his books you might like it. It's just a sort of light fiction about the war in Spain particularly about a small band of guerrilla fighters." **[2 PARAGRAPHS]** "All my love always" **[/]** "Johnny"

   **** To Miss Katherine Glenn, Box 190, Riverton, Wyo. (1/22 [sic]/42, 11:43 PM, Postmarked 1/22/42, 10:30 AM). Return Address: J. Sproule, 1309 Kearney, Laramie, Wyo. "Hello darling," **[2 PARAGRAPHS]** "One eye keeps going shut so I'd better get it to bed." **[/]** "All my love and kisses as always darling. Goodnight sweetheart" **[/]** "XXXXX" **[/]** "Johnny"

   **** To Miss Katherine Glenn, Box 190, Riverton, Wyo. (1/21/42, 11:59 PM, Postmarked 1/22/42, 10:30 AM). Return Address: J. Sproule, 1309 Kearney, Laramie, Wyo. "Hi darling," **[/]** "I've been plugging away here at my desk and I have become so sleepy that my efficiency is about zero." **[/]** "I think that I will get out of going to my Engineering classes Friday because of the Civil Engineers meeting being held in Cheyenne Friday and Sat. Thus I should have only one class to attend Friday. That v be a welcome relief." **[2 PARAGRAPHS]** "Remember I love you always" **[/]** "Johnny"

**** To Miss Katherine Glenn, Box 190, Riverton, Wyo. (1/23/42, 11:01 PM, Postmarked 1/24/42, 12:30 PM). Return Address: J. Sproule, 1309 Kearney, Laramie, Wyo. "Kay darling," **[/]** "I don't know what to t you about this mail business. I really don't—I thought you knew that I write to you every night. And I post your letters in just the same manner each week—I say each week because I mail your letters on week days (Mon. thru Fri.) in a collection box in the Engineering building from which the mail is collected at 8:25 a.m. (I mail your letters before I go to my 8 o'clock class). Then Saturday mornings I mail the letter I write on Friday night in a collection box in the opposite corner of the block—the mail is collected at 10:40 a.m. and I mail your letter as I go to work. Then on Sunday I walk down to the depot to mail the letter I've written Saturday night so it will go out on the train as there is no mail collection or delivery on Sunday." **[7 PARAGRAPHS]** "Good night darling. Remember I love yo with all my heart." **[/]** "All my love and kisses always" **[/]** "Johnny"

**** To Miss Katherine Glenn, Box 190, Riverton, Wyo. (1/24/42, 8:53 PM, Postmarked 1/24 /42, TR 27, OM. & OGDEN R.P.O.). Return Address: J. Sproule, 1309 Kearney, Laramie, Wyo. "Hello sweetheart," **[** "... I think I'll study for a couple hours and then he [Jimmy Jenson] and I will go to the midnight show." **[5 PARAGRAPHS]** "All my love + kisses" **[/]** "Johnny"

**** To Miss Katherine Glenn, Box 190, Riverton, Wyo. (1/26/42, 10:36 PM, Postmarked: indecipherable). Return Address: J. Sproule, 1309 Kearney, Laramie, Wyo. "Hello darling," **[/]** "Well last night after the bunch cleared out I went to work on my curves notebook but it took me until 6:30 this morning to get it finished. — There wasn't much use in going to bed then so I'm going to get to bed by 11 tonight. I won't get so far behind again I hope." **[2 PARAGRAPHS]** "All my love + kisses" **[/]** "Johnny"

**** To Miss Katherine Glenn, Box 190, Riverton, Wyo. (1/25/42, 11:17 PM, Postmarked 1/26/42, 8:30 AM). Return Address: J. Sproule, 1309 Kearney, Laramie, Wyo. "Hello darling," **[/]** ". . . After the dishes were washed Jimmy + I and a couple more fellows who eat here took a ride up to the Summit + watched the skiing for a while." **[1 PARAGRAPH]** "This has been one of my most idle weekends for last night Jimmy + I went to the midnight show. It was 'Johnny Eager' with Robert Taylor and Lana Turner. A sort of gangster show but it was good I thought." **[2 PARAGRAPHS]** "All my love + kisses" **[/]** "Johnny"

**** To Miss Katherine Glenn, Box 190, Riverton, Wyo. (1/27/42, 11:41 PM, Postmarked 1/28/42, 10:30 AM). Return Address: J. Sproule, 1309 Kearney, Laramie, Wyo. "Hello darling," **[/]** "You know, by damn, I was sleepier this morning when I got up after 8 hours of sleep than I was yesterday morning when I didn't have any—odd isn't it? **[1 PARAGRAPH]** "There were thirteen on the table tonight so it took a while longer than usual to get the dishes done." **[1 PARAGRAPH]** ". . . I know you said you'd write as often as I did, but as of today the score is 24 to 11. You probably have at least one more letter in the mail but you can see that you have been writing about half as often as I have." **[2 PARAGRAPHS]** "All my love + kisses" **[/]** "Johnny"

**** To Miss Katherine Glenn, Box 190, Riverton, Wyo. (1/28/42, 11:57 PM, Postmarked 1/29/42, 10:30 AM). Return Address: J. Sproule, 1309 Kearney, Laramie, Wyo. "Hello darling," **[1 PARAGRAPH]** "I did my tomorrows problems this afternoon so I didn't have any thing pressing that had to be done tonight. Jimmy + I and another fellow who eats here went to the show. We just got back. We saw 'Sun Valley Serenade' and 'Blossoms in the Dust.' Both were good shows. I liked 'S.V.S' the most because it was sort of a light musical comedy—a good kind for just entertainment when you don't want anything but some laughs and stuff." **[1 PARAGRAPH]**

"That job that Joe [Glenn] took shouldn't be too bad—cooks sometimes have to get up early but then they probably have time off during the day and they shouldn't have to work too hard. And then if he likes it better than what he was doing it will be much nicer." **[3 PARAGRAPHS]** "All my love + kisses"   **[/]**   "Johnny"

  **** To Miss Katherine Glenn, Box 190, Riverton, Wyo. (1/29/42, 11:34 PM, Postmarked 1/30/42, 11:00 AM). Return Address: J. Sproule, 1309 Kearney, Laramie, Wyo. "Dearest darling," **[2 PARAGRAPHS]** "Darling did you call me last night? Mrs. Buck said I had a long distance call from Riverton last night. If it was from you, I'm sorry as hell that I wasn't home. I don't usually go to the show in the middle of the week, or anyplace for that matter, but I did win a show ticket from Jimmy and since the shows were pretty good we went." **[1 PARAGRAPH]** "Yes Ray and Mary Jane are still going together. . . ." **[1 PARAGRAPH]** "All my love" **[/** "Johnny"

  **** To Miss Katherine Glenn, Box 190, Riverton, Wyo. (1/30/42, 11:33 PM, Postmarked 1/31/42, 2:00 PM). Return Address: J. Sproule, 1309 Kearney, Laramie, Wyo. "Hello my darling," **[/]** "It was wonderful to talk to you for a little while again even if we did have to do it via the telephone. I really liked it. I still get excited though and can't think of much to say. But its grand to hear your voice again." **[2 PARAGRAPHS]**

"Dearest I have your letter here where you say 'What do you feel exactly right now?'. Here it is—I won't hedge. I can see two mistakes that I've made, which I wish fervently that I hadn't. The greatest one was my staying out of school when I did that—I should have kept on no matter what. Further I've taken some courses down here that were not very valuable to me but that really isn't too serious—only that I should have spent my time on something more worthwhile." **[/]**

"About us I have no doubts—not the slightest ones. I love you and you love me and sweetheart we're going to have the greatest life together. I think that if two people have their love for each other, a reasonable amount of economic security, and the capacity or ability to see one anothers point of view, they can't miss having a wonderful successful marriage." **[/]**

"I'm working as fast as I can to finish up this college degree for it's the first long step. When I've got a job I'll probably learn as much again as I have here in school, but this school work is the foundation for the ability to learn + reason." **[/]** "After I'm through here and have gone to work it won't be long till we can be married." **[2 PARAGRAPHS]** "All my love sweetheart" **[/]** "Johnny"

**** To Miss Katherine Glenn, Box 190, Riverton, Wyo. (1/31/42, 11:49 PM, Postmarked 2/1/42, TR 9, OM. & OGDEN R.P.O.). Return Address: J. Sproule, 1309 Kearney, Laramie, Wyo. "Hello darling," **[/]** "A month has gone by and it has seemed like an age. This going to college seems like such a long drawn out process. I will really rejoice when it's over. I get damned tired of being on the go from 8 am to midnight—especially at such a low wage." **[/]** "But I'll feel better tomorrow after a good nights sleep. I usually react better when I'm not so tired." **[1 PARAGRAPH]**

"Since this is the last of the month I'll send you the calendar sheet for January which I referred to previously." [A calendar page {2" x 4"} is pasted in below with notation that a checkmark means days when JHS wrote a letter and then underlining refers to days when he received a letter from KVS.] "Total letters written—28 "Total letters received—15" **[1 PARAGRAPH]** "All my love sweetheart. 'Night." **[/]** "XXXXXX" **[/]** "Johnny "

**** To Miss Katherine Glenn, Box 190, Riverton, Wyo. (2/2/42, 1:51 AM, Postmarked 2/2/42, 10:30 AM). Return Address: J. Sproule, 1309 Kearney, Laramie, Wyo. "Hello sweetheart," **[1 PARAGRAPH]** "I've got Jimmy's radio while he's away on his honeymoon—he could only get 4 days off, 5 counting Sunday, from work— . . . I like to play the radio late 'cause then the programs are mostly popular music with few interruptions for commercials." **[/]** "Did you ever notice how songs can remind you of times or places? I've heard several songs this evening which recalled, oh!

ever so vividly, some of the grand times we've had together darling." **[1 PARAGRAPH]** "All my love + kisses" **[/]** "Johnny"

**** To Miss Katherine Glenn, Box 190, Riverton, Wyo. (2/2/42, 11:50 PM, Postmarked 2/3/42, 9:00 AM). Return Address: J. Sproule, 1309 Kearney, Laramie, Wyo. "Hello darling," **[3 PARAGRAPHS]** "I didn't get to bed last night till 2 so I'll have to do better tonight. . . ." **[/]** [JHS includes a heart drawing] "X's" **[/]** "Johnny"

**** To Miss Katherine Glenn, Box 190, Riverton, Wyo. (2/3/42, 11:49 PM, Postmarked 2/4/42, 10:30 AM). Return Address: J. Sproule, 1309 Kearney, Laramie, Wyo. "Hello darling," **[2 PARAGRAPHS]** "Honey I wish I had some of your spare time. I could sure use it—I seem to be busy most of the time but still my work seems to pile up—and then when the pile gets big enough I stay up all night some night + catch up on a good part of it. Even on ordinary evenings I never get to bed before midnight. Darling could you send me a pound (of your spare time)?" **[3 PARAGRAPHS]** "Goodnight my love" **[/]** "X X X" **[/]** "Johnny"

**** To Miss Katherine Glenn, Box 190, Riverton, Wyo. (2/4/42, 11:50 PM, Postmarked 2/5/42, 10:30 AM). Return Address: J. Sproule, 1309 Kearney, Laramie, Wyo. "Hello sweetheart," **[/]** ". . . I've been going to bed around midnight even if I don't have it all done—getting a regular amount of sleep makes it a lot easier to get up in the mornings and I haven't missed any classes so far this quarter." **[4 PARAGRAPHS]** "All my love X X X X" **[/]** "Johnny"

**** To Miss Katherine Glenn, Box 190, Riverton, Wyo. (2/6/42, 5:47 AM, Postmarked 2/6/42, 9:30 AM). Return Address: J. Sproule, 1309 Kearney, Laramie, Wyo. "Hello darling," **[1 PARAGRAPH]** "I tried a new tack—instead of studying till the late hour I came down last night and went to sleep early + then got up about 3 and did my bit of studying." **[/]** "It seems all right now but I don't think it would work for a general practice 'cause I might not always wake up." **[3 PARAGRAPHS]** "All my love + kisses" **[/]** "Johnny"

**** To Miss Katherine Glenn, Box 190, Riverton, Wyo. (2/6/42, 9:05 PM, Postmarked 2/7/42, 5:30 PM). Return Address: J. Sproule, 1309 Kearney, Laramie, Wyo. "Hello sweetheart," **[/]** "Well I haven't accomplished anything yet this evening except reading the current installments of a couple of stories in the Colliers." **[/]** "But I think I'll buckle down and do a little work pretty soon." **[4 PARAGRAPHS]** "All my love" **[/]** "Johnny"

**** To Miss Katherine Glenn, Box 190, Riverton, Wyo. (2/9/42, 2:10 PM, Postmarked 2/9/42, 5:00 PM). Return Address: J. Sproule, 1309 Kearney, Laramie, Wyo. "Hello my darling," **[/]** "Here I have an afternoon off—what do you think of that! I worked 8 hours Saturday so I didn't have to work as usual this aft. It's probably a good thing for I didn't sleep much last night. I went to bed at 12 + got up at 4—now deducting 1 hour for changing to 'War Time' leaves only 3 hr. I had to get up and finish some problems for today. I could have let them go but I hate to hand things in late." **[1 PARAGRAPH]**

"Well now you didn't seem to get the idea in the matter about S. A. [South America]—I thought of it only as a place where it would be warmer for it was terribly cold that night when I was writing you. That's all it was—just an unfunny joke." **[3 PARAGRAPHS]** "love + kisses" **[/]** "Johnny"

**** To Miss Katherine Glenn, Box 190, Riverton, Wyo. (2/9/42, 10:09 PM, Postmarked 2/10/42, 9:30 AM). Return Address: J. Sproule, 1309 Kearney, Laramie, Wyo. "Hello sweetheart," **[4 PARAGRAPHS]** "I asked him [Ray Berryman] when he was going to get married. He said there was nothing definite—but he's in favor of it. We got to talking about religion. His one query about Catholicism was about the prohibition of birth control." **[3 PARAGRAPHS]** "All my love + kisses" **[/]** "Johnny"

**** To Miss Katherine Glenn, Box 190, Riverton, Wyo. (2/10/42, 11:58 PM, Postmarked 2/11/42, 10:00 AM). Return Address: J. Sproule, 1309 Kearney, Laramie, Wyo. "Hello darling," **[/]** "Well this new time is a fine thing but is sure dark when I get up in the morning. It's nice to have the extra daylight in the evening and once it gets dark you never notice th difference." **[5 PARAGRAPHS]** "Love" **[/]** "Johnny"

**** To Miss Katherine Glenn, Box 190, Riverton, Wyo. (2/11/42, 11:33 PM, Postmarked 2/12/42, 10:30 AM). Return Address: J. Sproule, 1309 Kearney, Laramie, Wyo. "Hello darling," **[2 PARAGRAPHS]** "I went downtown with a couple of the fellows who eat here—one of them was looking for a tire. He bought a second hand one—a pretty good one though—for $9.00. Before the rationing, I'll bet you could have bought it for 4 or 5 dollars." **[4 PARAGRAPHS]** "Always" **[/]** "Johnny"

**** To Miss Katherine Glenn, Box 190, Riverton, Wyo. (2/13/42, 8:05 PM, Postmarked 2/13/42, OM. & OGDEN R.P.O.). Return Address: J. Sproule, 1309 Kearney, Laramie, Wyo. "Hello darling," **[5 PARAGRAPHS]** "Happy Valentine's day darling, for you are my valentine—and everything else in the world to me sweetheart!" **[1 PARAGRAPH]** "Yours always" ["Johnny"

**** To Miss Katherine Glenn, Box 190, Riverton, Wyo. (2/15/42, 10:37 PM, Postmarked 2/16/42, 8:30 AM). Return Address: J. Sproule, 1309 Kearney, Laramie, Wyo. "Hello darling," **[1 PARAGRAPH]** "I went t the basketball game last night— . . . and then fooled around for a while a didn't get anything done. Then this evening I went to the show with Dea Tunks, a fellow who boards here at the house. The show was 'Woman of the Year' with Hepburn + Tracy. It wasn't a bad show but its not all its advertised to be. . . ." **[/]**

"It usually works about the same each quarter—I'll work and work to kee caught up and then I'll let things slide for a while until I've absolutely got keep busy. . . ." **[1 PARAGRAPH]** "Did you get saddle pants to go with cowboy boots? What color did you get? I'll bet they look swell." **[/]** "Goodnight sweetheart." **[/]** "All my love" **[/]** "Johnny"

**** To Miss Katherine Glenn, Box 190, Riverton, Wyo. (2/16/42, 10:45 PM, Postmarked 2/17/42, 11:30 AM). Return Address: J. Sproule, 1309 Kearney, Laramie, Wyo. "Dear Darling," **[1 PARAGRAPH]** "What w being on war time for a week, I'm getting fairly used to it. It doesn't mak such a great deal of difference, but if it's a helpful measure then I'm for it." **[5 PARAGRAPHS]** "Goodnight sweetheart" **[/]** "All my love" **[/]** "Johnny"

 **** To Miss Katherine Glenn, Box 190, Riverton, Wyo. (2/17/42, 11:51 PM, Postmarked 2/18/42, 10:00 AM). Return Address: J. Sproule, 1309 Kearney, Laramie, Wyo. "Hello darling," **[2 PARAGRAPHS]** "It was only 15° below zero this morning as I went to school so you can see that spring has not sprung—yet anyhow." **[5 PARAGRAPHS]** "Goodnight sweetheart. I love you always" **[/]** "X X X X X" **[/]** "Johnny"

 **** To Miss Katherine Glenn, Box 190, Riverton, Wyo. (2/19/42, 10:47 PM, Postmarked 2/20/42, 10:30 AM). Return Address: J. Sproule, 1309 Kearney, Laramie, Wyo. "Hello darling," **[/]** ". . . God knows how I got so far behind, but I'm getting caught up a little at a time. I guess it was because I was working so much over at the lab the first of the quarter. I haven't worked over there since about the 10th when I had my hours for the month in. I'd just as soon not work there at all but the \$7.50 a month enables me to pay my room rent." **[/]** "Well now I was surprised to open your letter this afternoon and see the full page admonition. I didn't realize that I had fallen behind two letters, . . ." **[1 PARAGRAPH]**

"Yes darling I have been reading those books you sent. I have read through most of them and started in the other evening to learn the prayers in the Catechism. I have only learned the Lord's Prayer, the Angelical Salutations, the Apostles Creed and the Confiteor so far. What about all the questions and answers in the Catechism? Should I know all the answers as they are given or what about them? Thanks darling for your generous offer to help which I may need as I get further along." **[1 PARAGRAPH]** "That's swell that Anna [Glenn] just has a little way to go to work. I'd wondered if she ever had to walk way down there, for that would be quite a distance." **[/]**

"So far as I know I'll be able to finish here for I haven't heard anything different from the draft board." **[3 PARAGRAPHS]** "All my love and kisses" **[/]** "Johnny"

**** To Miss Katherine Glenn, Box 190, Riverton, Wyo. (2/21/42, 11:49 PM, Postmarked 2/22/42, TR 9, OM. & OGDEN R.P.O.). Return Address: J. Sproule, 1309 Kearney, Laramie, Wyo. "Hello darling," **[4 PARAGRAPHS]** "Darling I wish you a very happy birthday. It would be grand if we could be together and really celebrate it. . . ." **[/]** "It's getting cold as the devil here in my room and as its late I don't think I'll do any more tonight." **[2 PARAGRAPHS]** "All my love + kisses" **[/]** "Johnny"

**** To Miss Katherine Glenn, Box 190, Riverton, Wyo. (2/24/42, "(really F. 25 since it's almost 1 am)", Postmarked 2/25/42, 10:30 AM). Return Address: J. Sproule, 1309 Kearney, Laramie, Wyo. "Hello darling," **[/]** "I really hit the jackpot today after the unusually long period between mail deliveries for I received three letters from you today. That sort of put me behind again doesn't it? That is counting since Feb 1st." **[4 PARAGRAPHS]**

"I listened to the Presidents speech last night. He really laid it on the line didn't he? And he's right for a lot of people still don't realize what a serious situation we are in. And they're going to have to wake up. This next year is apt to see some improvement though—if of course, labor and industry will quit their petty squabbling over everything and concentrate on production and more production. This 8 hour day 5 day week is fine in peacetime, but we just haven't time for it now. By God I'll be glad when I can get a job—do some work and pay some taxes." **[5 PARAGRAPHS]**

"That's swell that you haven't felt any discomfort from giving up smoking. I've been smoking a pipe quite a bit lately for its easier and quicker than rolling a cigarette and pipes give a fine smoke when they are kept clean. The only thing I really use a lot of matches when I smoke a pipe." **[2 PARAGRAPHS]** "Always + forever yours" **[/]** "Johnny"

**** To Miss Katherine Glenn, Box 190, Riverton, Wyo. (2/25/42, Postmarked 2/26/42, 11:30 AM). Return Address: J. Sproule, 1309 Kearney, Laramie, Wyo. "Hello sweetheart," **[2 PARAGRAPHS]** "No I don remember ever reading 'The Road Back', but I seem to recall that it was something about the rehabilitation of German soldiers after World War I—

possibly by Remarque or possibly I'm thinking of some other book." **[4 PARAGRAPHS]** "Always" **[/]** "Johnny"

  **** To Miss Katherine Glenn, Box 190, Riverton, Wyo. (2/28/42, 8:45 AM, Postmarked 2/28/42, 2:30 PM). Return Address: J. Sproule, 1309 Kearney, Laramie, Wyo. "Goodmorning darling," **[/]** "I am writing you this morning instead of last night for I worked with Ray [Berryman] all night last night on details of a geological map—a part of his thesis. He had them worked up but not drawn so I helped him out by drawing them." **[2 PARAGRAPHS]** "At the moment I am sleepy but I'll get over that, for I've quite a bit to do yet today." **[2 PARAGRAPHS]**

"OK then darling, we'll celebrate your birthday in July. It will be much nicer weather I agree, and I can see where you would feel more like a celebration. **[/]** "Well now I guess that using my time more efficiently—spending less time just sitting around reading or gasing with some of the fellows—isn't what you'd termed a Lenten sacrifice, but I think my idea at that time was giving up my leisure time—what leisure time I have, that is." **[2 PARAGRAPHS]** "X X X X" **[/]** "Johnny" **[1 PARAGRAPH]** "PS.[2] I didn't 'lay it on' till you were 10 or 12 letters behind did I?" **[/]** "love again" **[/]** "J."

  **** To Miss Katherine Glenn, Box 190, Riverton, Wyo. (3/2/42, 2:01 AM, Postmarked 3/2/42, 10:30 AM). Return Address: J. Sproule, 1309 Kearney, Laramie, Wyo. "Hello darling," **[1 PARAGRAPH]** "Dean Tunks and I just got back from Greeley and Fort Morgan where we drove this afternoon. We stopped at Greeley and Dean saw a girl he knows there and then we went on down towards Fort Morgan where his folks live. It was a nice drive even if we did get stuck in a snow bank down at Dean's folks place." **[1 PARAGRAPH]**

"Out of the ten persons having their blood typed Saturday mine was the only one that would match. Consequently I donated a pint that afternoon. I'd never done that before and I wondered how it would be—it was really easy—nothing to it, I couldn't even tell the difference after the doctor finished taking it as compared with beforehand. I heard that professional donors get $25 a pint for blood—I wouldn't mind in the least being able to sell blood for $25 a pint for it would sure be an easy way to make $25 bucks. But at least I know that my blood is type 2 and that it is pure." **[2 PARAGRAPHS]** "You'll have a full set of Fiesta Ware one of these times now when you keep adding some from time to time." **[2 PARAGRAPHS]** "Goodnight sweetheart." **[/]** All my love" **[/]** "Johnny"

  **** To Miss Katherine Glenn, Box 190, Riverton, Wyo. (3/2/42, 11:58 PM, Postmarked 3/3/42, 11:30 AM). Return Address: J. Sproule, 1309 Kearney, Laramie, Wyo. "Kay darling," **[/]** "I'm so sorry that you don't see the merits of long letters. Personally I think they are o.k." **[2 PARAGRAPHS]** "All my love" **[/]** "Johnny"

  **** To Miss Katherine Glenn, Box 190, Riverton, Wyo. (3/4/42, Postmarked 3/5/42, 8:30 AM). Return Address: J. Sproule, 1309 Kearney, Laramie, Wyo. "Hello darling," **[1 PARAGRAPH]** "No on the contrary, when they had tapped me for a pint of blood, I couldn't even tell the difference—it was that easy—I think I told you I was type 2. Incidentally the transfusion didn't do much good for the old fellow died." **[4 PARAGRAPHS]** "Wyoming won a b.b. game last night. A loud time was had by all for it was close and a sort of grudge game like Riverton + Lander. They beat C.U. 40-39. Which may in some measure atone for this second place standing." **[3 PARAGRAPHS]** "X X X" **[/]** "Johnny"

  **** To Miss Katherine Glenn, Box 190, Riverton, Wyo. (3/6/42, 12:58 PM, Postmarked 3/6/42, 4:30 PM). Return Address: J. Sproule, 1309 Kearney, Laramie, Wyo. "Hello sweet," **[2 PARAGRAPHS]** "That's swell that the dentist passed you for the next six months without having to have any grinding or anything done." **[2 PARAGRAPHS]** "All my love" **[/]** "Johnny"

  **** To Miss Katherine Glenn, Box 190, Riverton, Wyo. (3/6/42, 11:45 PM, Postmarked 3/7/42, 12 M). Return Address: J. Sproule, 1309 Kearney, Laramie, Wyo. "Hello darling," **[1 PARAGRAPH]** "My chief sensation at this moment is sleepiness. If I'd gone to bed last night it probably wouldn't be so bad but I had about 10 days work on my curves notebook to do so - - -." **[/]** "That's too bad about Ken's car. They're fine to have but it doesn't look like a good time to own one right at the present—what with tire rationing etc." **[4 PARAGRAPHS]** "All my love" **[/]** "Johnny"

**** To Miss Katherine Glenn, Box 190, Riverton, Wyo. (2[sic]/10/42, 4:30 PM, Postmarked 3/11/42, 9:30 AM). Return Address: J. Sproule, 1309 Kearney, Laramie, Wyo. "Hello darling," **[2 PARAGRAPHS]** "Sunday night I went up to a party or open house or call it what you like—in celebration of the third anniversary of the opening of the Union. They had a number of games with prizes for the winners of the tournaments in those various games. I didn't get there in time to get in the pool or snooker tournament. So I entered the Chinese checkers tournament (I won it incidentally)." **[/]** "Sunday I put in a good day on my school work even though Dean and I went to the matinee. The show was 'The Louisiana Purchase'. A pretty good show." **[1 PARAGRAPH]**

"Ray passed his oral for his master's yesterday and has his thesis done—he's leaving for Los Angeles Thursday or Friday. He's supposed to report for work Monday morning the 16th." **[4 PARAGRAPHS]** "All my love" **[/]** "Johnny"

**** To Miss Katherine Glenn, Box 190, Riverton, Wyo. (3/11/42, Postmarked 3/12/42, 9:30 AM). Return Address: J. Sproule, 1309 Kearney, Laramie, Wyo. "Hello darling," **[3 PARAGRAPHS]** "Mary Jane had a dinner for Ray this evening. The folks where she stays (two old maid school teachers) absented themselves for the evening. She had fried chicken etc and cherry pie with ice cream. Very good-. **[/]** "That took up part of the evening—till 9:30—and then I started working on some problems and experiments." **[4 PARAGRAPHS]** "All my love" **[/]** "Johnny"

**** To Miss Katherine Glenn, Box 190, Riverton, Wyo. (3/12/42, Postmarked 3/13/42, 4:30 PM). Return Address: J. Sproule, 1309 Kearney, Laramie, Wyo. "Hello darling," **[1 PARAGRAPH]** "Today I did something I've been going to do for some time—Got a birth certificate. Dean had to go to Cheyenne to pay his income tax so I went along and got the certificate. Nice day + nice trip except for one flat tire." **[4 PARAGRAPHS]** "Love from" **[/]** "Johnny"

    **** To Miss Katherine Glenn, Box 190, Riverton, Wyo. (3/16/42, 12:30 AM, Postmarked 3/17/42, 4:30 PM). Return Address: J. Sproule, 1309 Kearney, Laramie, Wyo. "Hello darling," **[2 PARAGRAPHS]** "Well you never know how long things will stay the same nowadays—Ray and I have been reclassified 1A and they have lifted some of the requirements — it looks like Ray is going—I may be a little better off—I'm trying to get a deferment so I can finish my degree that is if I pass the physical. I haven't heard anything more lately but I should know more when I see you. Ray was over to Cheyenne Sat and then again today—I haven't seen him since Saturday so I don't know just what he found out. At least he isn't able to take that job in California. He was to have started work there this morning. Rather a rude blow for him." **[2 PARAGRAPHS]** "Night darling" **[/]** "All my love" **[/]** "Johnny"

    **** To Miss Katherine Glenn, Box 190, Riverton, Wyo. (3/18/42, 1:20 PM, Postmarked 3/18/42, 9:00 PM). Return Address: J. Sproule, 1309 Kearney, Laramie, Wyo. "Hello darling," **[1 PARAGRAPH]** "I called the Murphy girl about a ride and she said her folks were only coming to Rawlins and she was to meet them there, so I guess I'll go to Rawlins on the bus too and ride over from there with them. That will be Friday." **[3 PARAGRAPHS]** "All my love" **[/]** "Johnny"

    **** To Miss Katherine Glenn, Box 190, Riverton, Wyo. (3/24/42, 12:05 AM, Postmarked 3/25/42, 10:00 AM). Return Address: J. Sproule, 1309 Kearney, Laramie, Wyo. "Hello darling," **[/]** "Here I am back at the old stand and ready to begin work on the spring quarter." **[/]** "I miss being with you after having such a grand vacation with you but I remind myself that we love each other and that this separation won't last a hell of a lot longer and so I'm ready to buckle down and make the time go as fast as possible." **[1 PARAGRAPH]**

"Took a taxi home after phoning the house and finding that Dean and Gene [not Gene Sproule but one of JHS's roomates, apparently named Gene St.

Peter] had gone to the show then I went over to see Ray and went down town and had supper." **[4 PARAGRAPHS]** "XXXXX" **[/]** "Johnny"

    **** To Miss Katherine Glenn, Box 190, Riverton, Wyo. (3/25/42, Postmarked 3/26/42, 12:30 PM). Return Address: J. Sproule, 1309 Kearney, Laramie, Wyo. "Hello darling," **[/]** "I did quite a bit today even though I did get registered in a short time. I had to see about postponing payment of my fees till I see the loan committee tomorrow. Then I filed a change of curriculum from Mechanical engineering to General and wrote a petition to the Registrar asking for permission to take 24 hours this quarter." **[/]**

"I got my grades from my adviser today and they were nothing extra—they averaged 2.6." **[3 PARAGRAPHS]** [JHS provides a grid matrix of his class schedule 1-5, Monday-Friday; then lists the courses: "CE24y – Hydraulics / CE29c – Mechanics / ME26c – Factory Management / ME33 – General Heat Engineering / CE10 – Surveying" **[/]** "Thus I have 21 hours by classwork and I'll take a 3 hr correspondence course if my petition is okayed." **[2 PARAGRAPHS]** ". . . I remember you mentioning that I wrote so large that I didn't get much on a page so I tried to correct it." **[/]** "All my love" **[/]** "Johnny"

    **** To Miss Katherine Glenn, Box 190, Riverton, Wyo. (3/26/42, 11:55 PM, Postmarked 3/27/42, 11:00 AM). Return Address: J. Sproule, 1309 Kearney, Laramie, Wyo. "Hello darling," **[2 PARAGRAPHS]** "I applied for a loan of $60.00 this afternoon. The committee meets Tuesday so I should know about it by Wednesday." **[/]** "I did my Mechanics problems for tomorrow a little while ago. I wasn't particularly eager to do them, but I'm going to keep up this quarter and not have so much to do at the last moment. . . ." **[/]** "I'm going to begin a program of catching up on my sleep so I'd better go to bed if I expect the program to work out." **[1 PARAGRAPH]** "Night darling XXX J."

    **** To Miss Katherine Glenn, Box 190, Riverton, Wyo. (3/30/42, 2:25 AM, Postmarked 3/30/42, 10:30 AM). Return Address: J. Sproule, 1309 Kearney, Laramie, Wyo. "Hello darling," **[1 PARAGRAPH]** ". . . This afternoon Dean and Gene [St. Peter] and I drove around in Gene's car and then went to the show this evening. It was 'To Be or Not to Be' with Carole Lombard and Jack Benny. A pretty good show—sort of a war picture but not too serious and with a laugh or so to make it interesting." **[/]**

"I received another card from the draft board notifying me of another change of status. It said that I was 1A till August. I don't know exactly what that stands for—I took it to mean that I was deferred till then. I'll find out more about that and let you know when I do." **[1 PARAGRAPH]** "I have that one roll of film that I finished while I was home developed, but I haven't printed any pictures from it yet. . . . They were the ones taken when we climbed up on that hill and the ones taken up by that hole in the sandstone. . . . " **[/]** "Darling my monkey bites you gave me are about to disappear. I wish you could be here—I wish it so much I might even let you reinforce (2 e's?) them if you were." **[2 PARAGRAPHS]** "All my love always" **[/]** "Johnny"

**** To Miss Katherine Glenn, Box 190, Riverton, Wyo. (3/30/42, 7:45 PM, Postmarked 3/31/42, 5:30 PM). Return Address: J. Sproule, 1309 Kearney, Laramie, Wyo. "Hello darling," **[3 PARAGRAPHS]** "Yes 24 hours is quite a few about 8 more than average I should judge but I don't think it will be too tough even though I'll probably be busy to say the least. I won' have to take so many during the summer quarter." **[/]** "No, I'll keep on hashing, but I borrowed to pay my fees, books etc." **[4 PARAGRAPHS]** "All my love always" **[/]** "Johnny"

**** To Miss Katherine Glenn, Box 190, Riverton, Wyo. (4/1/42, 2:41 AM, Postmarked 4/1/42, 9:00 AM). Return Address: J. Sproule, 1309 Kearney, Laramie, Wyo. "Hello darling," **[3 PARAGRAPHS]** "It would be swell if A [Agnes Glenn] does come down for Easter—you could have a fine visit—maybe she could stay over a day or so." **[2 PARAGRAPHS]** "All my love" **[/]** "Johnny"

**** To Miss Katherine Glenn, Box 190, Riverton, Wyo. (4/1/42, 11:53 PM, Postmarked 4/2/42, 12:30 PM). Return Address: J. Sproule, 1309 Kearney, Laramie, Wyo. "Hello darling," **[3 PARAGRAPHS]** "This evening Dean, Gene [St. Peter], and I went down town and had a coke and played a couple games of snooker. Dean is working nights from 12 to 8 so he just left for work a little bit ago. That sort of broke up the bull session we were having. Gene [St. Peter] went to bed and I suspect I won't be long in doing the same." **[/]** "I got a notice that my loan was okayed but I haven't heard from my petition for extra hours. . . ." **[2 PARAGRAPHS]** "Always" **[/]** "Johnny"

    **** To Miss Katherine Glenn, Box 190, Riverton, Wyo. (4/5/42, 1:30 AM, Postmarked 4/6/42, 12:30 PM). Return Address: J. Sproule, 1309 Kearney, Laramie, Wyo. "Hello darling," **[/]** " . . . Friday afternoon was nice except for a little wind and so another fellow and I went out north of the campus and picked out a few—about three—possible locations for the half mile of highway that we have to lay out in our surveying class. . . . We are supposed to figure all the cuts and fills and balance them so that the dirt to be excavated would just fill in the grades to be filled in. Also we will have a curve to put in and we'll have to figure how much to bank it—just do everything so if it were to be actually constructed it would be all ready for the contractor to move in. . . ." **[1 PARAGRAPH]**

"Friday night the fellows here at the house—Dean Gene and a new fellow Karl Henneke and I went down and played a bit of snooker and then went over and bowled a line. I hadn't bowled for more than a year I'd guess but I made about 160 so I didn't think that was too bad. After that we came home and started a game of poker. And Dean had to go to work at 12 but Ray came over so we had enough players. We played till 5:30. No one won very much—I think the whole evening—bowling, snooker and poker cost me 40¢." **[1 PARAGRAPH]**

"I went to church this morning. I still didn't know all that's going on but it was nice. My suit came in time so I had it to wear. It's a lighter gray that it looked like in the catalog but I like it better than if it were darker." **[/]** "This afternoon Dean Gene Karl and I and a guy who works with Gene—Todd by name—drove over to Cheyenne. We drove out to the airport for a while and around Ft Warren; had a coke and went to the show. It was 'Captain of the Clouds' another airplane picture—but in technicolor and on the better side so I rather liked it." **[3 PARAGRAPHS]** "All my love always" **[/]** "Johnny"

**** To Miss Katherine Glenn, Box 190, Riverton, Wyo. (4/6/42, 11:55 PM, Postmarked 4/7/42, 10:30 AM). Return Address: J. Sproule, 1309 Kearney, Laramie, Wyo. "Hello sweetheart," **[4 PARAGRAPHS]** "I hope A [Agnes Glenn] was able to get there for Easter. How is she getting along now? You mentioned something about not knowing what to feed her so I took it to mean that she was still dieting." **[1 PARAGRAPH]** "Dean went to work a while ago and Gene went to bed so I think I'll go to bed soon too." **[1 PARAGRAPH]** "All my love and kisses" **[/]** "Johnny"

**** To Miss Katherine Glenn, Box 190, Riverton, Wyo. (4/8/42, 12:52 PM, Postmarked 4/8/42, 9:00 PM). Return Address: J. Sproule, 1309 Kearney, Laramie, Wyo. "Hello dearest darling," **[3 PARAGRAPHS]** "I'm glad A [Agnes Glenn] was able to be there for Easter. I know you were glad to see her. What kind of a diet does she have? I feel for her for I know I'd hate to have to follow one." **[2 PARAGRAPHS]** "X X X X" **[/]** "Johnny"

**** To Miss Katherine Glenn, Box 190, Riverton, Wyo. (4/9/42, 12:40 AM, Postmarked 4/9/42, 12:30 PM). Return Address: J. Sproule, 1309 Kearney, Laramie, Wyo. "Hello darling," **[2 PARAGRAPHS]** "Darling that was very thoughtful of you to send me a prayer book. Its swell and I thank you very much. It will be a big help to me." **[2 PARAGRAPHS]** "ALL my love and kisses" **[/]** "Johnny "

**** To Miss Katherine Glenn, Box 190, Riverton, Wyo. (4/10/42, 8:35 AM, Postmarked 4/10/42, 12:30 PM). Return Address: J. Sproule, 1309 Kearney, Laramie, Wyo. "Good morning sweetheart," **[2 PARAGRAPHS]** "Well Ray finally got started for California. He left last night about 5:45. I suppose he'll start work Monday. I'll miss him but I'm glad he finally got started to work." **[2 PARAGRAPHS]** "Johnny"

**** To Miss Katherine Glenn, Box 190, Riverton, Wyo. (4/10/42, 11:40 PM, Postmarked 4/11/42, 12:30 PM). Return Address: J. Sproule, 1309 Kearney, Laramie, Wyo. "Darling," **[2 PARAGRAPHS]** "I worked this afternoon and I'm going to work tomorrow. I'm always glad to get my hours for the month in on that job for then I don't have to think about it till next month." **[2 PARAGRAPHS]**

"No I didn't happen to be late to mass Easter. I have been though as I remember; I always try to be punctual, but sometimes there are conflicts it seems. I guess I'm getting along o.k., but I wish I had more time—24 hours and a couple jobs seem to take quite a bit of time." **[3 PARAGRAPHS]** "Always" **[/]** "Johnny"

  **** To Miss Katherine Glenn, Box 190, Riverton, Wyo. (4/14/42, 11:18 AM, Postmarked 4/14/42, 9:00 PM). Return Address: J. Sproule, 1309 Kearney, Laramie, Wyo. "Hello darling," **[1 PARAGRAPH]** "As usual I didn't get my studying done over the weekend so I worked all night Sunday and got quite a bit done. I can do about twice as much when everything's quiet at night like that as I can in the same amount of time during the day." **[/]**

"Last night then the guys here at the house and I went to the show down at the Crown—it was 20¢ night. One show was about some Dead End kids or something and the other was a Charlie Chan picture but I don't remember much about it for I was sort of sleepy. We had a cup of coffee then and came home and I laid down on the bed to read your letter again. I was just on the point of getting up and writing you when I fell asleep. I woke up enough at 4 o'clock to undress and get in bed properly. I managed to make my 8 o'clock this morning and I was only about 2 minutes late." **[2 PARAGRAPHS]** "Bye for now darling" **[/]** "All my love always" **[/]** "Johnny"

  **** To Miss Katherine Glenn, Box 190, Riverton, Wyo. (4/14/42, 7:55 PM, Postmarked 4/14/42, 12 M). Return Address: J. Sproule, 1309 Kearney, Laramie, Wyo. "Hello darling," **[1 PARAGRAPH]** "I just finished the dishes and I'm going to get my problems done and get to bed early. I was a little longer getting the dishes done tonight as there were 15 on the table and of course the pots + pans + and our dishes in the kitchen." **[1 PARAGRAPH]**

"I've been listening to the radio—I think Tuesday night is one of my favorites. I listen to Burns + Allen, Fibber McGee + Molly, Bob Hope and Red Skelton. I still have Jimmy Jensons radio. He loaned me his when he got married since his wife had one too and they only needed one in their apartment. I haven't seen Jimmy for quite a while. I haven't done a great deal of visiting lately." **[5 PARAGRAPHS]** "All my love and kisses" **[/]** "Johnny"

**** To Miss Katherine Glenn, Box 190, Riverton, Wyo. (4/16/42, 11:58 PM, Postmarked 4/17/42, 10:30 AM). Return Address: J. Sproule, 1309 Kearney, Laramie, Wyo. "Hello darling," **[3 PARAGRAPHS]** "I got a summer school bulletin today and by it I see that the first term of summer school starts June 13. The first term runs till July 17 and the second term from July 18 to August 21. Spring quarter final week is over June 10, but I should be able to finish up before that since most of my subjects are engineering and they usually try to get thru early." **[2 PARAGRAPHS]** "All my love and kisses" **[/]** "Johnny"

**** To Miss Katherine Glenn, Box 190, Riverton, Wyo. (4/19/42, 11:51 PM, Postmarked 4/20/42, 12:30 PM). Return Address: J. Sproule, 1309 Kearney, Laramie, Wyo. "Hello darling," **[/]** "Another week end has gone by—it hasn't meant anything except that the passage of time has reduced by so much the amount of time that will elapse before I can see you again." **[/]** "I didn't accomplish much this week-end except for what studying I did Friday night. The guys here went to the show or something but I decided I ought to get something done so I wouldn't be all night Sunday night doing my problems for Monday. . . ." **[4 PARAGRAPHS]** "All my love and kisses" **[/]** "Johnny"

**** To Miss Katherine Glenn, Box 190, Riverton, Wyo. (4/21/42, 1:15 PM, Postmarked 4/21/42, 5:30 PM). Return Address: J. Sproule, 1309 Kearney, Laramie, Wyo. "Hello darling," **[3 PARAGRAPHS]** "I had a card from Ray yesterday. He was in Los Angeles and had started working but was going to be transferred to Bakersfield. He didn't say much except that he would write when he got settled." **[2 PARAGRAPHS]** "Johnny"

**** To Miss Katherine Glenn, Box 190, Riverton, Wyo. (4/21/42, Midnight +, Postmarked 4/22/42, 4:30 PM). Return Address: J. Sproule, 1309 Kearney, Laramie, Wyo. "Hello darling," [2 PARAGRAPHS] "I've been working some problems and I'd worked + worked on the last one to get it to come out when I discovered that I had solved for the total answer instead of a certain part which the book asked for. That sort of thing disgusts me no end." **[/]**

"I think a couple of the fellows who work for Western Electric are going to be transferred to Cheyenne in a week or so, so it should be quieter around here then. And I should get my work done better too, for I do spend more time than I should just fooling around playing snooker or something equally unimportant." **[1 PARAGRAPH]** "All my love always" **[/]** "Johnny"

**** To Miss Katherine Glenn, Box 190, Riverton, Wyo. (4/26/42, 10:55 PM, Postmarked 4/27/42, 12:30 PM). Return Address: J. Sproule, 1309 Kearney, Laramie, Wyo. "Hello darling," [1 PARAGRAPH] "Mrs. Buck's son Frank came down the last of the week. He was about to be drafted—he was registered in Lander—so he came down to go over to Cheyenne to see what he could get into. He took his physical and will be inducted in the morning. I think he's getting into the engineers corps." **[/]** "And that's a peculiar thing to me—there seems to be a crying need for engineers and yet they draft them into the army. He wasn't going to be able to get deferred even though he had taken a job in Washington (State) and the firm had requested a deferment since it was defense work. He was going to report out there last Wed., but now he is in the army." **[10 PARAGRAPHS]** "All my love and kisses always" **[/]** "Johnny"

**** To Miss Katherine Glenn, Box 190, Riverton, Wyo. (4/29/42, 12:53 PM, Postmarked 5/1/42, 6:30 PM). Return Address: J. Sproule, 1309 Kearney, Laramie, Wyo. "Kay darling," [2 PARAGRAPHS] "Gilbert made me an interesting proposition the other day but I couldn't act on it. He said he was going to apply for leave from the University and would I be interested in running the bees while he was gone. It would have been ok but I'm going to be taking so much stuff this summer that I wouldn't have time to work so I turned it down." **[7 PARAGRAPHS]** "All my love and kisses" **[/]** "Johnny"

**** To Miss Katherine Glenn, Box 190, Riverton, Wyo. (5/2/42, 10:25 PM, Postmarked 5/3/42, TR2, OM. & OGDEN R.P.O.). Return Address: J. Sproule, 1309 Kearney, Laramie, Wyo. "Hello sweetheart," **[4 PARAGRAPHS]** "You are having quite a time with that birth certificate aren't you. They are very peculiar about changing those things but I don't see why you couldn't get it changed. <u>Question</u>: When did it say you were born?" **[3 PARAGRAPHS]** "All my love always darling," **[/]** "Johnny"

**** To Miss Katherine Glenn, Box 190, Riverton, Wyo. (5/4/42, 8:22 PM, Postmarked 5/5/42, 3:30 PM). Return Address: J. Sproule, 1309 Kearney, Laramie, Wyo. Hello sweetheart," **[4 PARAGRAPHS]** "That woul[d] be swell if you could get up to Cody to see A [Agnes Glenn]. You don't get to see her so often since she started working up there do you?" **[4 PARAGRAPHS]** "All my love always" **[/]** "Johnny"

**** To Miss Katherine Glenn, Box 190, Riverton, Wyo. (5/5/42, 7:34 PM, Postmarked 5/6/42, 10:30 AM). Return Address: J. Sproule, 1309 Kearney, Laramie, Wyo. "Kay darling," **[3 PARAGRAPHS]** "Sugar rationing is going on here too—four days of it starting Tuesday. I haven't gotten around to it yet but I have Thursday afternoon with no classes so I'll probably do it then." **[/]**

"I was figuring up the other day and it's going to cost me about $1000 to g[o] to summer school—$800 which I will lose by not working (there seems to be a lot of good paying jobs open) and $200 for school expenses—board + room etc since I don't think I'll have time to work and go to school too." **[2 PARAGRAPHS]** "All love + kisses" **[/]** "Johnny"

**** To Miss Katherine Glenn, Box 190, Riverton, Wyo. (5/6/42, 11:00 PM, Postmarked 5/7/42, 5:30 PM). Return Address: J. Sproule, 1309 Kearney, Laramie, Wyo. "Hello darling," **[2 PARAGRAPHS]** "[indecipherable] to get my ration book tomorrow [indecipherable] at a rooming house I don't think I'm supposed to use it. They've started puttin[g] sugar in individual portions up at the Union and when [?] get a cup of [?]

ask you whether or [?] much sugar but not using it in my coffee I don't notice it." [JHS scotch tapes a sample packet to the letter, 1 x 2 inches, on which is printed: "Sugar is being Rationed / We furnish this envelope to INSURE CLEANLINESS / Thank you"] **[2 PARAGRAPHS]** "All my love and kisses" **[/]** "Johnny" [Note that the tape has deteriorated and has greatly stained this letter as well as letters that had been stored in close proximity to it.]

**** To Miss Katherine Glenn, Box 190, Riverton, Wyo. (5/11/42, 5:52 AM, Postmarked 5/11/42, 9:30 AM). Return Address: J. Sproule, 1309 Kearney, Laramie, Wyo. "Good morning sweetheart," **[/]** "Yes it's morning now and I hear Mrs. Buck stirring around up stairs—she'll no doubt be down in a little while + holler around about me not staying up all night but it won't matter." **[5 PARAGRAPHS]** "All my love+ kisses" **[/]** "Johnny"

**** To Miss Katherine Glenn, Box 190, Riverton, Wyo. (5/12/42, "Early Tue. morning", Postmarked 5/12/42, 4:00 PM). Return Address: J. Sproule, 1309 Kearney, Laramie, Wyo. "Darling," **[/]** "That's absolutely perfect that you are coming down and I'll only be able to tell you how happy I am when you get here and I can tell you in person. I really can't think of anything nicer." **[/]** ". . . and finish our surveying—we're making a topographical map of a 20 acre tract. We were out yesterday afternoon and the wind was blowing a gale—which interfered some what." **[3 PARAGRAPHS]** "All my love and kisses" **[/]** "Johnny"

**** To Miss Katherine Glenn, Box 190, Riverton, Wyo. (5/17/42, Postmarked 5/18/42, 9:30 AM). Return Address: J. Sproule, 1309 Kearney, Laramie, Wyo. "Hello darling," **[/]** "It was grand to see you this week and I can't write how grand it was for there aren't enough words. The time till the end of the quarter will fly by now and it won't be but about three weeks till I see you again. **[/]** "I went to bed last night about 7 and didn't get up till noon so you can see that I really got some sleep." **[3 PARAGRAPHS]** "All my love and kisses" **[/]** "Johnny"

**** To Miss Katherine Glenn, Box 190, Riverton, Wyo. (5/18/42, 10:30 PM, Postmarked 5/19/42, 2:30 PM). Return Address: J. Sproule, 1309 Kearney, Laramie, Wyo. "Hello darling," **[3 PARAGRAPHS]** "Sweetheart you certainly didn't interfere with anything and I only wish you could have stayed longer. It was grand to see you as it always is and now I'm anxiously waiting for the end of the quarter when I'll see you again." **[1 PARAGRAPH]** "All my love and kisses" **[/]** "Johnny"

**** To Miss Katherine Glenn, Box 190, Riverton, Wyo. (5/21/42, 2:30 AM, Postmarked 5/21/42, 9:30 AM). Return Address: J. Sproule, 1309 Kearney, Laramie, Wyo. "Kay darling," **[3 PARAGRAPHS]** "Darling I hope that time just flies by until this quarter is over and I see you again. . . ." **[1 PARAGRAPH]** "All my love and kisses" **[/]** "Johnny"

**** To Miss Katherine Glenn, Box 190, Riverton, Wyo. (5/22/42, 12:50 PM, Postmarked 5/22/42, 5:30 PM). Return Address: J. Sproule, 1309 Kearney, Laramie, Wyo. "Hello darling," **[1 PARAGRAPH]** "I'm going over to school this afternoon and finish up the highway problem and hand it in. I will be caught up with everything this weekend I think and that gives me a feeling of satisfaction." **[4 PARAGRAPHS]** "All my love + kisses" **[/]** "Johnny"

**** To Miss Katherine Glenn, Box 190, Riverton, Wyo. (5/25/42, 10:00 PM, Postmarked 5/26/42, 5:00 PM). Return Address: J. Sproule, 1309 Kearney, Laramie, Wyo. "Hello sweetheart," **[2 PARAGRAPHS]** "Gene + Todd were transferred to Cheyenne today so things are quite calm here now since Dean is on his vacation. But since it's only 50 miles over there I wouldn't be surprised if they drop over once in a while." **[2 PARAGRAPHS]** "'Night darling." **[/]** "All my love and kisses" **[/]** "Johnny" **[/]** "P.S. Being caught up on my work now I can catch up on sleep." **[/]** "Night again darling" **[/]** "X X X X X" **[/]** "J."

**** To Miss Katherine Glenn, Box 190, Riverton, Wyo. (5/26/42, 11:50 PM, Postmarked 5/27/42, 4:30 PM). Return Address: J. Sproule, 1309 Kearney, Laramie, Wyo. "Kay darling," **[/]** "That was an especially grand letter I received from you this afternoon. I like nothing better than for you to tell me how much you love me! And I'll be kissing you so much there won't be any chance to get dizzy." **[3 PARAGRAPHS]** "All my love and kisses" **[/]** "Johnny"

    **** To Miss Katherine Glenn, Box 190, Riverton, Wyo. (5/27/42, 11:50 PM, Postmarked 5/28/42, 2:30 PM). Return Address: J. Sproule, 1309 Kearney, Laramie, Wyo. "Hello darling," **[3 PARAGRAPHS]** "Darling I quite realize how you feel about the prospect of being there [Riverton] with most every one you know gone. . . . [indecipherable] . . . the same with me here. . . ." **[2 PARAGRAPHS]** "All my love + kisses" **[/]** "Johnny"

    **** To Miss Katherine Glenn, Box 190, Riverton, Wyo. (5/28/42, 11:45 PM, Postmarked 5/29/42, 8 AM). Return Address: J. Sproule, 1309 Kearney, Laramie, Wyo. "Hello sweetheart," **[1 PARAGRAPH]** "This sure is a good place with my work caught up I hardly have anything to do. When the other fellows were here we used to shoot a little snooker or play cards, but now I just sleep and read. All I did today was sleep till noon and mow the lawn. Exciting? But no doubt when summer school starts I'll think back to this idleness and wish I could do it again." **[1 PARAGRAPH]**

"Sweetheart, with the aid of a couple books and an hour or so work I made out (I think) about 50% of your shorthand message. I love you very very much too darling and I'll be able to tell you much better when we're together." **[1 PARAGRAPH]** "All my love and kisses" **[/]** "Johnny"

    **** To Miss Katherine Glenn, Box 190, Riverton, Wyo. (5/30/42, 3:00 PM, Postmarked 5/30/42, 8 PM). Return Address: J. Sproule, 1309 Kearney, Laramie, Wyo. "Hello darling," **[1 PARAGRAPH]** "I've been working about the house today—scrubbing the ceilings of the kitchen + bathrooms, a job which I'm glad is over for its sort of hard on the neck + shoulders." **[3 PARAGRAPHS]** "All my love always"   **[/]** "Johnny"

    **** To Miss Katherine Glenn, Box 190, Riverton, Wyo. (6/3/42, 6:00 PM, Postmarked 6/3/42, TR 9, OMAHA & OGDEN R.P.O.). Return Address: J. Sproule, 1309 Kearney, Laramie, Wyo. "Kay darling," **[3 PARAGRAPHS]** "Dean got back from his vacation Sunday so it hasn't been so lonely around here. He's still working 12 to 8 and isn't enjoying it too much." **[1 PARAGRAPH]** "All my love always" **[/]** "Johnny"

Chapter 7. Onto the Air Force: Leaving Laramie, Arriving Dayton—June 11, 1942 to August 31, 1942

JHS reports a hectic final pace, comments on his having switched from hashing to restaurant dining, and reassures KVS that the beard grown for Frontier Days will soon disappear. With KVS heading to Portland, Oregon comes the specter of a longer separation. Commiseration to KVS on Bernard Glenn now in Army camp and convalescing from meningitis. Job applications loom large, and the draft board issues a 1A. And new changes unfold in quick succession: Commencement, a train ride to Dayton, Ohio, reporting to Wright Field, and impressions of a new town.

**** To Miss Katherine Glenn, Box 190, Riverton, Wyo. (6/10/42, Postmarked 6/11/42, 12:30 PM). Return Address: J. Sproule, 1309 Kearney, Laramie, Wyo. "Hello darling," **[/]** "We just got here a little while ago—about 1 am—and the others have gone on. I'm sort of sleepy now but I didn't sleep any on the way down." **[1 PARAGRAPH]** "It was grand being with you again darling and I'll get through this last separation by remembering the swell times we've had together and thinking of all the wonderful times we will have together." **[2 PARAGRAPHS]** "All my love always darling" **[/]** "Johnny"

**** To Miss Katherine Glenn, Box 190, Riverton, Wyo. (6/22/42, 9:05 PM, Postmarked 6/23/42, 10:30 AM). Return Address: J. Sproule, 1309 Kearney, Laramie, Wyo. "Kay darling," **[2 PARAGRAPHS]** "Saturday Dean + I worked on his car and then Sunday we went to the show. It was 'Reap the Wild Wind'. A fine show + improved by the technicolor photography of the sea scenes + the colorful dress. I think it was supposed to be of about 1840." **[/]**

"I imagine you are missing Anna now for she has always been with you. I hope she + Cleo have a nice trip. And they'll get to see Bernard which will be swell. I'm glad he likes it out there." **[1 PARAGRAPH]** "Dean + Gene [St. Peter] took out on a date a while ago so I've been studying calculus.

We're going to have an hour test in that in the morning." **[1 PARAGRAPH]** "'Night darling" **[/]** "All my love + and kisses" **[/]** "Johnny"

**** To Miss Katherine Glenn, Box 190, Riverton, Wyo. (6/23/42, 11:47 PM, Postmarked 6/24/42, 10:30 AM). Return Address: J. Sproule, 1309 Kearney, Laramie, Wyo. "Hello darling," **[1 PARAGRAPH]** "School is still the same—I've been going from 7:30 to about 5 or so + that isn't proving to be enough time. I guess I'll have to start going over in the evenings so I can keep up." **[1 PARAGRAPH]**

"I suppose if Ken is scheduled for the army the middle of next month he won't be doing much work between now + then. Who knows, maybe army life will do him good." **[2 PARAGRAPHS]** "Love always" **[/]** "Johnny"

**** To Miss Katherine Glenn, Box 190, Riverton, Wyo. (6/24/42, 12:30 AM, Postmarked 6/25/42, 10:30 AM). Return Address: J. Sproule, 1309 Kearney, Laramie, Wyo. "Kay darling," **[1 PARAGRAPH]** "This evening Dean Gene + I took a drive up to the summit + around after supper + then went to a circus which was making a one night stand. I know why it was only a one night outfit too, for it was really a flop." **[/]** "But there isn't a thing to do around here so mostly we just sit around the room + talk or go down town + play a game of snooker or some other equally simple amusement." **[/]**

"Dearest I know you're really glad that you won't be working at the phone office much longer. I have the same feeling when I can see the end of this school in sight." **[1 PARAGRAPH]** "Always Johnny"

**** To Miss Katherine Glenn, Box 190, Riverton, Wyo. (6/27/42, 11:30 PM, Postmarked 6/28/42, 12:30 PM). Return Address: J. Sproule, 1309 Kearney, Laramie, Wyo. "Hello darling," **[2 PARAGRAPHS]** "So Helen + Ken are going to get married— . . ." **[/]** "Have you heard from Anna yet? I suppose she's been there two or three days by now hasn't she?" **[2 PARAGRAPHS]** "'Night darling" **[/]** "Forever [heart drawing and "X's" **[/]** "Johnny"

**** To Miss Katherine Glenn, Box 190, Riverton, Wyo. (Tue. am 1:15 [6/30/42], Postmarked 6/30/42, 10 AM). Return Address: J. Sproule, 1309 Kearney, Laramie, Wyo. "Hello sweetheart," **[4 PARAGRAPHS]** "Darling you didn't say when exactly you were going to be thru working at the phone office so I figure where to send you some money to come down on. You are figuring on coming down before you take out for the coast aren't you?" **[2 PARAGRAPHS]** "All my love" **[/]** "Johnny"

**** To Miss Katherine Glenn, Box 190, Riverton, Wyo. (6/30/42, 11:45 PM, Postmarked 7/1/42, 11:30 AM). Return Address: J. Sproule, 1309 Kearney, Laramie, Wyo. "Hello my darling," **[3 PARAGRAPHS]** "Laramie is having a celebration the 10th and + 11th but I suppose it will be rather on the tame side too. It will break the monotony though + that's something." **[1 PARAGRAPH]** "I hope studying short hand isn't getting you down. I know from experience that this studying can be a bore." **[2 PARAGRAPHS]** "Forever" **[/]** "Johnny"

**** To Miss Katherine Glenn, Box 190, Riverton, Wyo. (7/1/42, 12:00 PM, Postmarked 7/2/42, 10:30 AM). Return Address: J. Sproule, 1309 Kearney, Laramie, Wyo. "Dearest," **[1 PARAGRAPH]** "It was quiet here though this evening for Dean + Gene went out on a date so I was able to study pretty good. Dean just went to work so that reminds me that I'd better get to bed so as to prepare for the morrow." **[2 PARAGRAPHS]** "All my love + kisses always" **[/]** "Johnny"

**** To Miss Katherine Glenn, Box 190, Riverton, Wyo. (7/2/42, 11:55 PM, Postmarked 7/3/42, 8:30 AM). Return Address: J. Sproule, 1309 Kearney, Laramie, Wyo. "Hello sweetheart," **[2 PARAGRAPHS]** "There won't be much going on around here over the 4th I don't suppose for Laramie is having a celebration the 10th + 11th. I've been growing a short beard as my contribution to the frontier atmosphere they're endeavoring to create. You'd like it no doubt—I'll take a picture before I cut it off so you can see whether you'd like it. I enclose a sample length [JHS tapes a 9/16th inch strand of hair] for your inspection." **[1 PARAGRAPH]**

"Well I haven't gotten tired of eating in restaurants yet, but it does seem expensive after earning board by hashing for a couple years. I like it though for I can eat whenever I like." **[2 PARAGRAPHS]** "All my love always" **[/]** "Johnny"

**** To Miss Katherine Glenn, Box 190, Riverton, Wyo. (7/4/42, 10:55 AM, Postmarked 7/4/42, OMA & OGDEN R.P.O.). Return Address: J. Sproule, 1309 Kearney, Laramie, Wyo. "Hello darling," **[/]** "This won't be much of a fourth without you. I remember all the good times we've had together and then I miss you more than ever." **[2 PARAGRAPHS]** "We were down to breakfast a little while ago and the town is sure empty." **[1 PARAGRAPH]** "All my love + kisses" **[/]** "Johnny"

**** To Miss Katherine Glenn, Box 190, Riverton, Wyo. (7/6/42, 1:15 AM, Postmarked 7/6/42, 5:30 PM). Return Address: J. Sproule, 1309 Kearney, Laramie, Wyo. "Darling," **[1 PARAGRAPH]** " . . . We decided to relax (or whatever you would term it) by driving down into the Colorado mountains. The weather was swell and the scenery nice and new to me so it was satisfactory—I could have written grand if you had been with me!" **[/]** "We went to the show tonight—it was 'Kings Row' and not very appealing in my opinion. So now I'm ready to get some work done. I'm not very sleepy as I think I'll put the rest of the night in on Shades + Shadows and that should about catch me up in that." **[/]**

"Sweetheart I don't want you to have the expense of the trip down here so let me send you the money and let me know when you're coming so I'll know when to send it. Now I know what you'll say—but you need the money you've been saving to go to the coast on. I even think you ought to let me help you with that + we can talk about that when you come down." **[1 PARAGRAPH]** "All my love + kisses" **[/]** "Johnny"

**** To Miss Katherine Glenn, Box 190, Riverton, Wyo. (7/7/42, 11:55 PM, Postmarked 7/8/42, 10:30 AM). Return Address: J. Sproule, 1309 Kearney, Laramie, Wyo. "Hello sweetheart," **[2 PARAGRAPHS]** "I'm not exactly surprised at Helen + Ken getting married, but as you say, I don't know why did they didn't do it sooner if they were going to do it. That ain't good—married one day and the groom in the army the next. But I hope they're very happy and that things will work out OK for them." **[/]**

"Never fear darling, this beard is coming off this weekend. I'd just as soon I'd never started it—but you know me—finish things out no matter what." **[/]** "I got a roll of color film and took some color pictures of some of the mountain scenery we observed over the 4th. It's sort of expensive $1.25 for the film + developing and 40¢ apiece for the prints. But I thought I'd try a roll to see if the pictures were worth it. I haven't finished the role yet cause you don't just shoot anything at that price. I don't right now anyhow." **[7 PARAGRAPHS]** "All my love + kisses" **[/]** "Johnny"

**** To Miss Katherine Glenn, Box 190, Riverton, Wyo. (7/11/42, 11:45 PM, Postmarked 7/13/42, 3 PM). Return Address: J. Sproule, 1309 Kearney, Laramie, Wyo. "Hello darling," **[/]** "I've been thinking of what you said in your last letter about coming down or rather I should say about not coming down—anyway I've been thinking of it all weekend and I still don't know what to tell you. You know I'd like to see you and of course I know that it would be too expensive for you since it will probably take quite a bit to go to Oregon—so sweetheart why won't you let me send you some money to come down on? . . ." **[5 PARAGRAPHS]** "All my love + kisses" **[/]** "Johnny"

**** **GROUP OF 7 LETTERS, 7/14/42 - 7/25/42 CONTAINED IN ONE ENVELOPE**: To Miss Katherine Glenn, 1216 SW Yamhill, Portland, Oregon (**SINGLE ENVELOPE,** Postmarked 7/25/42, 4:30 PM; "Via Air Mail," four 3¢ stamps). Return Address: J. Sproule, 1309 Kearney, Laramie, Wyo.

[1] July 14, 1942, 8:55 PM: "Darling" **[/]** "It was swell to be talking to you a few minutes ago, but it gave me the most desolate feeling when you said goodbye. I wish with all my heart that you were coming down but I guess it just can't be." **[/]** "I'm sorry I haven't written oftener the past few days but as I said I've been over my head in getting thru. This summer school is sure concentrated. But next term it will be easier I think for I'll only be carrying about two thirds as much work. . . ." **[1 PARAGRAPH]**

"I'm just realizing how far away you'll be sweetheart. I'd been thinking th I'd see you before you go, but now that you're leaving Thursday I—well I don't know what to say except that I'll miss you terribly and now that I know I won't see you it seems so very desolate here." **[/]** "Since I won't know where to write to you until I hear from you I guess I'll just save the letters I write and then send them when I know where you are." **[2 PARAGRAPHS]** "All my love + kisses" **[/]** "Johnny"

[2] July 16, 1942, 11:50 PM: "Kay darling" **[2 PARAGRAPHS]** "Tomorrow will be the last day of this first term and high time too I'd say. . ." **[/]** "I know you are glad to be getting out of Riverton—the only thin wish is that we were together! But we will be as soon as we can won't we darling and then everything will be just as it should be." **[3 PARAGRAPHS** "All my love + kisses always" **[/]** "Johnny"

[3] July 18, 1942, 11:50 PM: "Darling" **[3 PARAGRAPHS]** "I'm taking 10 hours this quarter—4 hours of machine design + 6 hours of calculus. I'll only have lab on Mon. Wed. + Friday afternoon instead of every day as before. The proffs aren't losing any time though for we were given assignments for Monday's classes just as though there were no difference between the terms—well I guess there isn't when you are taki a course that runs through both terms." **[2 PARAGRAPHS]** "All my love + kisses" **[/]** "Johnny"

[4] July 20, 1942, 11:00 AM: "Hello darling" **[1 PARAGRAPH]** "Today was school again so it really doesn't seem like a last term—only a continuation of the first. I got my grades today and they weren't too bad 1.76 average." **[3 PARAGRAPHS]**

"I don't know when I'll be in Riverton again—I wrote Mom asking if she + Gene [Sproule] could come down for Commencement Aug. 21—if they come down I might just go to work from here (that is if I have a job lined then—I'm getting some application letters started off). I would like to ge back to Riverton for a day or so to see everyone—but it's hard to say how things will work out a month from now." **[2 PARAGRAPHS]** "All my love" **[/]** "Johnny"

[5] July 21, 1942, 11:55 PM: "Kay darling" **[/]** "You are right in your classification of the summer—it hasn't been so good and that's an understatement if I ever made one. I'm sure getting tired of this school and tired of Laramie though none of it would be so bad if we were together—it will be over though in a month + will I rejoice when that month is over? I should say I will." **[5 PARAGRAPHS]** "All my love always" **[/]** "Johnny"

[6] July 23, 1942, 9:00 PM: "Hello darling" **[/]** "This has been a fairly busy week for me—there isn't any school tomorrow as it is Laramie Day at the Cheyenne Frontier Days—so on account of that I did a week's work in 4 days. I think I'll just sleep in tomorrow, that seems to me the best way I could take advantage of the vacation." **[4 PARAGRAPHS]** "All my love" **[/]** "Johnny"

[7] July 25, 1942, 10:45 AM: "Darling" **[4 PARAGRAPHS]** "That's too bad about Bernard + Hartzell losing their ratings. I think they will be able to work back up soon though. I guess I don't remember the accident you mentioned concerning Hartzell. I'll bet that you were glad to see Bernard though—it's been a long time since you saw him last. Tell him hello for me." **[5 PARAGRAPHS]** "All my love + kisses" **[/]** "Johnny"

**** To Miss Katherine Glenn, Roseland Hotel, 1216 SW Yamhill, Portland, Oregon (7/27/42, 10:22 PM, Postmarked 7/29/42, 10:30 AM; "Via Air Mail," two 3¢ stamps). Return Address: J. Sproule, 1309 Kearney, Laramie, Wyo. "Kay darling" **[5 PARAGRAPHS]** "I've got to go down + see the draft board in the morning—Wednesday it is insisted I see on looking at the card—anyway I don't know whether it will amount to much or not but I'll let you know." **[2 PARAGRAPHS]** "All my love + kisses" **[/]** "Johnny"

**** To Miss Katherine Glenn, Roseland Hotel, 1216 SW Yamhill, Portland, Oregon (7/28/42, 11:55 PM, Postmarked 7/29/42, 11:30 AM; "Via Air Mail," two 3¢ stamps). Return Address: J. Sproule, 1309 Kearney, Laramie, Wyo. "Kay darling" **[3 PARAGRAPHS]** "It will be a relief to just get out of here + do some work where I can feel that I'm accomplishing something." **[3 PARAGRAPHS]** "All love + kisses" **[/]** "Johnny"

**** To Miss Katherine Glenn, Roseland Hotel, 1216 SW Yamhill, Portland, Oregon (7/30/42, 4:05 PM, Postmarked 7/31/42, 3:30 PM; "Via Air Mail," two 3¢ stamps). Return Address: J. Sproule, 1309 Kearney, Laramie, Wyo. "Hello darling" **[1 PARAGRAPH]** "Well I went down to the draft board yesterday and they sent me over to a doc. I didn't find out anything though—a nurse drew out a blood sample and the doc. asked me if I had anything wrong with me except my eyes. I said I didn't think so and that was all there was to it. In my opinion it was a waste of time (I don't mind that so much, but it seems so damn inefficient) to go down—if it's a preliminary examination for classification it seems they ought to examine you." **[3 PARAGRAPHS]**

". . . Do you know why Ken was turned down by the Army? If he isn't going to be drafted he can probably get a defense job most anywhere—anyway I think he + Helen could fix things so they could be together." **[1 PARAGRAPH]** "All love always" **[/]** "Johnny"

**** To Miss Katherine Glenn, Roseland Hotel, 1216 SW Yamhill, Portland Oregon (8/1/42, 11:20 AM, Postmarked 8/1/42, TR 22, OM. & OGDEN R.P.O.; "Via Air Mail," two 3¢ stamps). Return Address: J. Sproule, 1309 Kearney, Laramie, Wyo. "Hello darling" **[1 PARAGRAPH]** "Here it is the first of August and that means three weeks more school—the prospect of which doesn't make me unhappy. Of course I have a hell of a lot of work to do to finish up everything, but if it's only three weeks more I can stand to work pretty hard. I wish I knew what I would be doing after that, but as yet I don't know anything definite. I gave up the idea of working at the airport—I only intended to work out there while I was f finishing up here—but I decided I wouldn't have time to work + go to school so I didn't do any more about it." **[8 PARAGRAPHS]** "All my love" **[/]** "Johnny"

**** To Miss Katherine Glenn, 1216 SW Yamhill, Portland, Oregon (8/3/42, 7:00 PM, Postmarked 8/4/42, 12:30 PM; "Via Air Mail," two 3¢ stamps). Return Address: J. Sproule, 1309 Kearney, Laramie, Wyo. "Hello darling" **[2 PARAGRAPHS]** "It rained quite hard for a while this afternoon along about quitting time so I called Dean + had him come by and pick me up to save walking home in the rain. We waited till Gene [roommate] got off work at 6 and then went down town and ate. I didn't see much of my roommates during the day, but we usually manage to eat supper together." **[/]** "Dean + Gene took off a bit ago—Dean is attending a night class in radio 3 nights a week and Gene had to go back to work. He's working 12 hours a day this week so that will pretty well keep him occupied." **[6 PARAGRAPHS]** "All my love always" **[/]** "Johnny"

**** To Miss Katherine Glenn, 1216 SW Yamhill, Portland, Oregon (8/5/42, 7:20 PM, Postmarked 8/6/42, 10:30 AM; "Via Air Mail," two 3¢ stamps). Return Address: J. Sproule, 1309 Kearney, Laramie, Wyo. "Hello darling" **[3 PARAGRAPHS]** "You know, I'd say you really did all right saving enough money for your trip in about a month. You always do o.k. whenever you decide to do something—you're a very capable person darling. . . ." **[4 PARAGRAPHS]** "All my love and kisses" **[/]** "Johnny"

**** To Miss Katherine Glenn, 1216 SW Yamhill, Portland, Oregon (8/7/42, 8:00 PM, Postmarked 8/8/42, 8:30 PM; "Via Air Mail," two 3¢ stamps). Return Address: J. Sproule, 1309 Kearney, Laramie, Wyo. "Hello darling" **[2 PARAGRAPHS]** "School hasn't changed any but it will be over in a couple weeks so it doesn't matter much. . . ." **[3 PARAGRAPHS]** "All my love + kisses" **[/]** "Johnny"

**** To Miss Katherine Glenn, 1216 SW Yamhill, Portland, Oregon (8/10/42, 8:30 PM, Postmarked 8/11/42, 4:30 PM; "Via Air Mail," two 3¢ stamps). Return Address: J. Sproule, 1309 Kearney, Laramie, Wyo. "Hello darling" **[2 PARAGRAPHS]** "I've been having a bunch of application blanks to fill out lately. Last night I filled out a pile (3 or 4 blanks) in reference to a civil service job as a Jr. Engineer. And tonight I filled out an application blank for the Glenn L. Martin Co. + one for North American Aviation. They came in response to some application letters I wrote. I know just what you meant when you spoke of filling out endless blanks when you were looking for a job. I'm not very fond of endlessly writing down the same old information on blank after blank." **[/]**

"I got a classification card of 1A last Saturday. I don't know whether that means I'm apt to be called soon or not but nothing would surprise me. It's all so damned indefinite. I saw in the paper where a graduate might be given a 60 day deferment to obtain a job so I think I'll ask about that. Won't hurt to ask about it anyway. I wish that I had a definite job lined up so I'd have an idea of what was going to happen but I've been scouting around and something definite may turn up one of these days." **[/]**

"I had a letter from Mom the other day. She said she was coming down for commencement. I don't know whether Gene [Sproule] will be able to come down or not—Mom talked like they were quite busy at the bee house." **[2 PARAGRAPHS]** "All my love + kisses" **[/]** "Johnny" **[/]** "P.S. Photo is a sample of an application picture I had taken."

**** To Miss Katherine Glenn, 1216 SW Yamhill, Portland, Oregon (8/12/42, 9:15 PM, Postmarked 8/13/42, 4:30 PM; "Via Air Mail," two 3¢ stamps). Return Address: J. Sproule, 1309 Kearney, Laramie, Wyo. "Hello darling" **[5 PARAGRAPHS]** "I was thinking of that song 'A Tisket, a Tasket' that you mentioned. It does seem a long long time ago. For some reason it reminds me of Reeps Cafe—funny isn't it, how songs will remind you of people or places?" **[2 PARAGRAPHS]** "All my love always" **[/]** "Johnny"

**** To Miss Katherine Glenn, 1216 SW Yamhill, Portland, Oregon (8/15/42, 11:48 PM, Postmarked 8/16/42, 7:30 PM; "Via Air Mail," two 3¢ stamps). Return Address: J. Sproule, 1309 Kearney, Laramie, Wyo. "Hello darling" **[2 PARAGRAPHS]** "Well I have another week of school to go thru and then if I pass everything I'll graduate I guess—the prospect of getting out of here and doing something constructive leaves me positively weak with joy." **[2 PARAGRAPHS]** "All my love + kisses" **[/]** "Johnny"

**** To Miss Katherine Glenn, 1216 SW Yamhill, Portland, Oregon (8/17/42, 11:55 PM, Postmarked 8/18/42, 11 AM). Return Address: J. Sproule, 1309 Kearney, Laramie, Wyo. "Sweetheart" **[4 PARAGRAPHS]** ". . . There was something in the paper a few days or so ago saying something about 60 day deferments for college graduates to enable them to find a job, but I don't know whether they are very available or not. I'll look into it though if I don't have something definite soon. I think I'll stay here and work out at the airport until I have a job located – if I don't have one by the time school is over." **[3 PARAGRAPHS]** "XXXXX" **[/]** "Johnny"

**** To Miss Katherine Glenn, 1216 SW Yamhill, Portland, Oregon (8/19/42, 9:45 PM, Postmarked 8/20/42, 9 PM). Return Address: J. Sproule, 1309 Kearney, Laramie, Wyo. "Hello darling," **[/]** "I've got the typewriter out, I've been typing out answers to some application letters and stuff so I thought that I'd type this. My typing is quite rusty from long disuse, but maybe you'll be able to make out most of it." **[/]**

"I finished up my school work today, though it kept my [sic] quite busy. I had a final to take this afternoon—it was a two hour exam and I was really glad when it was over. I also had some problems in Machine Design to get in which I did this morning, and that together with attending my last class took up most of the morning. Besides cramming a bit and taking the final this afternoon, I went down town, saw the draft board, took a badly needed haircut and picked up my pants from the cleaners." **[/]** "The last two items were necessities for attending a commencement dinner which the graduates were given this evening as [sic] 6:30. It was quite boring, what with the speeches and the fact that I hardly knew anyone there. Anyway after that I came home with a magazine and after I've written to you, I think I'll read a while and go to bed." **[/]**

"My interview with the draft board resulted in a 60 day deferment which will give me a bit of time to look around for a job. They also said that they would give me a classification of IIA or IIB if I got a job vital to national defense, depending upon the degree of vitalness. So that sounds as though I will be able to take a job. That together with the fact that I have finished up my school work makes me feel rather good tonight." **[1 PARAGRAPH]**

"I haven't any immediate plans except to locate a job. I've written a number or [sic] letters as I mentioned and they should be bringing in some results soon. One letter I received in answer to an application sounded rather promising, especially in view of the draft boards reaction, but it has one drawback—the company (Glenn L. Martin, builders of flying boats etc) is located in Baltimore Maryland and I don't think much of the East for two reasons—one, we would be twice or three times as far apart and another don't think much of the people from that part of the country from what I've seen of easterners out here." **[/]**

"I'll have a little time to make a choice, though now that I received that short deferment, so I won't have to take the first thing that pops up. My first choice of a job would be with Boeing at Seattle, if I can land a worthwhile job with them. I have an application in there and I filled out some blanks they sent me, but I haven't heard from them since I sent the blanks back. If that doesn't work out I hope to get out on the West coast on some other job, and I've applied to several other aircraft companies out there." **[/]** "If I don't have something definite in a day or so, I may go out to the airport and try to work out there for the contractor until I do accept some definite job. It probably wouldn't be the best job in the world, but I could make a little expense money while I'm waiting around here." **[2 PARAGRAPHS]** "All my love and kisses" [handwritten] **[/]** "Johnny"

[On October 16, 1942, six weeks after he had accepted a job as a Jr. Engineer at Wright Field in Dayton, Ohio, JHS finally received a job offer from the Boeing Aircraft Company, Seattle, Washington from J. Gehring, Assistant Personnel Manager—this to be "a Draftsman in our Renton Tooling Department at a beginning salary of $160 a month."]

**** To Miss Katherine Glenn, 1216 SW Yamhill, Portland, Oregon (8/23/42, 3:30 PM, Postmarked 8/24/42, 6:30 PM). Return Address: J. Sproule, 1309 Kearney, Laramie, Wyo. "Hello Darling," **[1 PARAGRAPH]** "Mom and Eugene came down Thursday night or possible [sic] one could call it Friday morning for it was two-thirty when they got here. They came down after Gene got off work Thursday evening. It was good to see them and we had time for a nice visit before they had to go back home. Dad was also able to be here so it was the first time in years that we were all together at one place. He was looking well and seemed to be getting along ok, but from what I gathered, his second marriage is breaking up. However, since it didn't concern me I didn't ask him about it." **[/]**

"Friday night was Commencement which lasted until about 9:30 and then after that we sat around and visited till rather late. Yesterday we didn't get up very early, but after I got up I sorted through a bunch of papers and such, preparatory to packing. I sent my books and such papers and problems as I wanted to keep home. I really had a lot of things to go through—the accumulation of several years. When I get located and have a place and find a need for any of my books or such, I can send for them then." **[/]** "Glenn and Elsie Kelly came down yesterday afternoon. There is a lodge convention being held here that they came to attend. We stopped in to see them and then stayed for dinner last night, so I had a chance to see the Kellys which I probably wouldn't have had otherwise since I'm not going to go home." **[/]**

"I have an offer of a Civil Service job with the Army Air Corps. which looks as good as anything else that I might turn up. I would be rated as a Junior Engineer.—pay $2000.00 per year which amounts to about $167 per month. Do you think we can live on that? The only drawback is that I would be located in Dayton, Ohio which is the wrong direction to be going for us to be together immediately. However darling, I don't know whether we would be able to see much of each other even if I were on the coast unless we were both in the same town. So this is what I think: I can take this job and if I'm out there where I wouldn't know a soul, I can really save my money—pay off the debts I have incurred by going to school this summer—and build up a bit of a surplus so we can get married. It looks to me like we could get married quicker that way than if I came out to the coast to work and used up any surplus cash coming to see you which I know I'd do if we were in the same part of the country. It will mean that it will be a while longer before we see each other, but it will also mean that this is our last separation. **[THIS PARAGRAPH CONTINUES]**

When I have saved some money, we we'll be married and won't be apart anymore. What do you think of this? Also, a request for deferment will be sent in when I report for duty. From what the draft board told me the other day, plus the fact that the job would be with the Army Air Corps, I think that this job would merit a deferment as long as there were any. I've thought about this all weekend and my decision is based on what I think will turn out best for us, so I hope you approve darling." **[/]**

"I will have to report at Dayton the first of September, so I'll probably leave here about Friday morning—the 28th—; that wil [sic] give me a little margin of safety to make bus or train connections and look around for a place to stay. . . ." **[2 PARAGRAPHS]** "All my love and kisses" [hand-written] **[/]** "Johnny"

  **** To Miss Katherine Glenn, 1216 SW Yamhill, Portland, Oregon (8/24/42, 2:55 PM, Postmarked 8/25/42, 8 PM). Return Address: J. Sproule, 1309 Kearney, Laramie, Wyo. "Hello Darling" **[/]** ". . . While the folks were here it seemed as though I had most of my time occupied though, for I hadn't seen them in some time and we seemed to have quite a bit of visiting to catch up on. Since they left Sunday afternoon though, I've surely been catching up on sleep, for yesterday I slept till 5:30 in the afternoon which made me about 15 or 16 hours sleep and then today I didn't get up till noon so that was another 12 or 13 hours." **[/]**

"You know, I find it difficult to realize that I finished school too, for as you said, it seems as though I have always been going to school. Anyway, I guess I did get through for they gave me a diploma reading Bachelor of Science and that would indicate that I have been able to fulfill the requirements for graduation." **[2 PARAGRAPHS]**

"I did pretty good in the line of graduation presents—Puss and Charlie [Clyda and Charley Burns] sent me a check, the folks gave me an electric razor, and I also got a belt, some socks, a necktie, a billfold and a combination cigarette case and lighter. They all remind me that I've graduated and that is a good feeling." **[2 PARAGRAPHS]**

"Since I've had this typewriter out writing application letters and that sort of thing my typing has had more use than it's had for years, but it still isn't any too good. It will go along in good shape for a time and then I'll make a whole bunch of errors in a row and I have difficulty making the right margin come out even—in fact I'd say it just doesn't come out even at all." **[2 PARAGRAPHS]** "All my love and kisses" [hand-written] **[/]** "Johnny"

**** To Miss Katherine Glenn, 1216 SW Yamhill, Portland, Oregon (8/27/42, 11:45 AM, Postmarked 8/27/42, 6 PM). Return Address: J. Sproule, 1309 Kearney, Laramie, Wyo. "Darling," [/] "I'm very sorry to hear that Bernard is sick. I know that you must have been quite worried to get a call from Anna hearing that he had spinal meningitis. I'm glad that you were able to call the doctor at camp and find out that treatments were having effect. I know Bernard will have the best of medical care, for they have specialists and the best of doctors in the Medical Corps. It's fine too that you are close and can go to see him. That will help a lot." **[/]**

"There hasn't been anything going on here as usual, so I've been catching up on sleep and just taking a good rest or vacation. According to instructions in the letter I had offering me the Jr. Engineer appointment, I had to notify them that I was 1A (though they should know that from all the blanks I had to fill in, and they also mentioned that a request for a deferment should be sent in). Anyway I sent them a letter telling them of my classification according to instructions, so now I'm waiting for a reply, telling me when to report. Consequently I don't know just when I'll leave here, but I rather think that I'll hear from them by tomorrow so I'll probably leave Saturday morning." **[1 PARAGRAPH]**

"Tunks went down to Denver this morning to see about getting into the Marines or something as his draft number is about up. So I got up this morning about 8:30 to see him off, as I'll probably be gone by the time he comes back. That was the earliest I've been up so far this week. But since I don't have anything in particular to do I guess it doesn't make much difference when I do get up. Anyhow it sure is nice to get caught up on sleep I missed out on the past months." **[1 PARAGRAPH]** "All my love always" [hand-written] **[/]** "Johnny"

**** To Miss Katherine Glenn, 1216 SW Yamhill, Portland, Oregon ("Somewhere on the train in Nebraska Sat. afternoon," Postmarked 8/29/42, 10:30 PM, "Via Air Mail," two 3¢ stamps, Omaha, Nebraska. Burlington station). [No return address.] "Darling" [/] "I can see that this writing on the train will not be any too readable but I want to let you know that I'm started on the way out to Dayton. I hadn't heard from the outfit back there in reply to my letter notifying them of my draft classification yet this morning so I decided to come on out anyway since it was just some red tape anyhow and since if I waited to hear about this I couldn't possibly make it out to Dayton to report the 1st as I was instructed." **[/]**

"At any rate I came to that decision last night about 11 pm so then I had to pack up the rest of my stuff that I hadn't sent home and make a bunch of arrangements for things I hadn't gotten around to doing. So all in all I didn't get to bed last night, but I did make the train ok. It left Laramie at 6:10 am so being rather early and combined with the fact that I'd had no sleep the night before, it wasn't long till I fell asleep. I had quite a long nap and that makes the time pass quickly for which I'm thankful. We'll get into Chicago about 8 something in the morning and then I'll change to the B + O to go on to Dayton arriving there about 6:30 tomorrow evening." **[4 PARAGRAPHS]** "All my love + kisses" **[/]** "Johnny"

**** To Miss Katherine Glenn, 1216 SW Yamhill, Portland, Oregon (8/30/42, 11:10 PM, Postmarked 8/31/42, 8 PM, "Via Air Mail" with two 3¢ stamps, Dayton, Ohio.) Return Address: J. Sproule, Holden Hotel, Dayton, Ohio. "Kay my darling," **[/]** "Do you remember me and how much I love you? I'm missing you very much sweetheart and I wish above everything else that we were together!" **[/]**

"This trip out here was what I'd say offhand as uneventful. I boarded the train yesterday morning at 6:10 at Laramie and then arrived here at about 8:30 this evening. But to fill in an odd detail or two—there wasn't much to see, I mean nothing distinguishing about the towns or countryside till we reached Omaha. There we had to change cars and there was a short stop over so I had time to step to the door of the station and look out, but that's about all. The depot at Omaha was quite large and very well finished in a sort of gray marble. After the train left Omaha there didn't seem to be much to see and then it wasn't long till it was dark so we passed quite a bit of country that I didn't get to see. But my general impression is that most of the country I passed through is rather flat and mostly farmland—chiefly devoted to raising corn. **[THIS PARAGRAPH CONTINUES]**

I spent most of the trip reading for lack of anything else to do. Last night I slept from about 11 pm to 6 am and I was able to do that mostly because I hadn't had any sleep the night before. This morning when I woke at 6 there was quite a thick fog about which effectively obscured the countryside, but it soon began to lift and by the time we reached Chicago the sky was clear except for the smoke from the numerous smokestacks. The train arrived at Chicago at about 8:15 am and then I had to transfer from the Union Pacific to the Baltimore + Ohio RR and there was a layover for an hour + a half so I had breakfast and walked around the 'big town' for a while—apparently having too little time to notice anything outstanding though there were a lot of big buildings. The thing that I noted particularly was the noise made chiefly by the elevated railway running through town. Considering that it was Sunday morning I can imagine that on weekdays this din would be terrific." [/]

"Leaving Chicago we passed a large number of industrial plants of one sort or another and then the outlook was mostly corn again. I had to wait for almost two hours at a little whistle stop called Dishlin (no bigger than Shoshoni) to change trains again and then we came on into Dayton—Getting here about 8:30." [/]

"I checked my baggage and scouted around for a conveniently located hotel and then picked up my suitcases and got a room. It certainly felt grand to clean up and get a shave. I have a nice room at the Holden Hotel on the third floor facing the main part of town costing $2.00 per—which isn't bad, but it would run into money after a few days. Anyhow after I cleaned up I went after something to eat and walked around town to familiarize myself with the streets a bit. I bought a map of the city which will no doubt be a big help." [/]

"My first impressions of the city is that it seems to be quite a nice town. The sidewalks are quite wide and the streets are good—of course there are trolley cars and busses and a considerable amount of traffic so you have to wait for the green light before crossing the street. There are about 8 or 10 theaters and of course a lot of stores of various kinds. The population is something over 200,000 which is big enough I'd say. I haven't seen very much of the town of course but I do like what I've seen. One thing about traveling by trains—you don't seem to see much of the country and your views of towns especially the bigger ones are mostly all from the back side." **[/]**

"I'll have tomorrow to rest up and look around a little and then Tuesday morning I'll see what gives about this job. One thing I've noticed about this town is that the blocks are a lot longer than the ones I've been used to. I think that about 11 blocks would make a mile in this town." **[/]**

"Since I'll see about my job Tuesday I'll probably be moved from here soon. I'll write again right away of course and let you know where a letter will reach me as soon as I know where I'll live as I'll be moved from here by the time you get this darling. I sure do miss your letters and it will be grand to hear from you again. I think we're far apart enough that it would save quite some time in getting each other's letters if we airmailed them. I'll airmail this out in the morning and you can notice how long it takes to arrive." **[/]**

"Darling I think I'll stop now—I seem to have written most everything I can think of at the moment—and I'm dead tired from a shortage of sleep uncomfortable riding on the train and walking around this evening so I think I'm about ready for bed." **[/]** "'Night sweetheart. Remember I love you always!"   **[/]** "All my love + kisses" **[/]** "Johnny"

Chapter 8. Dayton Days: A Bachelor in the Air Force—September 1, 1942 to December 29, 1942

JHS adjusts to Dayton—crowds, humidity and temperature, the prices and taxes, trolleys and ridesharing. JHS' work: design and testing, making reports, giving briefings, Army red tape, inspecting the array of airplanes on Wright Field's flight line, and trips to Edgewood Arsenal (Baltimore). Quotidian details of salary, schedule (including Saturday as a sixth work day), stores open late Mondays for shopping, trading up for a better rented room, very little free time for errands. JHS reports on wartime conditions including draft deferments, possible officer's training, and war news. Mentions of old friends from Wyoming and new colleagues at the Field. JHS looks forward to marriage—taking instruction in Catholicism, preparing a train schedule for KVS, buying the ring, planning a honeymoon, and the ongoing project to find an apartment amid the severe scarcity.

**** To Miss Katherine Glenn, 1216 SW Yamhill, Portland, Oregon (8/31/42, 11:00 PM, Postmarked 9/1/42, 10 AM, "Via Air Mail" with two 3¢ stamps, Dayton, Ohio). Return Address: J. Sproule, Holden Hotel, Dayton, Ohio. "Hello darling," **[2 PARAGRAPHS]** "After locating the place to report and getting something to eat I went to a show. The price was only 40 cents; that was the afternoon price—I think the evening price was 60 cents. However I think that the one I went to was the best one. There are a number of others and the price varies down to 15 cents, but that seemed to be a second run theatre." **[/]**

"Generally speaking, I'd say prices weren't too high. For example hamburgers in most places are 10 cents where they were mostly 15¢ in Laramie—a contrast though are soft drinks which are 7¢ a bottle—at least they were where I noticed. They have a somewhat different tax system here. There is a 1 cent tax on articles from 10¢ to 40¢; 2 cents on articles from 40¢ to 73¢ and 3¢ up to a dollar which makes it a higher tax than the 2% sales tax in Wyoming. They also give a tax receipt (I guess you'd call it) with purchases—I'll enclose a sample. Then too they have an additional cigarette tax (sample enclosed). The only other place I ever saw one like that was in South Dakota one time. I bought a carton of Luckies for $1.49 and so maybe the dealers absorb the extra tax—or maybe other places charge more." **[/]** "But I suppose in a town this size—there are high-priced places and low priced ones and it's a matter of knowing where to buy. I'm curious to know about room and board—as yet I haven't inquired about that for I don't know where I'll be working, but I should find out tomorrow. If I work out at Wright Field I hope I can find a place near there to live. It's about 4½ miles from the center of town. . . ." **[/]**

"My impression of the place [Dayton] so far has been quite favorable. That judgment is solely on the town though for I haven't been here long enough to have an idea as to what the climate will be like. So far it has been warmer that I'm used to—about 85-, but I have a fan in my room and by turning it on, opening the window and sitting here in my shorts I'm quite comfortable." **[/]** "The people here don't seem to worry about the rubber shortage from the way they drive in the city traffic though they might drive slower when they are out of town. Though I did see an ad in the nights paper—I'll see if I can find it—yes here it is (enclosed)—which would indicate that tires are hard to get—for it is easily twice what the tire could have been bought for before rationing. . . ." **[/]** ". . . I may be able to locate a boarding house or at least a room somewhere near—at least I hope so. This living in a hotel is ok but a little expensive. . . ." **[3 PARAGRAPHS]** "All my love" **[/]** "Johnny"

[JHS encloses three items along with the letter: (1) A 1½-inch square paper marked "State of Ohio" / "Prepaid Sales Tax" / "Consumer's Receipt" / "1 Cent" which contains a unique number printed on the side; (2) a strip of cellophane onto which is affixed a 1/2-inch square "Cigarette Tax" for 2 cents; (3) a 1-inch by 2-inch classified newspaper ad reading "WANTED WILL PAY $100 to $150 For five 6.00x16 Tires and Tubes New or Near New No Recaps PRIVATE PARTY AD-8062 TA-6193 Eve."]

**** To Miss Katherine Glenn, 1216 SW Yamhill, Portland, Oregon (9/2/42, 10:55 PM, Postmarked 9/3/42, 10 AM, "Via Air Mail" with one 6¢ Air Mail stamp, Dayton, Ohio). Return Address: J. Sproule, Holden Hotel,

Dayton, Ohio. "Kay darling," **[/]** "I'm now among the employed for I started to work this morning out at Wright Field. I'm a Jr. Engineer in the Experimental Engineering Division Armament section Bombing unit. That doesn't necessarily mean that I'll be doing any bombing, but rather that the work I'll be doing will be concerned with bombs, bomb racks + shackles etc." **[/]**

"As I said I'll work out at Wright Field which is about 5 miles out of Dayton but there is regular bus service out there—which is ok, the only thing is I have to get up a little earlier. I made it in time this morning so I'll try to do better in the morning. . . ." **[1 PARAGRAPH]** "Things are going rather well I'd say—I think the job is ok and this is rather a nice little (I guess it isn't very little) town though it is rather expensive for room and eats." **[/]**

"I ran into a fellow I used to room with at college here—Mack Erwin is his name—who also works in Experimental out at the field though in a different division. He's a nice fellow and it was good to see him. We ate lunch together today and I'll see him often I imagine since he is working on the floor below me." **[/]** "And that reminds me of something—I haven't as yet found a room but you can write me in care of Mack + I'll get the letters (J- S- % Mack Erwin, 63 Grafton Ave., Dayton, Ohio). . . ." **[2 PARAGRAPHS]** "All my love + kisses" **[/]** "Johnny"

   **** To Miss Katherine Glenn, 1216 SW Yamhill, Portland, Oregon (9/4/42, 10:55 PM, Postmarked 9/5/42, 9 AM, "Via Air Mail" with one 6¢ Air Mail stamp, Dayton, Ohio). Return Address: [none]. "Hello darling," **[2 PARAGRAPHS]** "My job is fine and I rather like it—of course I don't know a whole lot about it yet, there is so much to catch on to—procedures and that sort of thing and of course everyone is new and it takes a while to get acquainted but I'm getting along in good shape I'd say." **[/]**

"Yesterday evening the Armament division had a picnic after work and it was quite enjoyable. There were quite a few people there and I was introduced to about every one it seemed, but it's hard to remember names when you meet so many at one time. There was beer and lots of eats furnished and it only cost a dollar each." **[/]** "Tonight Mack + I had a couple beers and looked around town, but it was rather a quiet evening. . . ." **[/]**

"But then when I have to get up at 6 or a quarter after I don't care to stay out too late. I have to walk 7 blocks to the bus depot to ride out to work and then it's a 15 minute walk from the gate to the building where I work so it means I have to start early. There sure is a jam at the depot in the mornings and at night at the exit gate—they just run one big bus after another and then too there's lots of people who drive or catch rides otherwise so you can see that there are lots of people working out at the Field. I don't know how many, but it must be in the thousands." **[/]** "We start work at 8 and work till 4:30 with a half hour off for lunch, but with traveling back + forth it occupies my time from about 6:30 am to 6 pm." **[3 PARAGRAPHS]** "All my love + kisses" **[/]** "Johnny"

**** To Miss Katherine Glenn, 1216 SW Yamhill, Portland, Oregon (9/6/42, 11:24 PM, Postmarked 9/7/42, 11 AM, "Via Air Mail" with two 3¢ "Win The War" stamps, Dayton, Ohio). Return Address: J. Sproule, 701 North Ave., Dayton, Ohio). "Hello darling," **[/]** "One thing I have noticed is that board + lodging are quite expensive. A fair meal will cost at least 65¢ and from there up to a buck, but I suppose I judge from my own standards and I'd guess I eat more than average. This room I found today costs $7.00 per week and it isn't much so I don't suppose I'll stay here long—I should be able to do as good for 4 or 5 dollars a week. This is better than the hotel though which was costing $2.00 a day. This is a nice neighborhood though and I only live about 3 blocks from Mack. The address so you can write me is 701 North Avenue Dayton Ohio. Finding this room is about all I did today. After moving up here from the hotel and unpacking a bit, Mack + I went back down town and did a bit of shopping. There sure aren't very many places to eat here—oh there are a lot of hamburger joints and that sort of thing, but I mean there aren't many good restaurants or cafes." **[/]**

"I like my job quite well though I don't know all about it yet and have been doing quite simple work so far, but I'll no doubt get into more involved work as time goes on. The only unhappy feature is that I have to get up earlier to make it out to work on time since I have to take a bus, but I'll get used to that no doubt and so it isn't too bad." **[2 PARAGRAPHS]** "All my love + kisses" **[/]** "Johnny"

**** To Miss Katherine Glenn, 1216 SW Yamhill, Portland, Oregon (9/8/42, 10:28 PM, Postmarked 9/9/42, 4 PM, "Via Air Mail" with two 3¢ "Win The War" stamps, Dayton, Ohio). Return Address: J. Sproule, 701 North Ave., Dayton, Ohio. "Hello darling," **[2 PARAGRAPHS]** "I miss you very much darling and especially since I haven't heard from you for such a long time. I always miss you you know sweetheart, but somehow when I was getting a letter from you every other day you didn't seem so far away. I haven't had one of your grand letters for over two weeks now darling and that has been an endless length of time. But no doubt I'll hear from you soon at least I sure hope so. I know of course that you couldn't write when I hadn't given you any address,—. . . ." **[/]**

"The job is going along fine though of course I have a lot to catch on to—everything it seems has just a certain way in which it should be done—for example I had to send a couple copies of some work I did the other day to Washington and the letter I wrote to accompany it had a very precise form to be followed— . . . ." **[2 PARAGRAPHS]** "All my love + kisses J."

**** To Miss Katherine Glenn, 1023 SW Yamhill, Portland, Oregon (9/10/42, 10:03 PM, Postmarked 9/11/42, 11 AM, "Via Air Mail" with two 3¢ "Win The War" stamps, Dayton, Ohio). Return Address: J. Sproule, 701 North Ave., Dayton, Ohio. "Hello darling," **[/]** "I'm very happy tonight for I received a letter from you today the first in such a long time. It's really quite an event for it seems like months since I heard from you last." **[/]**

"Today was rather typical I'd say. I got up at 6 and was at the field by about 7:30—I ate breakfast out there and then walked on down to the lab or office I guess you'd call it—any way to the building where I work. I worked to 11:30 and then off for lunch. We're given a half hour, but it takes nearly an hour since we have to walk (except when we can catch rides) out to the administration building (which is about ¾ to a mile distant it seems—over a half mile I'm sure) where the cafeteria is located. So we just have to eat +

get back to work as soon as we can." **[/]** "At 4:30 then the working day over and we are free. I caught a ride into town with a fellow who works downstairs and then came on up here to my room. I sat around and read the evening paper and then went to bed. I came back to the room then and was looking at some ads in the paper for rooms to let when Mack dropped by with a letter from you." **[2 PARAGRAPHS]**

". . . This single room in a private home is costing $7.00 a week which is quite a sum it seems to me. Especially when I was getting a better room Laramie for $7.00 a month. I'll probably look around again this weekend see what is available. I really don't need such a fancy room anyhow for I' gone from 6 am to 6 pm, 6 days a week. About all I do is sleep here." **[/**

"I still like the job ok—there's a lot of activity and I see a lot of different kinds of airplanes. Enclosed is a clipping from the evening paper. The article only lists a few of the more famous 'foreign' planes mostly English There are all types of American planes here too." **[/]** "I have 10 or 12 more letters to write but not tonight for it's bed time again and I don't seem to hear the alarm if I don't get to bed at what seems a very early he by the standards of college days." **[1 PARAGRAPH]** "All my love + kisses always" **[/]** "Johnny"

[The enclosed clipping mentioned in the letter is headlined "British Bomb Being Examined At Wright Field"; it reads: "A giant British four-engined bomber, the Lancaster, of the type used by Britain to drop huge 'blockbuster' bombs on German industrial areas, was under study today by Wright Field engineers, following its arrival at the field late yesterday afternoon / The British plane, dwarfing in size everything on the Wright Field flying line except the monster Douglas B-19, the largest land plane i the world, was flown in by Captain Clyde Pangborn, veteran trans-Pacific flyer, now attached to the Royal Air Force ferry command. / It came here from Washington, where it was inspected by ranking officers of the Army Air Forces, including Lt. Gen. Henry H. Arnold, chief of the Air Forces. It v remain here two days for thorough examination at the air force experimental center. / The Lancaster, which can carry eight tons of bomb and is powered with 1600 horsepower engines, temporarily joins a stran assortment of other foreign planes here at Wright Field for study. Among them are Wellington twin-engine bombers, Spitfire and Hurricane fighters, Beaufighter and Boulton-Paul Defiant night fighters, and German Messerschmidt fighters and Heinkel bombers. . . ."]

**** To Miss Katherine Glenn, 1023 SW Yamhill, Portland, Oregon (9/11/42, 10:25 PM, Postmarked 9/12/42, 11 AM, "Via Air Mail" with two 3¢ stamps, Dayton, Ohio). Return Address: J. Sproule, 701 North Ave., Dayton, Ohio. "Kay darling," **[/]** "I'm feeling better and better, now I've had 4 letters from you. . . ." **[/]** "I'm getting more + more used to living and working here now and as I'm becoming more settled I notice that I don't have as much free time as I thought I would. For example my working hours are from 8:00 am to 4:30 pm—But I have to get up at 6 or a quarter after so I can get out to the field eat breakfast and clock in before 8—then in the evenings it's always after 5 and something nearer six when I get back to my room. Which doesn't leave a lot of time before bedtime rolls around again. . . ." **[/]**

". . . I'm through school now and have a job so the thing I'd like is for us to be married as soon as it's feasible (is that the right word?)—I mean as soon as things are so we can. These are some incidentals such as, I ought to pay back the money I borrowed to finish school and the fact that we're some 2500 miles or so apart, and I have some studying on Catholicism to do—a few things like that . . . I wish darling, that you would think, seriously about this and let me know what you're thinking about when we can be married, how much we'll need to live on etc. We've talked about this a little, but never anything definite and I think it's time we were making some definite plans, don't you darling? I imagine there will be things you'll want to know about the set up here and I'll answer as fully + completely as I can— . . . ." **[3 PARAGRAPHS]** "All my love + kisses always" **[/]** "Johnny"

**** To Miss Katherine Glenn, 1023 SW Yamhill, Portland, Oregon (9/13/42, 10:10 PM, Postmarked 9/14/42, 4:30 PM, "Via Air Mail" with two 3¢ stamps, Dayton, Ohio). Return Address: J. Sproule, 701 North Ave., Dayton, Ohio. "Hello darling," **[/]** ". . . Between 6 am + 6 pm my time is mostly occupied with work, getting ready for work, and going back + forth on the bus. I find it better to get on the early bus and eat breakfast at the field cafeteria than to eat and then go out for the busses are so crowded—they are always crowded it seems, but especially from 7 to 8. At night the busses line up one right after another at the main gate—they fill up, pull into town and then back again for another load. I don't know how many civilian employees there are at Wright Field (as a matter of fact, I suppose thats one of those military secrets) but I'm sure they must number in the thousands." **[/]**

"I'm becoming accustomed to the new surroundings and if I could find a good place to stay, a ride back + forth to work instead of riding on the bus and a number 1 place to eat I would have my immediate problems solved. **[/]** "As I mentioned I go to bed a lot earlier than I've been used to and ge up earlier too, but one advantage of having my time well occupied is that the days go by faster it seems. I've been here two weeks tonight and it hasn't seemed long these past two weeks. But when I think back to June when we were together last it seems an age." **[/]**

"Darling I miss you like everything! And as I write it that seems like such a simple sentence, but it holds such a world of meaning. It means that all these times we've been apart my loving you hasn't changed a bit. It mean also that I'll be happy and content only when we are married and togethe after all these separations. Dearest, as you may have gathered by now, m loving you is something everlasting that will never change as long as there is breath in my body." **[/]**

"In these unusual times our love is one thing that hasn't or won't change. We waited to get married till I finished school and now that's done. What the future will hold—how long the war will last no one can tell, but we are certain of one thing—that we love each other." **[2 PARAGRAPHS]** "Night now sweetheart. I love you!" **[/]** "Johnny"

**** To Miss Katherine Glenn, Apt. No. 2, 1023 S.W. Yamhill, Portland, Oregon (9/14/42, 8:30 PM, Postmarked 9/15/42, 7:30 PM, "Via Air Mail" with two 3¢ stamps, Dayton, Ohio). Return Address: J. Sproule, 701 North Ave., Dayton, Ohio. "Hello darling," **[/]** "Monday night, or evening I guess I should say, is shopping night here. The stores stay open much in the fashion that they stayed open late on Saturday nights back home. I take it they were finding that a lot of people (like me for instance) just couldn't make it to the stores during the regular shopping hours because of their working hours so they stay open late Monday evening and do quite a business from the appearance of the crowds on the street." **[1 PARAGRAPH]**

"Yes darling, I do agree that all in all this has been interesting and some fun too, to come back here to a strange place and take a job knowing nothing of the people, the town or the job." **[/]** "... I've fallen into sort of a routine where I get up, go to work, come home, spend my free hours writing letters, reading or some such and then go to bed + do the same thing the next day—at any rate my sphere of action is rather limited and I could just as well be in any town. If I were traveling about the countryside more I suppose I would be more aware of how far East this is." **[/]**

"Yes this is rather a defense town for there are the two fields Wright + Patterson with lots of civilian employees and lots of army too and I'd say they were doing defense work though the particular section or division I'm in is doing research + experimentation rather than production. Besides these of course there are several branches of General Motors here, National Cash Register, a small aircraft factory not far away and a large number of tool factories, foundries etc. which all have war contracts and are producing various war goods. So all in all it's quite a busy place." **[/]**

"Darling, I've mentioned in my last couple letters that I wanted to know what you were thinking about this situation of us being separated, . . . I more or less have a course of action I guess you could call it or a plan worked out in my mind and you probably have too as it would be an excellent idea to get things worked out I think." **[/]** "I have some letters to write that I've put off a couple weeks now so maybe I'll get some of them done tonight. I write to you first though so you'll hear from me if I never get anything else done." **[/]** "'Night darling" **[/]** "All my love + kisses always" **[/]** "Johnny"

**** To Miss Katherine Glenn, Apt. No. 2, 1023 S.W. Yamhill, Portland, Oregon (9/15/42, 10:15 PM, Postmarked 9/16/42, 10 AM, "Via Air Mail" with two 3¢ stamps, Dayton, Ohio). Return Address: J. Sproule, 701 North Ave., Dayton, Ohio. "Kay darling," **[/]** "Things are going well now for I've had letters from you quite regularly these past few days. . . ." **[/]** "I didn't get home till about 7 this evening for I ate before coming home. I ate in a cafeteria—there are several here and I've eaten in them all now I think. As a matter of fact there are only 3 or 4 places in which I've eaten more than once . . . I'm getting used to paying 75¢ or so for a meal which is more than I was paying in Laramie but about average around here I guess—that is for supper—I eat breakfast + lunch at the field and it runs from 25 to 45¢ depending on what I have." **[1 PARAGRAPH]**

"But with all the army affairs carried on in this region officers are quite common—from lieutenants on up. All that I've had any contact with have been quite friendly. I've heard that some officers like pomp + ceremony + such, but I don't think there are too many like that. Of course my observations are of their dealings with civilians and that possibly makes a difference." **[/]** "I suppose I do get up rather early but with things as they are it seems better to go to bed earlier + get up earlier + so avoid the rush. It's better, I find to have plenty of time instead of having to rush around. It's hot enough here without having to hurry. But I imagine that it seems hotter because of the lower altitude and increased humidity—from what I've heard of the winters around here I don't anticipate its being very harsh." **[/]**

". . . So far the things I've been doing have been fairly simple—but I expected that for just starting in, I have a lot of things to catch on to— procedures and such stuff. Being in Experimental Engineering means that we test equipment and such to find how strong it is, how long it will work or how it will work under adverse conditions such as extreme heat, pressure or cold—. . . For example when an airplane is built some equipment is govt. furnished and that is designed by us and then too we cooperate or assist commercial contractors with their problems especially when something new comes up. . . ." **[/]**

"Darling I think it would be ok for you to work for a while anyway when we get married for otherwise you wouldn't have much to do while I'm working. I know that when I haven't had anything to do—like the time between graduation + starting to work—I've gotten very bored with just doing nothing. Then too darling we could afford a few more things as we started our marriage. And you wouldn't be so dependent on my salary which would be better in these troubled times if anything should happen to me. In normal times this last wouldn't be significant." **[1 PARAGRAPH]** "All my love + kisses" **[/]** "Johnny"

    **** To Miss Katherine Glenn, Apt. No. 2, 1023 S.W. Yamhill, Portland, Oregon (9/16/42, 10:55 PM, Postmarked 9/17/42, 1 PM, "Via Air Mail" with two 3¢ stamps, Dayton, Ohio). Return Address: J. Sproule, 701 North Ave., Dayton, Ohio. "Hello darling," **[1 PARAGRAPH]** ". . . I'm working on about three different things now. Not all at the same time of course but I turn from one to another as delays come up. For instance I'm working on a design of an armorplate bracket for an incendiary grenade (it has to be armorplated in places to prevent accidental ignition by a chance bullet in combat)—anyhow I am held up on that now waiting for the drafting dept to get my design drawn up so we can have one made for testing purposes. So that's the way it goes and by having a number of things to work on I can always have something to do." **[/]**

"This weather here is something I'm not accustomed to yet. I drink gallons of water—it seems like I'm always thirsty—and the more I drink the more I perspire and the thirstier I get and on it goes—a vicious cycle they call it I think." **[/]**

"Lately I've been keeping more in touch with the war news and the Russian's last ditch stand at Stalingrad looks very serious. But it seems to me that winter must be fast approaching in Russia and last year the Russians made great counter attacks helped in large part by the snow and cold since they were more prepared for the cold + accustomed to it. Then too, there's the possibility of the opening of a second front which would prevent the Germans from concentrating on one particular attack—such as Stalingrad." **[2 PARAGRAPHS]** "All my love" **[/]** "Johnny"

**** To Miss Katherine Glenn, Apt. No. 2, 1023 S.W. Yamhill, Portland, Oregon (9/17/42, 9:45 AM, Postmarked 9/18/42, 11:30 AM, "Vi Air Mail" with two 3¢ stamps, Dayton, Ohio). Return Address: J. Sproule, 701 North Ave., Dayton, Ohio. "Hello darling," [/] ". . . I wrote the othe day agreeing with your views about you working, for a while anyhow, afte we're married so that is settled." [/] "You're probably right about us no feeling as we did several years ago—well mostly right anyhow for I know one thing that hasn't changed and that's the fact that I love you. That's something that will never change darling." [/]

"I'm wondering how long a time you had in mind when you said you couldn't leave Portland 'very soon, in fact for quite a while.' It occurs to r that could be a very varied length of time, depending on one's interpretation. So I'll ask how long will it be before you can come here?" [/] "I agree that having to talk this over in our letters isn't the most satisfactory way I can imagine, but if we can decide about when we'll get married and when you'll come out here—you know, the main items, we could make our final decisions about where we'll live, and whether we'll take a furnished apartment or take an unfurnished one and buy our own furniture, and other points like that later. I think it would be especially good if you could come out at least a couple weeks before we get married—or earlier if you could. But if you could come out a couple wee before we get married we could find a place to live and talk over and decide about anythings that are unsettled or that we didn't decide in our letters. What do you think about that?" [/]

"Have I told you how much I'm making at this job yet? In case I haven't I' tell you (whether it's again or not.) My salary is $2000 per year—which is about $167 per month, but we're working Saturdays and get overtime fo that which amounts to about 20% or $400 more per year the way they figure it out, which would make about $200 per month. However there is 5% deduction for the government's version of social security and there's 10% for war bonds, but the overtime will cover these deductions so we could figure a net salary of $165 to $170 per month. I owe about $250 which I'll be able to pay off in about 3 months I think. Maybe this 'financ

statement' will help you some darling in your figuring—I hope so anyway."
[/]

"Today we really kept busy. We were preparing for a demonstration of some of our equipment and work for some inspecting colonels + generals tomorrow. We were working like mad to get everything in shape when we were told this afternoon that the demonstration would be put off a week. So—I guess we have plenty of time to get ready now." [/] "I missed the early bus this morning and consequently didn't get to the field in time to eat breakfast before going on down to work. I got to work on time but I did miss breakfast so if I get to bed a bit earlier tonight maybe I can make it in time for breakfast tomorrow." [/] "'Night darling" [/] "All my love" [/] "Johnny"

   **** To Miss Katherine Glenn, Apt. No. 2, 1023 S.W. Yamhill, Portland, Oregon (9/18/42, 10:57 PM, Postmarked 9/19/42, 12 M, "Via Air Mail" with two 3¢ stamps, Dayton, Ohio). Return Address: J. Sproule, 701 North Ave., Dayton, Ohio. "Darling," [/] "I'm glad too that we are back as you say, on a regular writing schedule. It's swell to come back from work and have a letter from you. Having a letter from you gives the evening a lift or a special feeling that everything is going well. . . ." [/]

"Today was rather easier than yesterday for we weren't under such a pressure to get anything done—I did some more work on preparations for the demonstration and then worked on some sketches for a device to test a hoisting device. It's a part of the specifications (this device + means + manner of testing). I'm writing for this outfit so contracts can be bid for their manufacture." [/]

"Yes we get Sundays off—we work Saturdays same as the other days of the week only we get paid overtime for the Saturdays we work. We get an overtime check at the end of the month for our overtime the previous month. We also get checks the 13th + the 28th of the month which are our regular salary divided into two checks. Since it takes a while to get the payroll made up, our checks which we get on the 28th are for the pay period ending the 15th and the checks we get the 15th are for the pay period from the 15 to the 30th. Hence I'll get my first check the 28th since I started the first + thereafter I'll get checks at the regular intervals. The only overtime we get is Saturdays—if we work till 6 or so that's our contribution, but that doesn't happen very often—I haven't worked late so far and I don't expect I'll have to soon. I get paid for this month's overtime the last of October and after that I'll be getting the 3 checks each month. Which won't make me unhappy." **[/]**

"You hit the nail exactly on the head when you said 'there's not much sense in caring for each other and being apart all this time' which is exactly what I think darling. The sooner we are together the happier we'll both be I know—about by being sure of myself darling—I'm not always sure about everything, but there's one thing I do know and never have any doubts about and that is that I love you darling." **[/]** "You mentioned Jan Feb + March and asked what I thought—I think we can be married in January at the latest darling. I don't want to wait any longer than necessary do you sweetheart? It has been such a long wait already. . . ." **[2 PARAGRAPHS]** "Always + forever yours" **[/]** "Johnny"

**** To Miss Katherine Glenn, Apt. No. 2, 1023 S.W. Yamhill, Portland, Oregon (9/20/42, 11:10 PM, Postmarked 9/21/42, 11 AM, "Via Air Mail" with two 3¢ stamps, Dayton, Ohio). Return Address: J. Sproule, 701 North Ave., Dayton, Ohio. "Hello darling," **[/]** ". . . This has been the longest time we've been apart darling and it will be so wonderful to be together that words alone cannot express how good I'll feel when we are together." **[1 PARAGRAPH]**

". . . Saturday evening it started to rain like someone emptying a bucket just before I caught the trolley for the rest of the trip back from work so I stayed in the shelter of a store entrance with about 15 other people until the sudden shower was over. So I didn't get back to the room until after 6:30. I cleaned up and went back downtown to eat and then went to a show—'Holiday Inn' with Bing Crosby + Fred Astaire which wasn't bad—sort of a musical—very light and entertaining. Which reminds me that Fred Astaire, Ilona Massey + Hugh Herbert were here in Dayton Friday on a bon selling tour. Anyhow after the show I came home and went to bed (early—only about 11) as there didn't seem to be much else to do. . . ." **[/]**

"I had to go down town to eat today because the eating places in this neighborhood (and a lot of downtown too) close on Sunday. I read for a while this afternoon and took a nap. The captain (who is the other roomer here) and I had supper together and then came back to the room and talked + listened to the radio. So now the evening is over and it will be time for bed again soon." **[1 PARAGRAPH]**

"Yes that Eldon House was the fellow I came home with one time. He was Ray Berryman's roommate at school before Ray finished last spring. Which reminds me that I heard in a roundabout way that Ray and Mary Jane may be going to get married. I'll have to ask Ray about it—I haven't heard from him since I've been down here." **[1 PARAGRAPH]** "Love + kisses" **[/]** "Johnny"

**** To Miss Katherine Glenn, Apt. No. 2, 1023 S.W. Yamhill, Portland, Oregon (9/21/42, 9:38 PM, Postmarked 9/22/42, 11 AM, "Via Air Mail" with two 3¢ stamps, Dayton, Ohio). Return Address: J. Sproule, 701 North Ave., Dayton, Ohio. "Hello darling," **[1 PARAGRAPH]** ". . . As far as I know sweetheart, there isn't anything we don't agree on. It's just that we haven't exactly settled a couple of things; for instance, when you are coming out here and an exact date for us to be married." **[/]**

"Since tonight was shopping night, I ate down town and then bought some stationary and a crystal for my watch. It is rather nice to have the stores open late one night a week, but it is sort of hard to get anywhere in a hurry for the streets are jammed—both with cars + busses and with pedestrians." **[1 PARAGRAPH]** "Yesterday and today were the coolest it's been since I arrived here. They have been the only days I haven't sweat gallons. We have a couple coke dispensing machines in the building where I work and I've been holding myself down to 5 or 6 a day. To show how nice it was today—I only had two. The trouble is we're in a brand new building and they don't have the drinking fountains in yet, but they will soon no doubt." **[1 PARAGRAPH]** "Always yours" **[/]** "Johnny"

**** To Miss Katherine Glenn, Apt. No. 2, 1023 S.W. Yamhill, Portland, Oregon (9/22/42, 8:40 PM, Postmarked 9/23/42, 11 AM, "Via Air Mail" with two 3¢ stamps, Dayton, Ohio). Return Address: J. Sproule, 701 North Ave., Dayton, Ohio. "Hello honey," **[/]** ". . . The days go along better if I get to bed early and then too, there's the fact that I want to pay those bills as soon as I can and going to bed early is a good way to save money. And while I think about it darling, I'll send you some money for you to come out on. I know it will probably be expensive so I want to help." **[1 PARAGRAPH]**

"I don't think you need to worry about Joe's [Glenn] 1A classification right away for, from my experience, the draft boards every once in a while go through their lists and class every one as 1A irregardless." **[/]** ". . . I finished up a roll of color film and I should have them back in a week or so. They have to be sent to the Eastman Camera Co. to be developed and printed since the color process is sort of involved. . . ." **[2 PARAGRAPHS]** "All my love + kisses" **[/]** "Johnny"

**** To Miss Katherine Glenn, Apt. No. 2, 1023 S.W. Yamhill, Portland, Oregon (9/23/42, 11:25 PM, Postmarked 9/24/42, 11 AM, "Via Air Mail" with two 3¢ stamps, Dayton, Ohio). Return Address: J. Sproule, 701 North Ave., Dayton, Ohio. "Hello darling," **[2 PARAGRAPHS]** ". . . I don't think we need to worry about having too large a place to live. If anything the difficulty will lay more in the other direction, for from what I hear, apartments aren't any too plentiful. . . ." **[4 PARAGRAPHS]** "All my love always" **[/]** "Johnny"

**** To Miss Katherine Glenn, Apt. No. 2, 1023 S.W. Yamhill, Portland, Oregon (9/24/42, 11:40 PM, Postmarked 9/25/42, 12:30 PM, "Via Air Mail" with two 3¢ stamps, Dayton, Ohio). Return Address: J. Sproule, 701 North Ave., Dayton, Ohio. "Hello darling," **[1 PARAGRAPH]** ". . . This evening I met Mack and his girl downtown and had supper with them and then sat around and talked a while. . . . The captain who has the other room here came in. He had a roll of film to develop so I helped him with that. We had to go down town and get some stuff etc. so while with waiting for the fresh solutions we mixed up to cool and waiting for the negatives to develop and then washing them afterward we just finished up developing the roll of film. . . ." **[1 PARAGRAPH]**

"Tomorrow I won't have to ride the bus for which I'm glad. A couple of the fellows in the Bombing Unit who were riding with another fellow started driving to work today as the guy they were riding with went to the Navy. So I'll ride out + back with them—for a while anyhow. I don't know how long it will be before they make some other arrangement." **[1 PARAGRAPH]** "Love + kisses" **[/]** "Johnny"

**** To Miss Katherine Glenn, Apt. No. 2, 1023 S.W. Yamhill, Portland, Oregon (9/25/42, 11:45 PM, Postmarked 9/26/42, 10 AM, "Via Air Mail" with two 3¢ stamps, Dayton, Ohio). Return Address: J. Sproule, 701 North Ave., Dayton, Ohio. "Hello darling," **[1 PARAGRAPH]** "I'd like to call you too darling, but like you say, it's constantly told by the telephone co. that all the facilities are needed by war business. And then we just barely get to talking when 3 minutes is up and the cost begins to multiply. But anyhow I'd call you if the telephone business was normal darling—since it isn't though you'll know that I am wishing I could call you." **[3 PARAGRAPHS]** "This will be sort of short tonight for I was helping Patterson (the captain) print some pictures this evening and didn't get them till just a little bit ago and now it's gotten rather late." **[/]** "Night darling" **[/]** "All my love + kisses" **[/]** "Johnny"

**** To Miss Katherine Glenn, Apt. No. 2, 1023 S.W. Yamhill, Portland, Oregon (9/26/42, 9:30 PM [sic], Postmarked 9/26/42, 8:30 PM, "Via Air Mail" with two 3¢ stamps, Dayton, Ohio). Return Address: J. Sproule, 701 North Ave., Dayton, Ohio. "Hello darling," **[1 PARAGRAPH]** "The thing I want to write about first (and don't know just how to say it) is your coming out here. I was hoping you could come out sooner than the first of the year darling. I guess it is sort of hard to get away, as you wrote, and there doesn't seem to be much I can do about that. But you will come as soon as you can won't you sweetheart? I sure am looking forward to seeing you and it will be the nicest thing I know for us to be together again." **[2 PARAGRAPHS]**

"Which brings me to another thought. About our honeymoon darling—I can get 5 days off after I've been here three months so I was thinking how would it be if you didn't take a job till after we're married? That way we'd know that there wouldn't be any conflict in our both getting off at the same time. And I can surely support us both for that length of time don't you think? Then too, it will take a while to locate an apartment—as I wrote, it won't make much difference to me where we live as I'll have to ride to work anyhow, so I'd like to have a place that would be most convenient for you darling— . . . ." **[2 PARAGRAPHS]** "All my love + kisses" **[/]** "Johnny"

  **** To Miss Katherine Glenn, Apt. No. 2, 1023 S.W. Yamhill, Portland, Oregon (9/28/42, Postmarked 9/29/42, 12:30 PM, "Via Air Mail" with two 3¢ stamps, Dayton, Ohio). Return Address: J. Sproule, 701 North Ave., Dayton, Ohio. "Kay darling," **[1 PARAGRAPH]** "Tonight was shopping night so I didn't get home very early and then I got in on a poker game here at the house with the landlord + some friends of his—barbers out at Patterson Field—the landlord runs the barber shop at the PX out there." **PARAGRAPHS]** "All my love + kisses" **[/]** "Johnny"

  **** To Miss Katherine Glenn, Apt. No. 2, 1023 S.W. Yamhill, Portland, Oregon (9/30/42, 10:50 PM, Postmarked 10/1/42, 12:30 PM, "Via Air Mail" with two 3¢ stamps, Dayton, Ohio. Return Address: J. Sproule, 701 North Ave., Dayton, Ohio. "Hello darling," **[2 PARAGRAPHS]** "Honey are you sure you don't want me to help you with the expenses you'll have coming out here? I'll be glad too you know darling. And I'll get some time tables and see what sort of an itinerary I can map out for you. You mentioned something about making some stops. It would help me honey, I knew something of what you have in mind . . . ." **[1 PARAGRAPH]**

"Darling I was wondering—how soon will we be married after you get here? Something I'm not very clear on this publishing the banns (spelling?), and I seem to remember Gene St. Peter saying something about the time being increased from 3 weeks to 6 weeks. Do you know anything about that? Anyhow you can probably give me some idea as to what we'll do darling." **[2 PARAGRAPHS]** "All my love + kisses" **[/]** "Johnny"

**** To Miss Katherine Glenn, Apt. No. 2, 1023 S.W. Yamhill, Portland, Oregon (10/1/42, 10:00 PM, Postmarked 10/2/42, 12:30 PM, "Via Air Mail" with two 3¢ stamps, Dayton, Ohio). Return Address: J. Sproule, 701 North Ave., Dayton, Ohio. "Hello darling," **[2 PARAGRAPHS]** "Darling I've been looking + thinking about a ring for you. It's sort of complicated by our being apart—I mean picking out one you'll like. So this evening I looked in the catalogue + noted a few I thought you might like from what you've said. So darling if you could look in the Montgomery Ward catalogue—(I was looking in the Fall + Winter 42-43 Chicago edition, but I imagine they will have the same numbers in the catalogue distributed out there) pages 570 to 572 and look at the combination P + S top of page 571 or the combination U + W on the middle right side of page 570 or the designs L, M, and N on page 572. Let me know if you like any of them or if there are any others you like—just tell me what ever you think of the above or anything else that occurs to you about this." **[2 PARAGRAPHS]** "All my love + kisses" **[/]** "Johnny"

**** To Miss Katherine Glenn, Apt. No. 2, 1023 S.W. Yamhill, Portland, Oregon (10/2/42, 11:15 PM, Postmarked 10/3/42, 12:30 PM, "Via Air Mail" with two 3¢ stamps, Dayton, Ohio). Return Address: J. Sproule, 701 North Ave., Dayton, Ohio. "Hello darling," **[4 PARAGRAPHS]** "Honey I don't know offhand about a route through Denver, but I'll look into it thoroughly and let you know about it." **[3 PARAGRAPHS]** "All my love + kisses" **[/]** "Johnny"

**** To Miss Katherine Glenn, Apt. No. 2, 1023 S.W. Yamhill, Portland, Oregon (10/4/42, 11:50 PM, Postmarked 10/5/42, 1:30 PM, "Via Air Mail" with two 3¢ stamps, Dayton, Ohio). Return Address: J. Sproule, 701 North Ave., Dayton, Ohio. "Hello darling," **[2 PARAGRAPHS]** "I heard the other day that the coldest it ever got here was about 10 below. Which isn't bad, although that will probably seem colder than 10 below in Wyoming because it is a lot more humid out here. It's probably a lot like the winter out where you are I imagine." **[/]**

"Last night I went to the show and had supper with a fellow from the same sub-unit I'm in. Lately I've been riding out to work with him. He's from

New Jersey—Bernie Boyuk by name—and quite a likable fellow." **[4 PARAGRAPHS]**

"I haven't thought much about where we could go on our honeymoon darling—Florida is quite a distance (1200 miles) from here, New York is closer, but it's probably pretty cold in January being right on the coast, Niagara Falls is rather traditional maybe a little too much so. As for me sweetheart we could just go down to Cleveland or Cincinnati or someplace and just be together. What do you have in mind darling? Just being with you will suit me so anything you have in mind will be fine." **[1 PARAGRAPH]** "All my love and kisses" **[/]** "Johnny"

**** To Miss Katherine Glenn, Apt. No. 2, 1023 S.W. Yamhill, Portland, Oregon (10/5/42, 8:38 PM, Postmarked 10/6/42, 12:30 PM, "Via Air Mail" with two 3¢ stamps, Dayton, Ohio). Return Address: J. Sproule, 701 North Ave., Dayton, Ohio. "Hello darling," **[2 PARAGRAPHS]** "Tonight being shopping night I stopped down town + bought Eugene [Sproule] a sweater for his birthday. There was quite a crowd on the streets and this didn't help walking conditions any. . . ." **[/]** "Something else I got tonight was some time tables so I'll see what I can work out in the way of an itinerary for you darling." **[2 PARAGRAPHS]** "All my love + kisses always" **[/]** "Johnny"

**** To Miss Katherine Glenn, Apt. No. 2, 1023 S.W. Yamhill, Portland, Oregon (10/6/42, 9:14 PM, Postmarked 10/7/42, 11 PM, "Via Air Mail" with two 3¢ stamps, Dayton, Ohio). Return Address: J. Sproule, 701 North Ave., Dayton, Ohio. "Hello darling," **[/]** "Here it is another day gone by—it passed rather quickly too, for I was on the test all day. A colonel and a couple of his men from Edgewood Arsenal—chemical warfare—were at the field to check the installation of a couple of chemical tanks in various airplanes. I was getting releases on the planes + seeing about racks + hoists etc.—and I'll bet I walked 15 miles today without exaggeration." **[/]** "One thing about this job we get plenty of variation. Sometimes I'm working on two or three hot jobs at the same time. Anyhow I've found it all very interesting so far." **[3 PARAGRAPHS]** "Always" **[/]** "Johnny"

**** To Miss Katherine Glenn, Apt. No. 2, 1023 S.W. Yamhill, Portland, Oregon (10/7/42, 11:35 PM, Postmarked 10/8/42, 12:30 AM, "Via Air Mail" with two 3¢ stamps, Dayton, Ohio). Return Address: J. Sproule, 701 North Ave., Dayton, Ohio. "Hello darling," **[4 PARAGRAPHS]** "Oh yes, I'm working on the time table I got so maybe tomorrow night I can have some sort of iteniary sp? worked out for your inspection and approval or adaptation or revision or whatever seems necessary. And we can try to figure out just when you'll get here and etc." **[2 PARAGRAPHS]** "All my love always" **[/]** "Johnny"

**** To Miss Katherine Glenn, Apt. No. 2, 1023 S.W. Yamhill, Portland, Oregon (10/8/42, 9:58 PM, Postmarked 10/9/42, 1 PM, "Via Air Mail" with two 3¢ stamps, Dayton, Ohio). Return Address: J. Sproule, 701 North Ave., Dayton, Ohio. "Hi honey," **[/]** "Tonight I have been looking about train schedules and here's one—see if you like it." **[/]** "Leave Portland 9:40 PM Sunday on the Portland Rose-Pony Express." **[/]** "Arrive at Denver 11:55 AM Tuesday." **[/]** "Leave Denver 4:15 PM Tuesday" **[/]** "Arrive at St. Louis 2:15 PM Wednesday." **[/]** "Leave St. Louis 6:00 PM Wednesday on the Pennsylvania Limited." **[/]** "Arrive at Dayton 1:40 AM Thursday." **[/]** "I have figured the trip straight through, but the trains are daily so you can stop in Denver as many days as you like. . . ." **[2 PARAGRAPHS]** "All my love + kisses" **[/]** "Johnny" [Written by KVS on the outside of the envelope is the word "Schedule."]

**** To Miss Katherine Glenn, Apt. No. 2, 1023 S.W. Yamhill, Portland, Oregon ("Saturday-midnight," Postmarked 10/11/42, 2 PM, "Via Air Mail" with two 3¢ stamps, Dayton, Ohio). Return Address: J. Sproule, 701 North Ave., Dayton, Ohio. "Hello darling," **[2 PARAGRAPHS]** "I was very glad to have a letter from you this evening when I came home from work. I had begun to think I was only going to get 1 letter from you this week, but getting one tonight doubled that. I received the other one Wednesday." **[2 PARAGRAPHS]**

"Sure darling, I'll reserve you a room so you'll have a place to go when you get here in case I'm working. You'll note in the train schedule I sent, I figured it out so you'd get here in the evening, but maybe you won't care to get in at that time. Anyhow, let me know what you think of that train schedule. And in case I'm working, my phone number at the field is 2361 and here at home it's RA 1811. In case this last one changes due to my moving some time, I'll tell you when I send you a new address—if any." **[4 PARAGRAPHS]** "All my love + kisses" **[/]** "Johnny"

**** To Miss Katherine Glenn, Apt. No. 2, 1023 S.W. Yamhill, Portland, Oregon (10/12/42, 11:06 PM, Postmarked 10/13/42, 12:30 PM, "Via Air Mail" with two 3¢ stamps, Dayton, Ohio). Return Address: J. Sproule, 701 North Ave., Dayton, Ohio. "Kay darling," **[/]** "This week got off to a swell start for I had two letters from you when I came home this evening." **[4 PARAGRAPHS]**

"Darling, have you had a chance to look over those rings I mentioned?" **[/]** "You're sure right about how swell it will be to see each other after this long long separation darling— . . ." **[/]** "'Night now darling." **[/]** "All my love + kisses" **[/]** "Johnny"

[On the back of this envelope, KVS has written out a schedule, presumably her work at the telephone office, as follows: S – 9-130 + 6:30-10 / M – 1-6 + 7-10 / T – off / W – off / T – 8:30-12 + 4-8:30 / F – Same [as above] / S – {blank}.]

**** To Miss Katherine Glenn, Apt. No. 2, 1023 S.W. Yamhill, Portland, Oregon (10/13/42, 9:40 PM, Postmarked 10/14/42, 11:30 PM, "Via Air Mail" with two 3¢ stamps, Dayton, Ohio). Return Address: J. Sproule, 701 North Ave., Dayton, Ohio. "Hello darling," **[/]** ". . . I'm about ready for bed—6 o'clock comes pretty early, I find. And I heard today that we'll start to work earlier, the last of the week or the first of next week— from 7:30 to 4 instead of 8 to 4:30—which will mean getting up even earlier. It will be ok with me though for it's dark when I get up anyhow, and getting off a half hour earlier will mean I can get into the stores after coming in from work in the evening." **[/]** "Today was payday so that was a cheery note to brighten the day." **[/]**

"I found a fine way to get a nice cold coke. We were testing some equipment in a cold box today and as the cokes from the dispensing machine weren't very cold we just put them in our cold box. We were using dry ice and had the temperature down to -105°F so the cokes got cold enough." **[3 PARAGRAPHS]** "All my love and kisses" **[/]** "Johnny"

**** To Miss Katherine Glenn, Apt. No. 2, 1023 S.W. Yamhill, Portland, Oregon (10/14/42, 10:59 PM, Postmarked 10/15/42, 2:30 PM, "Via Air Mail" with two 3¢ stamps, Dayton, Ohio). Return Address: J. Sproule, 701 North Ave., Dayton, Ohio. "Hello darling," **[2 PARAGRAPHS]** ". . . Your idea about me sending you a couple pages from the catalogue is ok honey only it will take me a bit of time to locate another catalogue as the one I was looking at was one the people here had borrowed and have since returned. However I'll look up one and send you a couple or so pertinent pages for your selection and comment. Something else that just occurred to me—will our ceremony be one—I think it's called a double ring ceremony—where we'd both have wedding rings?" **[3 PARAGRAPHS]**

"About going through Billings—you could undoubtedly go through there for one can go to almost any town of any size if time + money are not considered. But from the map I have for the Union Pacific it looks to me like it would be about a 1000 miles further. You would take the UP to Pocatello Idaho and thence to Butte where you would take the Northern Pacific to Billings. Leaving Billings you'd take the Chicago, Burlington + Quincy to Casper where you would change to the Chicago + Southern to go to Cheyenne. Then you'd switch back to the Union Pacific to go to Denver + St. Louis and so on like that other schedule I mentioned—. . . ." **[5 PARAGRAPHS]** "All my love + kisses" **[/]** "Johnny"

**** To Miss Katherine Glenn, Apt. No. 2, 1023 S.W. Yamhill, Portland, Oregon (10/16/42, 8:36 PM, Postmarked 10/17/42, 12:30 PM, "Via Air Mail" with two 3¢ stamps, Dayton, Ohio). Return Address: J. Sproule, 701 North Ave., Dayton, Ohio. "Hello darling," **[3 PARAGRAPHS]** "To avoid the standing on the corner and waiting for a bus that I've been doing, I'm going to move out of here and over to where another fellow I work with lives. He has a car and drives to work so that should be an improvement—besides lowering my room rent to $5.00 a week. Norm— Norm Milde is his name—said he'd lived there for 2 years so it will probably be a good enough place to stay. I'll move out Sunday when I'll have time pack. The address is 2000 North Main.—oh yes, and the phone is RA 179 in case you need to call me when you come out here—like if you should arrive while I'm at work." **[3 PARAGRAPHS]** "All my love" **[/]** "Johnny"

  **** To Miss Katherine Glenn, Apt. No. 2, 1023 S.W. Yamhill, Portland, Oregon (10/18/42, 12:40 AM, Postmarked 10/19/42, 10:30 AM, "Via Air Mail" with two 3¢ stamps, Dayton, Ohio). Return Address: J. Sproule, 2000 N. Main, Dayton, Ohio. "Darling," **[/]** "It's awfully late fo me to be up and still get up at 6 but I moved to 2000 N. Main this evening and I just got my things sort of straightened out." **[5 PARAGRAPHS]** "All my love + kisses" **[/]** "Johnny"

  **** To Miss Katherine Glenn, Apt. No. 2, 1023 S.W. Yamhill, Portland, Oregon (10/19/42, 9:50 PM, Postmarked 10/20/42, 1:30 PM, "V Air Mail" with two 3¢ stamps, Dayton, Ohio). Return Address: J. Sproule, 2000 North Main, Dayton, Ohio. "Hello darling," **[/]** ". . . I really kept o the go.—I got out a report, three letters, a couple of drawing releases, ha a couple of drawings changed and did some testing." **[5 PARAGRAPHS]** "All my love and kisses" **[/]** "Johnny"

  **** To Miss Katherine Glenn, Apt. No. 2, 1023 S.W. Yamhill, Portland, Oregon (10/20/42, 8:30 PM, Postmarked 10/21/42, 11:30 AM, "Via Air Mail" with two 3¢ stamps, Dayton, Ohio). Return Address: J. Sproule, 2000 North Main, Dayton, Ohio. "Hello darling," **[/]** "I just car from town a little while ago. I went down after I ate supper with Norm, a wanted to see if I could locate some shells for Gene [Sproule]. He wrote the other day and said it seems like shells are awful hard to get out there Most of the stores were closed by the time I got downtown, but I did not that there weren't many cartridge displays. I'll try some of those stores when they're open and see what I can do for him." **[/]**

". . . Sometimes it seems like it's hard to get anything done, but a lot of th things I work at take quite a bit of time like for example running cold test hot tests, vibrator tests etc. on some new item. So when I'm working on something like that, one day's work doesn't net a great deal of visible results." **[3 PARAGRAPHS]** "And kisses too" **[/]** "Johnny"

  **** To Miss Katherine Glenn, Apt. No. 2, 1023 S.W. Yamhill, Portland, Oregon (10/22/42, 10:10 PM, Postmarked 10/23/42, 2 PM, "Via Air Mail" with two 3¢ stamps, Dayton, Ohio). Return Address: J. Sproule, 2000 North Main, Dayton, Ohio. "Hello sweetheart," **[1 PARAGRAPH]** "Last night I didn't get to bed very early as I went to a party—a very informal sort of one cooked up to welcome home a friend of Marge's (Mack's girl). It was ok, but it did make me a bit short of sleep. . . ." **[1 PARAGRAPH]**

"And seeing about a ring sweetheart—it isn't too much trouble at all, it will just take a little bit more time. I've been wanting to get you one for a long long time honey, but not having such a great income while I was going to school was quite a hindrance." **[3 PARAGRAPHS]** "All my love and kisses" **[/]** "Johnny"

  **** To Miss Katherine Glenn, Apt. No. 2, 1023 S.W. Yamhill, Portland, Oregon (10/23/42, 9:40 PM, Postmarked 10/24/42, 1 PM, "Via Air Mail" with two 3¢ stamps, Dayton, Ohio). Return Address: J. Sproule, 2000 North Main, Dayton, Ohio. "Hi darling," **[/]** "The arrangement I have now is rather convenient for Norm and I eat breakfast together at a little place a couple blocks from here and then come back to Norm's car, pick up the other passengers and head out for the field." **[/]** ". . . Boy, when I was living over on North Ave. I was paying as much per week ($7.00) as I was paying in Laramie per month. Now that I'm paying $5.00 per week for room rent, it represents a saving and hence is more acceptable, though analyzing it is still quite a bit; but it's about as good as one can do here now conditions + stuff being as they are." **[/]**

"And along that line, I've been thinking lately that it would be a good idea for me to start looking for an apartment for us, rather than waiting till you get here and then hunting for one. Everyone I talk to mentions how scarce they are so it seems smart to get it, least have a place to live. Then honey, if, after you're here and get a little acquainted with the place, you find that our domicile could be improved by a move we'll hunt another. In the meantime darling, I wish you'd give me an idea as to what to look for. We'll want a furnished place, I know, but as to the detailed requirements you'd like I'm sort of hazy. My idea is a small place so our housekeeping will be kept to a minimum. What do you think of housekeeping or studio rooms (I think their called)? Anyhow darling, give me your ideas about this so I'll know what you think about it." **[/]**

". . . But this month has been going along fairly fast so maybe November + December will hurry by too. I'm hoping they pass quickly. 1943 is the first year I've ever looked forward to with such great anticipation. But that's because I've never had anything so swell to look forward to. Always before, January has meant that I'd be back in school and that we'd be apart. Now though it will mean we'll be together and that is really one swell thought." **[6 PARAGRAPHS]** "Always" **[/]** "Johnny"

**** To Miss Katherine Glenn, Apt. No. 2, 1023 S.W. Yamhill, Portland, Oregon (10/25/42, 11:00 PM, Postmarked 10/26/42, 10:30 AM, "Via Air Mail" with two 3¢ stamps, Dayton, Ohio). Return Address: J. Sproule, 2000 North Main, Dayton, Ohio. "Hello darling," **[2 PARAGRAPHS]** ". . . Norm and I had dinner with the Stouffers—the landlord + landlady—today. I thought it was nice of them to have us down and the home cooked meal tasted fine. After we ate Norm + I went out to the field and got in a few hours work. I finished up a report so I can give it to the stenographer in the morning and have it off my mind. . . ." **[4 PARAGRAPHS]** "'Night darling" **[/]** "All my love always" **[/]** "Johnny"

**** To Miss Katherine Glenn, Apt. No. 2, 1023 S.W. Yamhill, Portland, Oregon (10/26/42, 9:52 PM, Postmarked 10/27/42, 1 PM, "Via Air Mail" with two 3¢ stamps, Dayton, Ohio). Return Address: J. Sproule, 2000 North Main, Dayton, Ohio. "Hello darling," **[3 PARAGRAPHS]** "I haven't been home very long this evening. Right after supper I went downtown and hunted for some shells for Gene. I finally found a box and took them over to the express office only to discover that they had to be shipped in a wooden box." **[/]** "So I started home and thought I'd go by the Simpsons to see if I had had any mail come there today. While I was there I

mentioned having to have a wooden box for the shells and Mrs. Simpson said there were some boards in the basement + why didn't I go down + make one so I did that, nicely solving my problem. The Simpsons were quite nice and I liked living there—about the only reason I moved was because the rent was $7.00 and transportation to the field was a problem."
[2 PARAGRAPHS]

"NO darling I haven't yet seen about taking instructions—I mean seen a priest. I've been thinking the best way would be to get as much from the books you sent me as I can before I see the priest—. So I've been studying the prayers in the spare time I have. And as yet I haven't had any difficulty. But soon I'll see the priest + say 'this is what I know, what do I do next?'."
[/] "Here I am at the end of the page and I needs must write the folks before I go to bed so I'll close for now + write again tomorrow night darling. 'Night sweetheart. All my love and kisses Johnny"

**** To Miss Katherine Glenn, Apt. No. 2, 1023 S.W. Yamhill, Portland, Oregon (10/28/42, 10:48 PM, Postmarked 10/29/42, 10:30 AM, "Via Air Mail" with two 3¢ stamps, Dayton, Ohio). Return Address: J. Sproule, 2000 North Main, Dayton, Ohio. "Hello sweetheart," **[2 PARAGRAPHS]** "Honey, the package you sent arrived this evening and is now safely stored in my closet. That's an easy way to get your things out here so don't hesitate to send anything else you want out of the way." **[/]** ". . .This afternoon as I came from work it was a swell fall day and it just seemed made to order for a football game—a real calm, neither cold nor hot afternoon. That's one thing I like about this place—the wind doesn't blow very much." **[/]**

"Well today was a sort of screwy day and I didn't get much done. We put on a demonstration of some of our stuff this afternoon for about 30 members of the National Inventor's Council, or some such, and some other higher ups (army + navy) including an Admiral, a Major General, some assorted colonels, lieutenant colonels etc. Remind me sometime to tell you what I think of that sort of thing." **[2 PARAGRAPHS]** "Always" **[/]** "Johnny"

**** To Miss Katherine Glenn, Apt. No. 2, 1023 S.W. Yamhill, Portland, Oregon (10/29/42, 7:30 PM, Postmarked 10/30/42, 11 PM, "Via Air Mail" with three 2¢ stamps, Dayton, Ohio). Return Address: J. Sproule, 2000 North Main, Dayton, Ohio. "Kay darling," **[1 PARAGRAPH]** "Somehow or other I've caught a cold and I'm not feeling the best I ever have. . . . But don't worry honey, I'll be feeling tiptop by the time you get this." **[3 PARAGRAPHS]** "All my love and kisses" **[/]** "Johnny"

**** To Miss Katherine Glenn, Apt. No. 2, 1023 S.W. Yamhill, Portland, Oregon (10/30/42, 11:30 PM, Postmarked 10/31/42, 1 PM, "Via Air Mail" with three 2¢ stamps, Dayton, Ohio). Return Address: J. Sproule, 2000 North Main, Dayton, Ohio. "Hello darling," **[/]** "I'm feeling considerably improved tonight— . . . ." **[/]** "This rationing is quite a business, but it will help win the war, I'm all for it. And I guess that's the idea behind the freezing of workers to their jobs. Hey, you won't be frozen to your job and prohibited from coming out here will you?" **[1 PARAGRAPH]** "Dayton isn't bad to live in, it's sort of like a little country town grown up. When we are together darling any place seems swell to me. . . ." **[2 PARAGRAPHS]** "All my love + kisses" **[/]** "Johnny"

**** To Miss Katherine Glenn, Apt. No. 2, 1023 S.W. Yamhill, Portland, Oregon (10/30/42, 11:30 PM, Postmarked 11/2/42, 11:30 AM, with a 6¢ "U.S. Postage Via Air Mail" stamp printed on the envelope having borders strips of alternating red, white, and blue, Dayton, Ohio). Return Address: J. Sproule, 2000 North Main, Dayton, Ohio. "Hello darling," **[3 PARAGRAPHS]** "I went to a show last night, being as everyone else around here was gone and I didn't relish just sitting here—it was 'Icecapades' or some such—a skating picture with Sonia Henie. It wasn't bad at all—they (skating shows) used to be quite frequent, but I hadn't seen one for a long time." **[4 PARAGRAPHS]** "All my love + kisses" **[/]** "Johnny"

**** To Miss Katherine Glenn, Apt. No. 2, 1023 S.W. Yamhill, Portland, Oregon (11/2/42, 10:10 PM, Postmarked 11/3/42, 1:30 PM, "Via Air Mail" with a 6¢ Air Mail stamp, Dayton, Ohio). Return Address: J. Sproule, 2000 North Main, Dayton, Ohio. "Hello darling," **[/]** "I'm really feeling on top of the world and no fooling after such a grand long letter from you as was waiting for me tonight when I came home from work." **[/]** "... and the rest you have planned sounds like it will just match perfectly. I'll have to be getting a new suit to match your splendor darling—what color do you suggest honey, so it will go well with your new outfit? And you sure aren't boring me when you talk about your clothes darling—everything about you is of interest to me." **[1 PARAGRAPH]**

"Yes, the folks know we're going to get married, but they don't know exactly when. According to a letter you wrote about a month ago you thought you'd have this about Sunday the 3rd and get here about Monday the 11th and then that we could be married the coming Saturday which would be the 16th. Is that still your plan darling?...." **[/]** "I wish you were here darling, not to help me—though it would help a lot, but I can get all this studying done—...." **[/]**

"I'm terribly sorry to hear that Helen + Ken didn't get along—I sort of thought that when they got married they had everything fixed up, but I guess not. They used to get along sort of funny at times, but I thought that was just their way." **[/]**

"Anyhow darling, that doesn't have anything to do with the way we love each other, ... but anyhow we've always been able to work things out and being married it will be ever so much easier if anything comes up, for us to talk it over and work it out. Like you said darling, we may get irked once in a while, but that's just human nature and doesn't mean at all that we don't get along together—'cause we do get along well and we both know it. It would be even easier when are married 'cause we'd be together where in the past we've had to separate every once in a while. And having endured all these long long separations and still love each other like we do, shows pretty well I think darling, how permanent our love for each other is." **[4 PARAGRAPHS]** "All yours always" **[/]** "Johnny"

**** To Miss Katherine Glenn, Apt. No. 2, 1023 S.W. Yamhill, Portland, Oregon (11/4/42, 9:30 PM, Postmarked 11/5/42, 11 AM, "Via Air Mail" with a 6¢ Air Mail stamp, Dayton, Ohio). Return Address: J. Sproule, 2000 North Main, Dayton, Ohio. "Hello darling," **[1 PARAGRAPH]** "Today was rather a busy day for me. I worked a couple hours overtime and still didn't get thru. I had some hoisting to do in a couple bombers—test installations of a couple of aircraft mines to determine suitability, clearances etc. There was a Navy man and a fellow from Washington in to witness these tests and as the Navy man had to go back tonight we worked overtime to finish up. When we got thru we just quit so tomorrow I'll have the straightening up and paper work to do." **[/]**

"I've been trying to get a haircut for days now and don't seem to get to it for one reason or another. . . ." **[2 PARAGRAPHS]** "Sure doesn't seem like I get much done sometimes except work + sleep. . . ." **[1 PARAGRAPH]** "All my love + kisses" **[/]** "Johnny"

**** To Miss Katherine Glenn, Apt. No. 2, 1023 S.W. Yamhill, Portland, Oregon (11/5/42, 9:30 PM, Postmarked 11/6/42, 12 M, "Via Air Mail" with a 6¢ Air Mail stamp, Dayton, Ohio). Return Address: J. Sproule 2000 North Main, Dayton, Ohio. "Hello darling," **[1 PARAGRAPH]** "Norm I drove uptown and ate after we came in from work—usually we walk but the rain wasn't conducive to walking. I finally made it to the barber shop this evening and obtained a haircut. . . ." **[5 PARAGRAPHS]** "And all my kisses too" **[/]** "Always" **[/]** "Johnny"

**** To Miss Katherine Glenn, Apt. No. 2, 1023 S.W. Yamhill, Portland, Oregon (11/7/42, 8:30 PM, Postmarked 11/9/42, 3:30 PM, "Via Mail" with a 6¢ Air Mail stamp, Dayton, Ohio). Return Address: J. Sproule 2000 North Main, Dayton, Ohio. "Hello darling," **[2 PARAGRAPHS]** "It's peculiar how people travel so much by train in this region. It's always be unusual for me to go anywhere by train—but here it seems to be the accepted mode of travel. I guess it will become even more the common way to travel once the rationing of gasoline begins." **[/]**

"The headlines tonight are proclaiming a British victory in Egypt which is encouraging. Though last year when the English were claiming an overwhelming defeat of Rommel's Africa Korps, the Germans turned and drove to within 80 or 90 miles of Alexandria. If the English can wipe out the Germans in Egypt it might be possible that they would open a second front along the Mediterranean somewhere. At any rate it's encouraging to hear of Allied victories." **[/]**

"Yes and like you said the Republicans are increasing their membership in Congress too. But I'm not caring so much who's in Congress as how they prosecute the war. For victory over the Japs and Germans is the most important thing." **[/]** "That doesn't sound like a bad idea wearing slacks to work. In a time like this the question of what one wears to work is not so important as how much work gets done. Like you say though, some of the gals haven't a figure suited to the wearing of slacks." **[3 PARAGRAPHS]**

". . . I don't have as much time as I'd like so I haven't seen many opportunities to look for an apartment. But things are getting more so that I have my free time better organized—I mean that I know better now how much time I have off and can plan accordingly and then use the time I have off more efficiently. By the way honey, what is a flat? I've heard the term but as to knowing just what a flat consists of I'm stumped. I guess my experience in hunting a place to live has been rather limited." **[/]** ". . . Norm + I went to the show Friday night and I didn't get to bed as early as I usually do. The show wasn't bad though—it was Here We Go Again with Edgar Bergen, Charlie McCarthy, Fibber McGee + Molly Ginny Sims etc—just a comedy, so all it required was watching." **[2 PARAGRAPHS]** "All my love and kisses" **[/]** "Johnny"

**** To Miss Katherine Glenn, Apt. No. 2, 1023 S.W. Yamhill, Portland, Oregon (11/9/42, 9:30 PM, Postmarked 11/10/42, 1:30 PM, "Via Air Mail" with a 6¢ Air Mail stamp, Dayton, Ohio). Return Address: J. Sproule, 2000 North Main, Dayton, Ohio. "Hello darling," **[/]** "Today was the weekly meeting of the 'ok, hell its Monday' club. I didn't get much done today judging from output. I spent the whole day getting some blueprints + studying them in preparation for some work I'll have to do later on." **[/]** "This evening I helped Norm fix the fog lights on his car and take the numbers off his tires in preparation (the last mentioned) for his registration for gasoline rationing." **[/]** "After eating supper I took my laundry + cleaning out. Gad I had a bunch. I hadn't taken any out for 3 weeks so I'll bet it costs 6 or 7 bucks this time." **[1 PARAGRAPH]**

"I got a letter from my draft board in Laramie saying they were giving me another 90 days deferment to get the official papers sent in—'in order that your employers may submit the regular forms for your deferment.' It said to quote them. So I'm now deferred till near the last of January." **[/]** "And speaking of deferments reminds me that the war news sounds as though the Allies were beginning to get in the saddle. For which I'm glad—it's good to hear of some retaliation against our foes as they been handing it out for so long." **[1 PARAGRAPH]**

"It was a swell evening out tonight and the crowds on the streets really bore out that fact. And the trolleys too—they were really jammed—at least the one I came home on was. I stood all the way. The seats were all filled and all the standing room was taken too." **[1 PARAGRAPH]** ". . . He [Ray Berryman] talked like maybe he was going into the army in a few weeks. He thought he would get a deferment (one would have been plenty) but I'd guess he was getting tired of the suspense." **[3 PARAGRAPHS]** "All my love + kisses" **[/]** "Johnny"

**** To Miss Katherine Glenn, Apt. No. 2, 1023 S.W. Yamhill, Portland, Oregon (11/12/42, 1:35 AM, Postmarked 11/12/42, 1 PM, "Via Air Mail" with a 6¢ Air Mail stamp, Dayton, Ohio). Return Address: J. Sproule, 2000 North Main, Dayton, Ohio. "Hello darling," **[3 PARAGRAPHS]** "I'll bet you are glad to get a Saturday off after so long a time. I've been working every Saturday + will continue to do so for quite some time—indefinitely as a matter of fact as far as I know. Sunday is always our day off. Ordinarily working for the gov't. one gets all holidays off, but not so now. I doubt if we even get Xmas off." **[3 PARAGRAPHS]** "All my love + kisses always" **[/]** "Johnny"

**** To Miss Katherine Glenn, Apt. No. 2, 1023 S.W. Yamhill, Portland, Oregon (11/12/42, 10:05 PM, Postmarked 11/13/42, 12 M, "Via Air Mail" with a 6¢ Air Mail stamp, Dayton, Ohio). Return Address: J. Sproule, 2000 North Main, Dayton, Ohio. "Hello darling," **[2 PARAGRAPHS]** "One thing though the war news has been on the brighter side lately and I'm hoping it stays that way. It's good to realize that the U. is able to get in the saddle and get some action and results." **[/]**

"Hey tomorrow's Friday the 13th! But then I never was a superstitious sort and it will just be another day as far as I'm concerned. As a matter of fact I'll consider it a fine day 'cause it's payday—and that $79.16 will look good in my pocket—if it could be seen when it's in there." **[/]** "Darling I've got to scribble the folks a few lines and get to bed so I'll say goodnight kiss now." **[/]** "All my love and kisses" **[/]** "Johnny"

**** To Miss Katherine Glenn, Apt. No. 2, 1023 S.W. Yamhill, Portland, Oregon (11/13/42, 11:07 PM, Postmarked 11/14/42, 1 PM, "Via Air Mail" with a 6¢ Air Mail stamp, Dayton, Ohio). Return Address: J. Sproule, 2000 North Main, Dayton, Ohio. "Hello darling," **[/]** "Well this Friday the 13th didn't bring much in the way of excitement etc. About the only thing worthy of note was the announcement of a meeting to be held in connection with classifying our status and the likelihood of our future contacts etc. with selective service. Since it will undoubtedly be discussed on the morrow I'll be in a much better position to tell you what it's all about then so I won't say anything more about it tonight." **[/]**

"And ok yes being Friday it reminds me that I've been practicing (successfully too) abstaining from eating meat on Friday. It's not at all difficult as the only problem lays in remembering that it is Friday which isn't hard at all to do." **[/]** "I haven't done much this evening. Norm and I ate early—soon after we got home from work—and then I went and picked up my laundry + cleaning. Norm + I sat + listened to a bunch of records he has. . . ." **[1 PARAGRAPH]**

". . . the means which are being recommended to ensure that the personnel of Experimental Engineering Section, of which I am a member are kept at Wright Field. Anyhow it looks like the head men—the higher ups are beginning to do something for us." **[1 PARAGRAPH]** "All my love + kisses"   **[/]** "Johnny"

**** To Miss Katherine Glenn, Apt. No. 2, 1023 S.W. Yamhill, Portland, Oregon ("Sunday night," Postmarked 11/16/42, 12:30 PM, "Via Air Mail" with a 6¢ Air Mail stamp, Dayton, Ohio). Return Address: J. Sproule, 2000 North Main, Dayton, Ohio. "Hello Kay darling," **[2**

PARAGRAPHS] "Today the landlady had Norm + I down for Sunday dinner—a very welcome + pleasant change from restaurant cooking. Norm went away on a business trip for a few days—he left this evening early—so I'll have to catch a bus in the morning. That will mean getting up a bit earlier etc. Another disadvantage of the ride sharing business. . . ." **[/]**

"It appears that deferments are becoming very scarce or 'a thing of the past' as one might say. So the higher ups have been arranging thru Washington to get appointments for commissions (none above the grade of 1st Lieut. + mostly 2nd Lieut.) for the civilian engineers." **[/]** "In this there will be 2 groups, those above 30 + those under 30. Apparently those above 30 (not many of them) won't have too much trouble in getting appointments to attend officers training school at Miami for 6 weeks after which they will be sent back to the Field to work at their present job." **[/]** "For the under 30 group (there are quite a bunch in this group) the chances of getting an appointment are a bit smaller (there being so many in this group, I guess) but each application will be decided upon on its own merits. Those successful in getting an appointment will do as above." **[/]**

"Now for those getting the go by on their application there are a couple of other things that can be done. One is to apply for technical training and if accepted be placed on the enlisted reserve list. One would then continue working as at present until called to take the training which would be at Chanute or Lowery Fields and last about 12 weeks I understand. This would result in a commission and the higher ups would request that you be sent back to Wright Field to continue on your old job only in uniform. One engineer out there in our office just left on the above basis. His draft board had been after him and he had applied for this technical training. I guess he had been on the enlisted reserve for 6 or 7 months before he was called. It apparently takes several months before one is called to take this training as the schools are pretty crowded." **[/]**

"Another method of induction is imminent or close at hand is to enlist in the Wright Field Detachment and then either request officers training as a private + get through the officers school + come back to your old job. Or I'd guess one could take up the old job with out the additional officers training. I don't know but seems like all the things have additional ramifications and possibilities like—what will your civil service status be etc." **[/]** "And then finally of course if you are drafted the higher ups can request that you be sent to Wright Field so you can work at the job you've been doing." **[/]** "Well darling it would appear that I've gone on about this at some length but I wanted to explain what I know about what's happening. I'm applying for one of the commissions as the logical first thing to do. I expect it will take some time to find out about this as the applications have to go through Washington and I can imagine how everything is knee deep in the proverbial red tape there." **[/]**

"Dearest darling I still feel the same—that I love you with all my heart just as I always have and that I want to marry you. I feel the same too about becoming a Catholic too. I think it's the thing to do and I like it fine. The only thing, I get a little discouraged as I study when I see that I'm trying to learn by the next month and a half or so, all that you have learned and been associated with since you were a child." **[6 PARAGRAPHS]** "All my love and kisses" **[/]** "Johnny"

    **** To Miss Katherine Glenn, Apt. No. 2, 1023 S.W. Yamhill, Portland, Oregon (11/17/42, 11:30 PM, Postmarked 11/18/42, 4:30 PM, "Via Air Mail" with a 6¢ Air Mail stamp, Dayton, Ohio). Return Address: J. Sproule, 2000 North Main, Dayton, Ohio. "Hello darling," **[/]** "I had some outside work to do on an airplane—sketch up some brackets + take some measurements for an installation—but I put it off till tomorrow and worked on some other stuff that was needing attention. One beauty of this job is that I'm not doing exactly the same thing every day—the work is varied so that I can move around a bit. When working at the desk becomes tiring I have other things I can see about that take some moving around. Or vice versa—when the weather is bad I can stay in and do some desk work—correspondence, reports etc." **[/]**

"I've been having to get up about half or ¾ of an hour earlier so far this week since Norm is away on a trip. Consequently I have to catch a trolley and ride down town—walk 3 blocks to the bus depot and catch a bus out to the field. When I do this I usually eat at the field cafeteria instead of breakfasting before leaving town as I do when I ride with Norm. It doesn save any time, but it gives me a little more leeway if the bus should be a little late." **[2 PARAGRAPHS]** "All my love + kisses" **[/]** "Johnny"

**** To Miss Katherine Glenn, Apt. No. 2, 1023 S.W. Yamhill, Portland, Oregon (11/18/42, 7:11 PM, Postmarked 11/19/42, 11:30 PM, "Via Air Mail" with a 6¢ Air Mail stamp, Dayton, Ohio). Return Address: J Sproule, 2000 North Main, Dayton, Ohio. "Hello darling," **[/]** "Your sleeping in the other day reminds me that I did too this morning. It was broad daylight when I woke up and my clock said 9:30. I could hardly believe it. The alarm had run down and I'd slept right through. And I got bed by midnight too—that's what puzzles me. Well anyhow I got up and went to work even though it was 10:15 when I clocked in." **[/]** "That wi be deducted from my annual leave I guess—. . . ." **[3 PARAGRAPHS]**

"Like I said I was given 90 days more to get the official request for deferment sent in and would be the last of Jan. However with the President's little message which I saw in the paper this morning, things aren't any too settled I'd say. I have an idea that I will eventually be in a uniform, but still work at the same job. With this commission deal comin up I don't see why I can't get some more time to see about that even if th draft board should get anxious. So I really don't think I'll be in the army t after January darling. Now if this setup appears confusing honey just ask and I'll try to explain it better or more fully or something. Anyhow I wan you to know what's happening. The main thing I think is that the higher ups seem to want us to keep on working at our present jobs whether we civilians or in the army—and that looks pretty good." **[3 PARAGRAPHS]** "All my love and kisses always darling" **[/]** "Johnny"

**** To Miss Katherine Glenn, Apt. No. 2, 1023 S.W. Yamhill, Portland, Oregon (11/19/42, 9:10 PM, Postmarked 11/20/42, 9:30 AM, " Air Mail" with a 6¢ Air Mail stamp, Dayton, Ohio). Return Address: J. Sproule, 2000 North Main, Dayton, Ohio. "Hi sweetheart," **[2 PARAGRAPHS]** "Today was rather an uneventful day it seemed like. Anyhow I didn't seem to accomplish much. I sat in on some movies—training films—this morning along with some of the other fellows in the unit. It was our purpose to view the films with an idea as to making suggestions for any additional films needed to illustrate new equipment developed and supplement the films on hand—noting omissions of things of importance in the present ones etc." **[2 PARAGRAPHS]**

"I owe a half dozen letters or more that I should answer—I won't get them all this evening but maybe I can write a couple before I get sleepy." **[1 PARAGRAPH]** "All my love and kisses" **[/]** "Johnny"

 **** To Miss Katherine Glenn, Apt. No. 2, 1023 S.W. Yamhill, Portland, Oregon (11/20/42, 11:15 PM, Postmarked 11/21/42, 9 PM, "Via Air Mail" with a 6¢ Air Mail stamp, Dayton, Ohio). Return Address: J. Sproule, 2000 North Main, Dayton, Ohio. "Kay darling," **[2 PARAGRAPHS]** "I thought I'd go down town and see a show this evening, but I didn't get around to it. I read the Colliers for a while and then it was a little late so I just took a nap. . . ." **[/]** ". . . I don't mind working Saturdays but it's been hard to get used to not having as much free time since I've started working here. Always before I could arrange things somewhat but the hours are rigidly fixed now and that's all there is to it. . . ." **[4 PARAGRAPHS]** "All my love and kisses" **[/]** "Johnny"

 **** To Miss Katherine Glenn, Apt. No. 2, 1023 S.W. Yamhill, Portland, Oregon (11/22/42, 11:10 PM, Postmarked 11/23/42, 3 PM, "Via Air Mail" with a 6¢ Air Mail stamp, Dayton, Ohio). Return Address: J. Sproule, 2000 North Main, Dayton, Ohio. "Hello sweetheart," **[1 PARAGRAPH]** "I went to the show last night. It was 'The Major and Minor' with Ginger Rogers and Ray Milland. Not a bad show—interesting and sort of funny though it was a little far fetched." **[1 PARAGRAPH]** "Bob Rhodes, the other fellow who lives here, stopped in and we shot the breeze for a while. He works nights and Norm + I don't see him only on weekends. He gets to bed before we get up in the morning and leaves for work before we get home from work in the evenings." **[1 PARAGRAPH]**

"There was a news broadcast on the radio earlier this evening describing Italy's losses and from that it would sound as though the Italians were rather hard pressed. Which sounds good for any weakening of the Axis helps the Allies. And it will sure be a happy day when this war is over." **[3 PARAGRAPHS]** "All my love and kisses" **[/]** "Johnny"

**** To Miss Katherine Glenn, Apt. No. 2, 1023 S.W. Yamhill, Portland, Oregon (11/23/42, 11:45 PM, Postmarked 11/24/42, 6:30 PM, "Via Air Mail" with a 6¢ Air Mail stamp, Dayton, Ohio). Return Address: J. Sproule, 2000 North Main, Dayton, Ohio. "Hello darling," **[1 PARAGRAPH]** "Tonight was shopping night so I went down and picked up a few odds and ends—stationary, stamps, shoestrings a comb—just stuff. It rained a bit this evening, but not hard so the shopping crowd was as thick as ever." **[1 PARAGRAPH]**

"Dearest this draft situation is just something that's hard to figure out. We get a lot of rumors, sort of, around the office, but nothing definite. There was talk that this officers training business had fallen thru and then some one said it hadn't so one just can't tell I guess—until we're told definitely one way or the other. The officers training wouldn't be bad I'm sure—one would undoubtedly be damned busy as they no doubt have a lot of stuff in the course but I wouldn't mind. As a matter of fact, I don't know just how to say it—anyhow I won't care what happens as long as we can be together. From what I can discover, my bum eye will disqualify me for what could be called active service so the thing I've been figuring on is to keep on at the job in a military or civilian capacity and do what I can to further the war effort, AND we can be with each other too then darling which will be heavenly, swell, grand—all the nicest words there are." **[/]**

[And in fact, JHS's final Army physical reconfirmed the results from his previous medical examinations, namely that, in addition to generally poor eyesight, he was blind in one eye—this a consequence of a detached retina which came about from a gymnastics accident sometime around 1940.]

"Honey, find out about the Connors moving [in Riverton]—I mean when and stuff. If they'll be moving before we have a place out here I can write Gene [Sproule] and he can get them and take them down to the place and keep them there till we'd send for them. . . ." **[3 PARAGRAPHS]** "I'll be working Thanksgiving but it won't matter because I wouldn't be doing anything any way. It's not so much a holiday as some of the other days as you mentioned." **[2 PARAGRAPHS]** "All my love and kisses" **[/]** "Johnny"

**** To Miss Katherine Glenn, Apt. No. 2, 1023 S.W. Yamhill, Portland, Oregon (11/24/42, 10:35 PM, Postmarked 11/25/42, 12:30 PM, "Via Air Mail" with a 6¢ Air Mail stamp, Dayton, Ohio). Return Address: J. Sproule, 2000 North Main, Dayton, Ohio. "Hello darling," **[1 PARAGRAPH]** "I've just been listening to the radio. Bob Hope put on his program from Patterson Field tonight—that's just a little ways from Wright Field where I work. It was just for the soldiers or I would have liked to go—not much use in going out if you couldn't attend." **[/]** "There was also a dance at Wright Field this evening. Tony Pastor played + I think the program was broadcast over some programs. This too was for the military." **[/]**

"I'm going out to the Edgewood Arsenal tomorrow afternoon (that's a ways out of Baltimore Maryland) for a few days—I'll be back about Friday I think. I'm going out to witness some tests being made out there that require the approval of our office." **[3 PARAGRAPHS]** "All my love and kisses sweetheart" **[/]** "Johnny"

**** To Miss Katherine Glenn, Apt. No. 2, 1023 S.W. Yamhill, Portland, Oregon (11/25/42, 11:25 PM, "Approaching Pennsylvania," Postmarked 11/26/42, 4 PM, "Via Air Mail" with a 6¢ Air Mail stamp, Baltimore, MD). Return Address: J. Sproule, 2000 North Main, Dayton, Ohio. "Kay darling," **[/]** "As if you wouldn't be able to tell by just looking at this page, I'm riding along now in my berth while I'm writing this. . . ." **[2 PARAGRAPHS]** "Well the first thing to come up—along about 5 minutes before time for the train to pull out—was the news that the train was an hour late. So then I ate a bit of supper and read the evening paper—well the whole upshot of the deal was that I finally left Dayton at 7:35—2½ hours late." **[/]** "That will no doubt play hell with my connections in Baltimore to proceed on to Edgewood. . . ." **[2 PARAGRAPHS]**

"And that reminds me—we had a meeting this afternoon (as a matter of fact I just rushed away from the meeting when it concluded to come into town) on the same old business of Selective Service inroads on the engineering and other key personnel." **[/]** "These points were brought out: (I'll try to make this just a summarization as the actual information given was somewhat brief.) a—it is still possible to get deferments on the basis of being a key man—if your draft board is agreeable." **[/]** "b—the commission deal is not operative, but attempts are being made in Washington by the higher ups to change this." **[/]** "C—it is still possible to enlist in the Wright Field Headquarters Squadron as a private and either stay on doing the same work or as a non-com or private or apply for officers training as an enlisted man and return after the completion of your training, if your application is successful, to your same job as a 2nd Lieut. . . ." **[3 PARAGRAPHS]** "All my love and kisses" **[/]** "Johnny"

**** To Miss Katherine Glenn, Apt. No. 2, 1023 S.W. Yamhill, Portland, Oregon (11/26/42, 11:50 EWT, "On the train again somewhere in Pennsylvania," Postmarked 11/27/42, 3 PM, "Via Air Mail" with a 6¢ Air Mail stamp, Dayton, Ohio). Return Address: J. Sproule, 2000 North Main, Dayton, Ohio. "Hello sweetheart," **[1 PARAGRAPH]** "It was the screwiest thanksgiving for me though. When I finally got to Baltimore this morning I was (the train was I mean) 3 hours late. It was 10:00 am and I should have been out to the Arsenal at 8 or so. Well I inquired about connections to Edgewood and the first train on out there was at 3:45 pm. So I called up the Colonel so he'd at least know I was in the country and proceeded to try to catch a bus on out. When it was 10 and I thought I could catch an 11 o'clock bus, but it left at 10:30 instead so I missed it and had to wait till 12 (noon) and I finally got out to Edgewood at 1:30." **[1 PARAGRAPH]** "I say 'at least sleep' for with all the rushing around today I only managed to get one meal. But I'll make up for that tomorrow so that doesn't worry me." **[3 PARAGRAPHS]** "All my love and kisses" **[/]** "Johnny" **[/]** "P.S. (or PC re card)" [Here JHS draws a postcard complete with his return address, a stamp, KVS's address, and a message sending love.]

**** To Miss Katherine Glenn, Apt. No. 2, 1023 S.W. Yamhill, Portland, Oregon (11/29/42, 11:30 PM, Postmarked 11/30/42, 10 AM, "Via Air Mail" with a 6¢ Air Mail stamp, Dayton, Ohio). Return Address: J. Sproule, 2000 North Main, Dayton, Ohio. "Hello darling," **[/]** "The trip wasn't bad, but I was so busy I was really tired when I got back Friday night. . . ." **[/]** ". . . I celebrated the day by putting out a good bit of work. I didn't even have time for a Thanksgiving dinner. I got a bit of breakfast when I got into Baltimore and then got on out to Edgewood Arsenal as fast as I could. I had to take the bus out as the next train didn't go till 3 something that afternoon (I'd missed my connection due to the train arriving late into Baltimore). As I was late getting out to Edgewood I went without lunch and was busy until it was time to leave so I could get back to town and pick up my reservation for the trip back. I had time to eat supper before leaving Baltimore though so I concentrated on that." **[/]** "Saturday was a busy day too as I had a couple jobs which came up while I was away to line up plus getting out a report on the trip and then the usual stuff too. So I worked today and endeavored to get caught up a bit." **[/]** "That, then, messed up my plan to talk to the priest about taking instruction. So I'll do it after work instead—. . . ." **[3 PARAGRAPHS]**

"As yet I haven't located an apartment—I'm discovering that, just like I've heard, they are sort of scarce. I'm hoping to have one when you get here though darling." **[3 PARAGRAPHS]** "Honey you didn't say any more about the Connors' leaving Riverton—do you want me to write + have Gene take your things from there + move them down to the farm?" **[2 PARAGRAPHS]** "All my love and kisses darling" **[/]** "Johnny"

**** To Miss Katherine Glenn, Apt. No. 2, 1023 S.W. Yamhill, Portland, Oregon (12/1/42, 11:18 PM, Postmarked 12/2/42, 12 M, "Via Air Mail" with a 6¢ Air Mail stamp, Dayton, Ohio). Return Address: J. Sproule, 2000 North Main, Dayton, Ohio. "Hello sweetheart," **[1 PARAGRAPH]** "When I wrote that I just stopped and remembered how long it's been since we saw each other darling—gee it's been the longest time on record. . . ." **[2 PARAGRAPHS]** "This evening I managed to get my laundry + cleaning down to the cleaners and to get a haircut ({note}—though no doubt I'll have had a couple more by the time you get here—anyhow I won't be too shaggy I'm sure}}. . . ." **[2 PARAGRAPHS]** "All my love and kisses" **[/]** "Johnny"

**** To Miss Katherine Glenn, Apt. No. 2, 1023 S.W. Yamhill, Portland, Oregon (12/2/42, 11:24 PM, Postmarked 12/3/42, 9 AM, "Via A Mail" with a 6¢ Air Mail stamp, Dayton, Ohio). Return Address: J. Sproule 2000 North Main, Dayton, Ohio. "Hello darling," **[4 PARAGRAPHS]** "Nor took a short vacation (the last of last week + first part of this one) and jus arrived here about the same time I was getting home... We sat + listene to a bunch of his records and shot the breeze for the duration of the evening. We just braved the storm and went out + got a sandwich + a cu of coffee a little bit ago." **[3 PARAGRAPHS]** "All my love and kisses" **[/]** "Johnny"

**** To Miss Katherine Glenn, Apt. No. 2, 1023 S.W. Yamhill, Portland, Oregon (12/4/42, 11:50 PM, Postmarked 12/5/42, 3 PM, "Via A Mail" with a 6¢ Air Mail stamp, Dayton, Ohio). Return Address: J. Sproule 2000 North Main, Dayton, Ohio. "Hello darling," **[/]** "I haven't done much this evening seems like, but here it is time for bed already. I read a while and shot the breeze with Norm a while." **[4 PARAGRAPHS]** "All my love + kisses" **[/]** "Johnny"

**** To Miss Katherine Glenn, Apt. No. 2, 1023 S.W. Yamhill, Portland, Oregon ("Sunday night," Postmarked 12/7/42, 12 M, "Via Air Mail" with a 6¢ Air Mail stamp, Dayton, Ohio). Return Address: J. Sproule 2000 North Main, Dayton, Ohio. "Hello sweetheart," **[/]** "I have to get earlier with Norm gone since I have to take a trolley down town and then catch a bus out to the Field." **[1 PARAGRAPH]**

"... I spent quite a bit of time looking for an apartment—but as yet have located one. And I've been endeavoring to contact a priest but as yet haven't succeeded. I thought I could see him after mass today but that didn't work—I went down this evening but no one was about. My main attentions are on this though sweetheart, and frustrations aren't discouraging me. It just seems like I don't have enough time to get things done as I'd like. ..." **[2 PARAGRAPHS]** "All my love + kisses" **[/]** "Johnny" **[/]** "P.S. Yes honey I have a sugar card. I got it when everyone registered—I haven't even had a coupon torn out yet so I'd guess it's as good as new."

**** To Miss Katherine Glenn, Apt. No. 2, 1023 S.W. Yamhill, Portland, Oregon (12/7/42, 11:15 PM, Postmarked 12/8/42, 11 AM, "Via Air Mail" with a 6¢ Air Mail stamp, Dayton, Ohio). Return Address: J. Sproule, 2000 North Main, Dayton, Ohio. "Hello darling," [/] "Guess want I got done tonight—you know that item that's been heading my list of things to do—that's right, I saw the priest this evening. Of course I would arrive right at supper time, so I didn't talk to him—Father [William S.] Staudt, rather a young man very pleasant from my first impressions—very long, but here's what I know so far. [Staudt is assistant pastor of Corpus Christi Parish in Dayton.] He has an instruction class Tuesday and Thursday evenings which I will begin to attended tomorrow night. Apparently it's customary to take instructions for three months, 2 hrs a week (1 hr each night), totaling 24 hrs of instruction. BUT it's not impossible to get the 24 hrs of instruction in a shorter time by going oftener or staying longer—so that's what I'll be doing. . . ." **[9 PARAGRAPHS]** "All my love + kisses" [/] "Johnny"

**** To Miss Katherine Glenn, Apt. No. 2, 1023 S.W. Yamhill, Portland, Oregon (12/8/42, 10:45 PM, Postmarked 12/9/42, 11 AM, "Via Air Mail" with a 6¢ Air Mail stamp, Dayton, Ohio). Return Address: J. Sproule, 2000 North Main, Dayton, Ohio. "Hello darling," [/] "Today was just an average day distinguished only by my first formal attendance of the instruction class. It was really easy tonight—if tonight was typical I sure don't have any worries on that score. I'll have to miss the Thursday class since I'll be away. I mentioned that to the priest so he wouldn't think I was defaulting and he didn't mind any. He's quite ok I think and I'm sure everything will go along in good shape." [/]

"I had a letter from Vernon Kelly the other day. Had you heard that he'd picked up a spot of tuberculosis on a lung? He's getting along fine and is feeling perfect he says. He's in a sanitarium in Hot Springs South Dakota now. He was discharged from the army and when he leaves the sanitarium he'll go home with a $75/month pension he said. Boy the Kelly family has sure had some tough breaks." [/] "I'm hoping it will have warmed up a bit by the time I get back from Baltimore. It hasn't been very cold really but it has been quite comfortable to wear a coat." **[4 PARAGRAPHS]** "All my love + kisses" **[/]** "Johnny"

**** To Miss Katherine Glenn, Apt. No. 2, 1023 S.W. Yamhill, Portland, Oregon (12/9/42, "In Penn somewhere," Postmarked 12/10/42, 5:30 PM, "Via Air Mail" with a 6¢ Air Mail stamp, Baltimore, MD.) Return Address: J. Sproule, 2000 North Main, Dayton, Ohio. "Hello darling," **[/]** ". . . The reason for the scribble being the unevenness of the Penn. RR's roadbed combined with the fact that I have an upper this trip and it seems even harder to write up here than in a lower as I had last time." **[1 PARAGRAPH]** "Just arrived at Baltimore and have made my reservation for going back tonight and found that I will be able to catch a train on out to Edgewood in about 30 minutes. So things are working out ok so far." **[1 PARAGRAPH]** "I expect that by now you know that I've seen a priest and that anything on that line is going along in good shape so you can proceed with your arrangements." **[3 PARAGRAPHS]** "All my love + kisses" **[/]** "Johnny"

**** To Miss Katherine Glenn, Apt. No. 2, 1023 S.W. Yamhill, Portland, Oregon (Edgewood Arsenal Maryland, 12/10/42, 5:15 PM, Postmarked 12/12/42, 12 PM, "Via Air Mail" with a 6¢ Air Mail stamp, Baltimore, MD). Return Address: J. Sproule, 2000 North Main, Dayton, Ohio. "Hello darling," **[/]** "Here I am supposedly hard at work and can't get much done. The weather here today was so foggy it could have been cut with a knife. Consequently no aircraft went aloft here today and as a result I'm having to stay over since the job requires that an airplane participate." **[/]** "So tonight I'm staying at what is termed Gunpowder Mess. Where it got that title I can't imagine and yet that's its name. . . ." **[1 PARAGRAPH]**

"It is rather fun to go on trips like these though. There's new country + things to see (when the weather permits). And then I meet a lot of people too. Colonels, Lieut. Cols. and so on down—really a lot of the big shots." **PARAGRAPH]** "I've eaten now and am feeling fine. There were 8 of us at the table—no one (except myself) was of lower rank than a major. Everyone was quite cordial—it seemed no different than eating with any other group of men." **[/]** "I was finally able to get a call through to Baltimore canceling my reservation on tonight's train. The weather looked alright when I was in Baltimore this morning so I had gone ahead and made my reservations + had my Pullman ticket for the trip back tonight. Then when this weather situation was so adverse I had to get my ticket canceled so I could exchange it for another tomorrow night. At least I'm hoping I will be able to leave here tomorrow night." **[1 PARAGRAPH]**

". . . I suppose that by today you have received my letter saying I'd seen a priest and that everything looked ok." **[/]** "So that should consist now of attending the instruction class and arranging the extra instruction period. Tuesday night after the class was over Father Staudt asked me if I would be there again tonight. When I said I'd have to be out of town on business he [said] that was ok and that we'd arrange the extra instruction after the next class." **[2 PARAGRAPHS]** "All my love and kisses always"   **[/]** "Johnny"

**** To Miss Katherine Glenn, Apt. No. 2, 1023 S.W. Yamhill, Portland, Oregon (12/13/42, 11:25 PM, Postmarked 12/14/42, 2:30 PM, "Via Air Mail" with a 6¢ Air Mail stamp, Dayton, Ohio.) Return Address: J. Sproule, 2000 North Main, Dayton, Ohio. "Hello darling," **[5 PARAGRAPHS]** "Boy this sure is a small world—as I got on the train in Baltimore, who should I meet but George Baxter, a fellow I went to school with a couple years ago. Were we ever surprised! We had a lot of things to talk about and it sure made the trip pass quickly." **[3 PARAGRAPHS]** "All my love + kisses" **[/]** "Johnny"

**** To Miss Katherine Glenn, Apt. No. 2, 1023 S.W. Yamhill, Portland, Oregon (12/14/42, 11:03 PM, Postmarked 12/15/42, 12 M, "Via Air Mail" with a 6¢ Air Mail stamp, Dayton, Ohio). Return Address: J. Sproule, 2000 North Main, Dayton, Ohio. "Hello darling," **[1 PARAGRAPH]** "Tonight was shopping night so I went back downtown after I got home from work. The crowds were really filling the streets and stores—everywhere. I met one of the fellows from the office and we shopped around together and then had supper." **[3 PARAGRAPHS]** ". . . I get a happy glow every time I think that in less than a month you'll be here." **[1 PARAGRAPH]** "All my love and kisses always" **[/]** "Johnny"

**** To Miss Katherine Glenn, Apt. No. 2, 1023 S.W. Yamhill, Portland, Oregon (12/15/42, 9:25 PM, Postmarked 12/16/42, 2:30 PM, "Via Air Mail" with a 6¢ Air Mail stamp, Dayton, Ohio). Return Address: J. Sproule, 2000 North Main, Dayton, Ohio. "Hello sweetheart," **[1 PARAGRAPH]** "Tonight I shopped downtown and got some stamps so I could send some Xmas cards. . . . I attended the instruction class again tonight. . . ." **[6 PARAGRAPHS]** "All my love + kisses" **[/]** "Johnny"

**** To Miss Katherine Glenn, Apt. No. 2, 1023 S.W. Yamhill, Portland, Oregon (12/17/42, 10:30 PM, Postmarked 12/18/42, 10 AM, "Via Air Mail" with a 6¢ Air Mail stamp, Dayton, Ohio). Return Address: J. Sproule, 2000 North Main, Dayton, Ohio. "Hello darling," **[2 PARAGRAPHS]** "We had a bit of good news at the office today—saying that we wouldn't have to work Christmas day, which doesn't make me a bit mad as I'm always glad to get a day off. I hope you don't have to work either darling—. . ." [3 PARAGRAPHS] "All my love + kisses always" **[/]** "Johnny"

**** To Miss Katherine Glenn, Apt. No. 2, 1023 S.W. Yamhill, Portland, Oregon (12/16/42, 10:15 PM, Postmarked 12/17/42, 5 PM, "Via Air Mail" with a 6¢ Air Mail stamp, Dayton, Ohio). Return Address: J. Sproule, 2000 North Main, Dayton, Ohio. "Hello sweetheart," **[2 PARAGRAPHS]** ". . . Darling I'm really counting the days till I see you! When it's a long time till I'll see you, I can try to keep from thinking how long it will be till we'll see each other—but now that it won't be so long till you're here honey, that's all I'm thinking of." **[3 PARAGRAPHS]** "All my love and kisses" **[/]** "Johnny"

**** To Miss Katherine Glenn, Apt. No. 2, 1023 S.W. Yamhill, Portland, Oregon (12/20/42, 10:30 PM, Postmarked 12/21/42, 1:30 PM, "Via Air Mail" with a 6¢ Air Mail stamp, Dayton, Ohio). Return Address: J. Sproule, 2000 North Main, Dayton, Ohio. "Hello sweetheart," **[/]** "First let me thank you for the swell Christmas present darling! Being the curious type and not finding any 'Do not open till Christmas' seals on it I opened it when it came. It's a swell robe darling and I like it very much." **[/]** "Honey, I'm going to get your Christmas present when you get here. That

way darling you can pick out just what you like. Want to know what it will be? Ok—it's a comb, brush + mirror set made of that new Lucite plastic."
[/]

". . . Norm's folks were down over the weekend. I met them last night + they + the Stouffers + Norm + I sat + talked till midnight or so. They had Sunday dinner down at the Biltmore Hotel before they left today and invited me—which was very nice I thought. Then after they left this morning Norm + I sat around listening to the radio + shooting the breeze."
[/]

"Darling that's swell that you have your resignation put in so the Tel. Co. knows you are leaving. . . ."   **[/]** "Sweetheart it will be so wonderful to see you! I'm so happy that I'll be with you soon—that you'll be here, and we'll be together after this terribly long separation—Dearest I'm so happy that words alone cannot describe it!" **[1 PARAGRAPH]** "Sweetheart I'll write again tomorrow night. I've some Xmas cards to send yet and I should be sending them if they are to arrive anywhere near Christmas." **[/]** "All my love and kisses always" **[/]** "Johnny"

**** To Miss Katherine Glenn, Apt. No. 2, 1023 S.W. Yamhill, Portland, Oregon (12/22/42, 12:30 AM, Postmarked 12/22/42, 5 PM, "Via Air Mail" with a 6¢ Air Mail stamp, Dayton, Ohio). Return Address: J. Sproule, 2000 North Main, Dayton, Ohio. "Hello sweetheart," **[3 PARAGRAPHS]** "I've been trying to keep real busy cause it sure makes the time pass a lot faster. Today went by very quickly and I hope the rest of the intervening days pass as fast so it will soon be the day that you'll arrive." **[5 PARAGRAPHS]** "All my love and kisses" **[/]** "Johnny"

**** To Miss Katherine Glenn, Apt. No. 2, 1023 S.W. Yamhill, Portland, Oregon (12/23/42, Postmarked 12/24/42, 11 AM, "Via Air Mail" with a 6¢ Air Mail stamp, Dayton, Ohio). Return Address: J. Sproule, 2000 North Main, Dayton, Ohio. "Kay darling," **[/]** "I really am floating on air after talking to you. It was wonderful beyond words to hear your voice again and to hear you say you love me. It will be the grandest, swellest time ever when you get here darling and we are together again after this long time." **[3 PARAGRAPHS]**

"By getting the papers I told you about (the dispensation to permit the mixed marriage, based on a well founded hope of conversion and a letter of delegation permitting Father Ansburg to witness the ceremony) it's possible for us to be married having a mixed ceremony—Thus we can be married as we planned. Meanwhile I will keep right on with the instructions and when they are completed and I can be baptized a Catholic we can have a nuptial mass said—which as I understand is the expression of the Church's blessing on our marriage." **[1 PARAGRAPH]**

"Just think darling in about 450 hours I'll be seeing you! We'll be together darling and we can start making up for these long long months we've been apart." **[1 PARAGRAPH]** "Johnny" **[/]** "PS. I hope I was able to explain the situation sufficiently clear tonight so you know how it is. That will be perfectly ok for Father Spillane to send a letter to me and I'll take them down to Father Ansburg. And in the meantime I'll be seeing about our license and so on darling. Also making a hotel reservation for you for the 10th—and along with everything counting the hours till you arrive sweetheart. XXXXXXX J."

  **** To Miss Katherine Glenn, Apt. No. 2, 1023 S.W. Yamhill, Portland, Oregon (12/25/42, Postmarked 12/26/42, 7:30 PM, "Via Air Mail with a 6¢ Air Mail stamp, Dayton, Ohio). Return Address: J. Sproule, 2000 North Main, Dayton, Ohio. "Hello darling," **[/]** "Merry Christmas sweetheart! I hope that everything was swell for you today." **[/]** "I did have to work today so I slept rather late. Then this afternoon I had Christmas dinner over at a friend's house—one of the fellows from the office—Bernie Bayuk by name. This evening he and I went to the show. It was 'Seven Days Leave' with Victor Mature + Lucille Ball—a sort of comedy musical with a military keynote. Rather good I thought." **[4 PARAGRAPHS]** "All my love and kisses always" **[/]** "Johnny"

  **** To Miss Katherine Glenn, Apt. No. 2, 1023 S.W. Yamhill, Portland, Oregon (12/27/42, 11:55 PM, Postmarked 12/28/42, 10 AM, "V

Air Mail" with a 6¢ Air Mail stamp, Dayton, Ohio). Return Address: J. Sproule, 2000 North Main, Dayton, Ohio. "Hello sweetheart," **[2 PARAGRAPHS]** "A number of us fellows out at the office had to work today—not to make up for having Christmas day off, but to prepare a demonstration for some big shots who are coming in Monday sometime. So we went out today so we'd have it ready for tomorrow." **[/]**

"Mrs. Stouffer had Bob and I down for a fine steak & spaghetti supper tonight. I really appreciated not having to go out for supper tonight after putting in a somewhat strenuous day out at the Field." **[/]** "Norm went home for Christmas and is leaving from Cleveland on a short trip so I'll be taking the bus in the morning. . . ." **[3 PARAGRAPHS]** "All my love & kisses" **[/]** "Johnny"

  **** To Miss Katherine Glenn, Apt. No. 2, 1023 S.W. Yamhill, Portland, Oregon (12/28/42, 8:25 PM, Postmarked 12/29/42, 11:30 AM, "Via Air Mail" with a 6¢ Air Mail stamp, Dayton, Ohio). Return Address: J. Sproule, 2000 North Main, Dayton, Ohio. "Kay darling," **[/]** ". . . I think I explained that the crux of this matter is that (as you gathered) I won't be able to finish the instructions by the 16th due to (a) the priest in charge of the instruction class requiring 24 hours of instruction and (b) his inability to arrange extra periods of instruction as was planned so I could finish for the 16th. Of course I'm continuing right along with the regular classes of instruction, it's just that I can't get in the extra instructions necessary to complete the required amount before the 16th." **[1 PARAGRAPH]**

"Dearest it is swell of you and I appreciate very much your writing to Father Spillain about getting it arranged so we can be married as we planned." **[/]** "Of course I understand that you want to know what's happening before you leave darling and I hope I've been able to explain it ok—briefly again it's this: a dispensation permitting our mixed marriage and a letter of delegation from Father Spillain permitting or authorizing Father Ansburg to witness our marriage will enable us to be married as we planned. This is necessary since I won't have the instructions completed by the 16th, but I'm going right on with the instruction darling and I will complete them just as soon as possible." **[/]**

"Sweetheart there is no way for things to turn out differently than we planned other than my becoming a Catholic after our marriage. . . ." **[1 PARAGRAPH]** ". . . Right now it's about 330 hours till you'll arrive as I figure it—I wish it were only 30 hours—I wish it were only 30 minutes!" **[1 PARAGRAPH]** "I did get one important thing done though honey—I reserved a room for you at the Hotel Miami (like in Miami Beach) for Sunday, January 10. So you won't arrive here without any place to stay darling." **[5 PARAGRAPHS]** "All my love and kisses always" **[/]** "Johnny"

[It's not clear exactly when KVS arrived in Dayton; but she was toasted at a celebratory dinner at Denver, Colorado's Edelweiss Café by her friend, Ruth, and others on January 6, 1943.]

Chapter 9. Eglin Field Testing—March and April 1944

Eglin Field, Florida—the cots and bunks, PX cokes and USO shows. What a climate in which to test airplane equipment—heat, thunderstorms, power failures, faulty fuel pumps, and Army red tape. But the income taxes are done and KVS reports on prospects of a new Dayton apartment. Mystery of the stolen sheets. A side trip to Pensacola.

**** To Mrs. J. H. Sproule, 1728 W 1st St., Dayton 7, Ohio ("Eglin Field, Fla.," 3/2/44, 9:40 PM, Postmarked 3/3/44, 10 AM, "Via Air Mail" with a 6¢ Air Mail stamp, Pensacola, Fla.). Return Address: J. H. Sproule, % V. O. Q., Eglin Field, Florida. "Hello darling," **[/]** "Here I am as you will have noted by the postmark. Arrived here this evening about 5:30, checked in, got a temporary pass (good till 9:00 in the morning when I will get a less temporary one) and a bunk in the V.O.Q. (Visiting Officers' Quarters) and that will be my address while I'm here—just Mr. J. H. Sproule % V. O. Q Eglin Field, Florida." **[/]**

"When I brought my stuff over to the quarters I met Charlie Wright from our unit who is also staying here at the VOQ. When I'd cleaned up a bit we had supper together. We went to a little place a few miles from the field with a manufacturer's representative who had a car which made it very handy." **[/]**

"The trip down was quite uneventful and not too bad although I didn't get to sleep till about 12 last night as the porter didn't get my berth made up till after 11. Consequently I think I'll be going to bed pretty soon—that is as soon as I've written to you and taken a shower." **[4 PARAGRAPHS]** "All my love and kisses" **[/]** "Johnny"

**** To Mrs. J. H. Sproule, 1728 W 1st St., Dayton 7, Ohio ("Eglin Field, Fla.," 3/5/44, 8:35 PM, Postmarked 3/6/44, 6:30 PM, "Via Air Mail" with a 6¢ Air Mail stamp, Pensacola, Fla.). Return Address: J. H. Sproule, % V. O. Q., Eglin Field, Florida.

[The printed return address on the envelope is: WAR DEPARTMENT / Army Air Forces / Materiel Command / Wright Field, Dayton, Ohio.]

"Hello sweetheart," **[1 PARAGRAPH]** "We moved into some new quarters today. We were staying in a barracks building of this same architecture as the barracks buildings of the GI's. We had cots with a thin pad for a mattress which wasn't so springy but one could sleep without danger of falling out because of the ample sag which developed when one laid down. The present arrangements feature individual rooms, some single and some double, with beds (not cots) having both springs and mattresses. Bob Rey (a fellow from another branch in the Armament Lab) and I took a double room. This has two beds as described above, a chest of drawers, two chairs, a mirror and two clothes closets. The rent for this is $10.00 per month as compared to 25¢ per day for the other place which is not bad at all. The only drawback to this arrangement is that these quarters are 1 mile distant from the others and hence also further from the PX, the theater, and the various offices and places in which I have business." **[/]**

"The theater which I mentioned is a standard War Dept theater, programs change 4 times per week, fairly new films and admission price 15¢. Thus, the maximum amount which one can squander on this pastime is 60¢ per week. Quite a sum isn't it honey?" **[/]**

"Here is a tidbit that occurred this morning. I was standing in church this morning and I did notice that it was rather hot—I was perspiring a bit and having had no breakfast and having stood on one spot for almost a half hour, anyway I thought to myself that if it were anywhere, but church, I'd step out and get some fresh air. Well the next thing I know I'd had a mild faint and toppled over. Very humiliating and embarrassing. I nicked my chin a bit on falling—nothing serious—so to add to everything when anyone asks me what I did to my chin, they look rather doubtful when I make the explanation." **[/]**

"Business has progressed rather slowly so far. Saturday was fairly well occupied for the people here by giving a demonstration for some one. I never did find out who. That's always the way with such things—no one ever knows exactly who it's being given for. Rumor always has it anyone from the president on down." **[5 PARAGRAPHS]** "Yours always with all my love and kisses" **[/]** "Johnny"

 **** To Mrs. J. H. Sproule, 1728 W 1st St., Dayton 7, Ohio ("Eglin Field, Fla.," 3/6/44, 8:07 PM, Postmarked 3/7/44, 6-PM, "Via Air Mail" with a 6¢ Air Mail stamp, Pensacola, Fla.). Return Address: J. H. Sproule, % V. O. Q., Eglin Field, Florida. [The printed return address on the envelope is: WAR DEPARTMENT / Army Air Forces / Materiel Command / Wright Field, Dayton, Ohio.] "Hi sweetheart," **[/]** "Just a few lines to remind you that I love you!" **[2 PARAGRAPHS]**

"An interesting phenomenon here at the field is the lighting system. I've never seen it fail that whenever it rains the lights go out. It's almost as sure a thing as it getting dark when the sun goes down. Usually with the third or fourth crack of thunder the lights go out for a period of five to fifteen minutes—usually nearer five. . . . And sure enough the lights soon come on again all over the field [JHS pens four musical notes]. But then it's not long till they're off again for a bit and then back again. About the third or fourth time they stay off for an hour or so. . . ." **[3 PARAGRAPHS]** "Yours always with all my love" **[/]** "Johnny" **[/]**

"P.S. As I address this envelope for this the thought just came to me that maybe by now we might have a new address. Did anything come of that prospect of renting the apartment that the [Eddie A.] Moraski's had? (Pause for the lights to come on again.) Anyhow good luck on your apartment hunting honey! (Pause for lights again.) I'd better get to bed before they go off permanently. This on and off is getting to [sic] frequent." **[/]** "Night again darling" **[/]** "All my love and kisses" **[/] **"J."

 **** To Mrs. J. H. Sproule, 1728 W 1st St., Dayton 7, Ohio ("Eglin Field, Fla.," 3/8/44, 10:13 PM, Postmarked 3/9/44, 6-PM, "Via Air Mail" with a 6¢ Air Mail stamp, Pensacola, Fla). Return Address: J. H. Sproule, % V. O. Q., Eglin Field, Florida. [The printed return address on the envelope is: WAR DEPARTMENT / Army Air Forces / Materiel Command / Wright

Field, Dayton, Ohio.] "Hello honey," **[1 PARAGRAPH]** "Things are pretty quiet around here. Oh, there's quite a bit of activity, but this place is pretty well spread out so it gives an impression more of sleepy time down south than of a beehive of activity." **[/]**

"I've been busy enough so far. I've been observing and reporting on the progress and results being accomplished on a couple of tests other than the ones I am more directly concerned with. This hasn't overburdened me though as the tests which are my principal concern are progressing very slowly. It looks like it will work out pretty good for by that time the ones I'm concerned with are in full swing the others should be completed." **[/]**

"One of the other fellows from our unit came down last night on yet another test. I thought probably he would be coming down but I didn't know when. He (Lt. [Jack A.] Chandler), one of the new fellows who came to the lab a month or so ago) said that his test was not getting off to any phenomenal start. I guess all these tests start up slow. The testing personnel here have to get acquainted with the equipment, decide how they want to test it and so on." **[/]**

"I went to the show last night. It was a double feature, but they didn't have any cartoon or other extras. One was a western and the other a nonsensical B grade show of which I have already forgotten the name—or I guess it's title was 'Week End Pass'—something about a shipyard worker and naval officers granddaughter who wanted to join the Wacs. . . ." **[4 PARAGRAPHS]** "All my love and kisses" **[/]** "Johnny"

  **** To Mrs. J. H. Sproule, 1728 W 1st St., Dayton 7, Ohio ("Eglin Field, Fla.," 3/9/44, 10:27 PM, Postmarked 3/10/44, 6-PM, with a preprinted Air Mail stamp of 6¢, Pensacola, Fla.). Return Address: J. H. Sproule, % V. O. Q., Eglin Field, Florida. "Hello darling," **[1 PARAGRAPH]** "From what you said about the apartment not being ready for a couple weeks or so, it appears as though there's no rush. I agree that it's not ideal, but as you say it is better than what we have. And we can still look for something that we'd really like to have." **[/]**

"Quite a number of the fellows, representatives of various companies etc, that I've seen around here the past couple days have been working or getting ready to work on their income tax returns. There were three here in the place this evening working on them. Makes me glad we've got ours all finished." **[1 PARAGRAPH]**

"Progress today was about average. I've battled this red tape buck passing army in so many ways that I've finally fallen into a mode of operation in which I contact officialdom as little as possible and head for a short cut whenever possible. This is not any horrible place to get anything done—I mean it's not just the place, but rather that it's just the army. I'll bet I'd make a hell of a soldier." **[5 PARAGRAPHS]** "All my love and kisses always" **[/]** "Johnny"

   **** To Mrs. J. H. Sproule, 1728 W 1st St., Dayton 7, Ohio ("Eglin Field, Fla.," 3/11/44, 9:19 PM, Postmarked 3/12/44, 6-PM, with a preprinted Air Mail stamp of 6¢, Pensacola, Fla.). Return Address: J. H. Sproule, % V. O. Q., Eglin Field, Florida. "Hi darling," **[3 PARAGRAPHS]** "If you're wondering whose pen I'm writing with it's Eddie Refenbark's. [This 3-11-44 letter is distinctly easier to read than prior ones because the ink is darker.] Bob Rey went home yesterday so Eddie moved in with me this afternoon." **[/]**

"I hope honey that the weather up there is improving so you won't be having the mess of the fire to contend with so much. And darling, I do sympathize with your being so thirsty in the middle of the night and one not there to get you a drink (with some grape flavoring and sugar in it). **[4 PARAGRAPH]** "All my love and kisses always" **[/]** "Johnny"

   **** To Mrs. J. H. Sproule, 1728 W 1st St., Dayton 7, Ohio ("Eglin Field, Fla.," 3/13/44, 9:57 PM, Postmarked 3/14/44, 5:30 PM, with a preprinted Air Mail stamp of 6¢, Pensacola, Fla.). Return Address: J. H. Sproule, % V. O. Q., Eglin Field, Florida. "Hello sweetheart," **[3 PARAGRAPHS]** "Boy I'm sure getting enough walking. I'll bet I average at least 5 or 6 miles a day and that's just the minimum amount I can get by with for I sure don't do any extra hiking just for fun." **[/]**

"I sure have a feeling of isolation—of being out in the woods out of touch with everything. Haven't seen a newspaper less than three days old, and without the daily bombardment of radio news broadcasts I sure am getting behind on the world news." **[/]** ". . . But honey it's quite a blow to be subjected to the vagaries of the cafeteria here after your swell cooking. You have no idea how dull and unimaginative the menu is at that cafeteria." **[3 PARAGRAPHS]** "All my love and kisses" **[/]** "Johnny"

**** To Mrs. J. H. Sproule, 1728 W 1st St., Dayton 7, Ohio ("Eglin Field, Florida," 3/14/44, 9:10 PM, Postmarked 3/15/44, 10:30 AM, with a preprinted Air Mail stamp of 6¢, Pensacola, Fla.). Return Address: J. H. Sproule, % V. O. Q., Eglin Field, Florida. "Dear Wife," **[2 PARAGRAPHS]** "The attached cartoon expressed, rather well I thought, the universal predicament over the tax situation so am passing it on hoping it will give you a chuckle or two, honey."

[Caption of the cartoon is illegible due to deteriorated tape used to affix it to the page; the visual shows a couple each reading the paper with one making a comment about paying taxes.] **[1 PARAGRAPH]**

"But the worst thing honey, is the sleep situation. Now here when I could be going to bed at 8 o'clock or so and really get plenty I find that I don't get sleepy till 10:00 or 10:30 or so depending on how early I get up. I've been getting up about 7 so that doesn't add up to much more than 8 or 9 hours sleep. Horrible situation isn't it when I could get 12 or 13 hours sleep if I could go to sleep." **[/]** "Eddie has been offering to buy me a coke so I guess we'll see if a couple civilians can get a coke over at the USO which is the nearest likely place at this hour. . . ." **[/]** "One thing this place lacks is a drinking fountain and the tap water is full of chlorine and not at all tasty even if one is thirsty." **[3 PARAGRAPHS]** "All my love and kisses" **[/]** "Johnny"

**** To Mrs. J. H. Sproule, 1728 W 1st St., Dayton 7, Ohio ("Eglin Field, Fla.," 3/15/44, NOON, Postmarked 3/15/44, 5:30 PM, with a preprinted Air Mail stamp of 6¢, Pensacola, Fla.). Return Address: J. H. Sproule, % V. O. Q., Eglin Field, Florida. "Kay darling," **[1 PARAGRAPH]**

"That sounds swell about the new place—new furniture and all. The only thing I don't like is that I'm not there to help you with a packing and moving." **[/]** "Fifteen dollars a week is not much more than we have been paying and we will have a much better place I'm sure. It all sounds very nice, except as I said the part about you having to do the moving alone. I hope you can overcome the urge to discard a portion of our things." **[1 PARAGRAPH]**

"Naturally a lot of questions occur about how this or that will be, but most of them can wait till I get home. Mostly now I'm wondering about what the phone arrangement is (what is the number?) and is there an ice box or a refrigerator? A refrigerator I hope. Will the downstairs be occupied by the Browns or someone else? Oh there is a lot to find out about a new place isn't there? But as I said, most of it can wait till I get there—the above are just a few questions that occurred to me at the present." **[1 PARAGRAPH]** "And when I get back I'll really go through a lot of that stuff I've got that I really don't need. But as I was saying before I left honey some of it is worth keeping especially those two electric motors (one of which came from that mixer) which are in that low cupboard in which the sink is located." **[4 PARAGRAPHS]** "All my love and kisses" **[/]** "Johnny"

  **** To Mrs. J. H. Sproule, 1728 W 1st St., Dayton 7, Ohio ("Eglin Field, Fla.," 3/15/44, 11:13 PM, Postmarked 3/16/44, 10-AM, with a preprinted Air Mail stamp of 6¢, Pensacola, Fla.). Return Address: J. H. Sproule, % V. O. Q., Eglin Field, Florida. "Darling," **[3 PARAGRAPHS]** "You know honey that coal dust may be just the thing that was causing my hair to get so dirty. I'd never thought of it but it sure sounds like it could be the cause." **[3 PARAGRAPHS]**

"Yes darling we sure have had a swell year. And loving each other as we do makes me know that everything will always be wonderful with us. Sweetheart I love you so very very much!" **[/]** "By now you'll know that I'm getting your letters, and it is really grand to get them!" **[3 PARAGRAPHS]** "All my love and kisses" **[/]** "Johnny" **[/]** "P.S. I don't know when I should start addressing letters to 348 Forest Ave. so I'll send this to 1728 W 1st and from then on to the other place for as I estimate the travel of the mail you should be over there by the time the next letter will get there." **[/]** "P².S.² I'm not low on money yet honey, but I expect I will need some more before I leave here so I guess you'd just as well send me $50.00." **[/]** "Night again darling" **[/]** "XXXXX" **[/]** "Johnny"

**** To Mrs. J. H. Sproule, 348 Forest Ave., Dayton, Ohio ("Eglin Field, Fla.," 3/16/44, 10:17 PM, Postmarked 3/17/44, 11-AM, with a preprinted Air Mail stamp of 6¢, Pensacola, Fla.). Return Address: J. H. Sproule, % V. O. Q., Eglin Field, Florida. "Hello sweetheart," **[4 PARAGRAPHS]** "With the means of entertainment here being a rather limited, Eddie and I have sure been catching up on our reading, but too much of that gets tiresome too." **[2 PARAGRAPHS]** "All my love and kisses" **[/]** "Johnny"

**** To Mrs. J. H. Sproule, 348 Forest Ave., Dayton, Ohio ("Eglin Field, Fla.," 3/17/44, 11:50 PM, Postmarked 3/18/44, 9:30 AM, with a preprinted Air Mail stamp of 6¢, Pensacola, Fla.). Return Address: J. H. Sproule, % V. O. Q., Eglin Field, Florida. "Hello sweetheart," **[1 PARAGRAPH]** ". . . That steak you mentioned sounded mighty good. I'm glad the dinner went well, but it couldn't help being anything but good with such a wonderful hostess namely you. It is a lot of work though I know honey, to come home from work and then get a big dinner. However the attached illustration shows one means of overcoming this difficulty."

[Taped to this page of the letter is a cartoon showing 8 elegantly dressed people sitting around a table with the host saying "After an hour of sparkling dinner conversation you'll all be our guests around the corner at Joe's Diner."] **[/]**

"When I get home darling, let's have a big steak for just us two what say?" **[1 PARAGRAPH]** "I spent the whole day getting some data for a fellow from the lab who is out on the coast for a few days. He called up down here yesterday and wanted some stuff that I couldn't easily lay my hands on. I was going to teletype it to him but it turned out to be a little long for a teletype (about 5 single spaced pages) so we'll compromise on an airmail special delivery." **[2 PARAGRAPHS]** "Always your" **[/]** "Johnny"

**** To Mrs. J. H. Sproule, 348 Forest Ave., Dayton, Ohio ("Eglin Field, Fla.," 3/19/44, 10:52 PM, Postmarked 3/20/44, 10 AM, with a preprinted Air Mail stamp of 6¢ onto which has been pasted an additional 10¢ postage (three 3¢ stamps and one 1¢ stamp), with handwritten "SPECIAL DELIVERY AIR MAIL," and also stamped in two places "VIA AIR MAIL / Special Delivery," Pensacola, Fla.). Return Address: J. H. Sproule, % V. O. Q., Eglin Field, Florida. "Hello sweetheart," **[2 PARAGRAPHS]**

". . . Got up about 11 and went to 12 o'clock mass. After that it was time to eat so met Eddie at the at the cafeteria and had lunch. As it had been looking like rain we decided to go to the afternoon show. It was 'See Here, Private Hargrove' and not bad—a rather above average comedy. After the show it wasn't long till it was time for supper so back to the cafeteria we went for another attempt at the standard Sunday menu: fried chicken, sweet potatoes and peas—the peas weren't bad." **[1 PARAGRAPH]** "This evening we sat around shooting the breeze and doing some more reading. That together with going over to the USO for a cup of coffee and taking a shower and washing my hair completed the activity for today." **[/]**

"I'm hoping that if everything goes as it should I'll be able to come home about the middle of the week. There's a plane leaving here Wed morning for Wright Field which I hope to be able to make. If so I should get up to Wright Field in the middle of the day some time, finish out the working day and be in town at the usual time after work. I'll alert you Tuesday evening if I expect to get out of here Wednesday morning in that plane. I'm thinking that I'd better send this special delivery air mail so this will get there Tuesday." **[2 PARAGRAPHS]** "All my love and kisses" **[/]** "Johnny"

**** To Mrs. J. H. Sproule, 348 Forest Ave., Dayton 5, Ohio (4/2/44, Friday 12:00 Midnight, Postmarked 4/2/44, 4 PM, "Via Air Mail" with an 8¢ Air Mail stamp, Eglin Field, Fla.). Return Address: J. H. Sproule, % V. O. Q., Eglin Field, Fla. "Hello darling," **[1 PARAGRAPH]** "I've just finished working on my notes bringing them up to date and I'm really feeling sleepy. . . ." **[1 PARAGRAPH]** "I'm hoping that I'll be able to come up on the Tuesday mail plane from here. I asked for a seat on it and I sure intend to be sitting in it when the plane leaves here if it's at all possible." **[/]** "We didn't get too much done today due to the airplane being out of commission all afternoon. But I always look forward to the next day with hope." **[2 PARAGRAPHS]** "All my love and kisses" **[/]** "Johnny"

**** To Mrs. J. H. Sproule, 348 Forest Ave., Dayton 5, Ohio (4/13/44, 10:45 PM, Postmarked 4/14/44, 8 AM, "Via Air Mail" with a 6¢ Air Mail stamp and a 2¢ stamp, Eglin Field BR., Fla.). Return Address: J. H. Sproule, % V. O. Q., Eglin Field, Fla. "Hello sweetheart," **[1 PARAGRAPH]** "We arrived here about 6:30 and then I got a temporary pass from the O. and got a room. Eddie Rifenbark had fixed it for me to get in with him—there's four of us, Eddie + Jim Shroyer and Charlie Wright in this one room We have two double decker bunks—since I am the last one to arrive I fell heir to an upper, but that won't bother me for I really feel ready for a night's sleep." **[3 PARAGRAPHS]** "All my love and kisses always" **[/]** "Johnny"

**** To Mrs. J. H. Sproule, 348 Forest Ave., Dayton 5, Ohio (4/14/44, 10:35 PM, Postmarked 4/15/44, 8 AM, "Via Air Mail" with a 6¢ Air Mail stamp and a 2¢ stamp, Eglin Field BR., Fla.). Return Address: J. H Sproule, % V. O. Q., Eglin Field, Fla. "Hello darling" **[/]** "This was a typic Eglin Field day—I mean a lot of hiking back and forth without accomplishing a great deal. I checked in at the necessary offices this morning and obtained a pass and all that stuff. That took up most of the morning and then the afternoon went by with nothing much accomplishe except some talking and some observing done on dispersion tests—that i tests to determine that the bullets from the machine guns in the turrets on not dispense over too great a space due to some inherent characteristics the installation." **[/]** "Well that's how the day went—a lot of energy expended with a none too startling quantity of results. The more I see of army business the more unweildy (sp?) I'm convinced it is." **[/]**

"The evening went by in the typical gabfest that a bunch of guys always g into. We cussed and discussed Eglin Field, income tax, draft boards, the Govt. and so on. It rained buckets for a little while this evening and then tapered off to a halt an hour or so ago—Jim, Eddie and I took advantage the lull to go over to the PX for some ice cream. We hadn't been back fro the PX long till it started to rain and it hasn't stopped completely yet. The wind is blowing at a great rate so maybe by morning it will have blown over. Hope so anyhow!" **[2 PARAGRAPHS]** "All my love and kisses" **[/]** "Johnny"

**** To Mrs. J. H. Sproule, 348 Forest Ave., Dayton 5, Ohio (4/15/44, 11:45 PM, Postmarked 4/16/44, 2:30 PM, "Via Air Mail" with a 6¢ Air Mail stamp and a 2¢ stamp, Pensacola, Fla.). Return Address: J. H. Sproule, % V. O. Q., Eglin Field, Fla. "Hello sweetheart" **[/]** "How's everything with my darling tonight? There was very little going on around here this evening. The show was some horse yarn so that was not at all appealing. We finally decided to get up a small poker game between the four of us. We started after supper and played till about 9:30 and then went over to the PX for some ice cream. The ice cream was on me as I'd won about $2.50. I also bought a pipe with my loot as Jim and Ed had pipes so I could hold my own in the smoke cloud making. We came back and played a while more during which time I won another 6¢—some stuff-eh? Got to make expenses somehow honey!" **[/]**

"I think maybe tomorrow we'll go over to Pensacola about 50 miles distant to sort of vary the monotony of things—that is if it's a nice day." **[/]** "We finished getting the airplane ready today—that is it's ready now to be started in on the various tests and if the weather will only permit we'll get something done for a change. It didn't rain today, but the ceiling was so low that very little flying was done by anyone. This part of Florida has about the poorest weather imaginable—especially when compared to the mental picture that one has of Florida—you know, palm trees flowers grass beach girls in bathing suits etc. Most of the time I've been here at Eglin Field both this time and in the past, the weather has been bad at least 50% of the time." **[4 PARAGRAPHS]** "All my love and kisses" **[/]** "Johnny"

**** To Mrs. J. H. Sproule, 348 Forest Ave., Dayton 5, Ohio (4/17/44, 11:15 PM, Postmarked 4/18/44, 8 AM, "Via Air Mail" with an 8¢ Air Mail stamp, Eglin Field BR., Fla.). Return Address: J. H. Sproule, % V. O. Q., Eglin Field, Fla. "Hello sweetheart" **[/]** "I love you darling! I love you every minute and I miss you too, I always miss you something awful whenever I am away from you!" [/] "We had some of the usual luck today—on the first flight, a gasoline pump developed a leak and that put the airplane out of commission for the rest of the day for repairs. I hope it will be fixed tomorrow so we can start getting something done." [/] "For the second day in a row the weather has been nice—no rain, just a nice sunny day." [/]

"Sunday the four of us took the bus into Pensacola about 10 in the morning. It was a fairly long ride since it's about 60 miles away and those GI busses don't make very good time. We ate lunch and then Charlie and Eddie went to a show and Jim and I were going to get out to Pensacola beach. After Charlie and Eddie went on Jim and I went down towards the bus depot where he had checked his swimming trunks. On the way I stopped in a drug store and bought a pair of sunglasses. When we got back to the hotel from which the bus to the beach left, there was a crowd getting on the bus already. We stood out at the edge and estimated that if we were able to elbow aside all the women and children and small men we would be able to get within five feet of the bus by the time it got full. So we gave up and went to a picture too. It was an old one—something about the Dead End Kids that we'd both seen but it was cool inside the theater so we stayed on." [/]

"After that we went down to the docks and watched the fury from the Naval Air Station dock. We went back to the hotel then and met the other guys. We had supper, saw another show and took the long ride back again. Very thrilling—I'm glad we went though because now if any one suggests going to Pensacola I can say I've already been there." [/]

"Charlie Wright got a notice in the mail today informing him that he was now in 1-A. He's wanting to get back to see what he can do about it—he's thinking of trying for a commission in the navy. I suppose if he goes back I'll get stuck with his stuff too." **[2 PARAGRAPHS]** "All my love and kisses" [/] "Johnny" [/] "P.S. I guess it's a good thing we didn't get out to the beach as we'd probably be as sunburned as everyone else today. I'd like to get a bit of tan, but I'm sure going to take it in easy stages. Love again J."

**** To Mrs. J. H. Sproule, 348 Forest Ave., Dayton 5, Ohio ("Tuesday" [4/18/44], 11:10 PM, Postmarked 4/19/44, 8 AM, "Via Air Mail" with an 8¢ Air Mail stamp, Eglin Field BR., Fla.). Return Address: J. H. Sproule, % V. O. Q., Eglin Field, Fla. "Hello sweetheart" **[/]** "Any rain up your way? Eddie, Jim, and I just swam back from the show a little bit ago. Boy is it raining here—and it's been at it since about 2:30 this afternoon and I heard that we were going to have this sort of weather for a couple days—. . . ." **[/]** "This horrible weather is one of the main reasons why it is so hard to get anything done down here. What with the rain shutting everything down here this afternoon I didn't get a great deal done today." **[1 PARAGRAPH]**

"One unusual thing has happened anyhow—the lights haven't gone off even once yet. As a usual thing they would have been off and on three or four times and by now would have been off for the evening." **[/]** "As I mentioned we went to the show this evening—it was a double feature, a rootin tootin western and the other a show I saw in Schenectady that wasn't much better. We had been trying to amuse ourselves with a little three handed poker after supper, but three is almost too few to make a good game so we stopped and went to the show." **[3 PARAGRAPHS]** "All my love and kisses always" **[/]** "Johnny"

**** To Mrs. J. H. Sproule, 348 Forest Ave., Dayton 5, Ohio ("Wednesday" [4/19/44], 11:23 PM, Postmarked 4/20/44, 8 AM, "Via Air Mail" with an 8¢ Air Mail stamp, Eglin Field BR., Fla.). Return Address: J. H. Sproule, % V. O. Q., Eglin Field, Fla. "Hello darling " **[/]** "I hope this past week has gone better for you than for me. Today was the old story again rain rain rain!—and consequently no accomplishments. It's bad enough to have to come down here let alone sitting around day after day getting nothing done. . . ." **[1 PARAGRAPH]** "As usual there wasn't anything to do except to go to the show this evening so Ed Jim and I hiked over and plunked down our 15¢ and sat through 'Four Jills in a Jeep'. It was not very exciting, but perhaps it was worth 15¢." **[3 PARAGRAPHS]** "All my love and kisses" **[/]** 'Johnny"

**** To Mrs. J. H. Sproule, 348 Forest Ave., Dayton 5, Ohio (4/20/44, 11:40 PM, Postmarked 4/21/44, 8 AM, "Via Air Mail" with an 8¢ Air Mail stamp, Eglin Field BR., Fla.). Return Address: J. H. Sproule, % V. O. Q., Eglin Field, Fla. "Hello darling " **[1 PARAGRAPH]** "Today as usual it rained in the afternoon and was foggy in the morning so didn't accomplish much. Also some major general flew our airplane down to Orlando and back this afternoon thus making doubly sure that we wouldn't do anything this afternoon." **[1 PARAGRAPH]**

"We went to a free USO show tonight. It wasn't bad—the usual collection of singing dancing and comedy acts that they get-together for these groups. They had one fellow, a juggler, who put on a pretty good act." **[/]** "After the show we came back and sat around cussing this region the weather and the various officers around here whom we think the place could get along very well without. . . ." **[4 PARAGRAPHS]** "All my love and kisses" **[/]** "Johnny"

**** To Mrs. J. H. Sproule, 348 Forest Ave., Dayton 5, Ohio (4/21/44, 9:33 PM, Postmarked 4/22/44, 8 AM, "Via Air Mail" with an 8¢ Air Mail stamp, Eglin Field BR., Fla.). Return Address: J. H. Sproule, % V. O. Q., Eglin Field, Fla. "Darling " **[/]** "I received your letter written the 18th today and honey I was so very glad to hear from you! It has been over a week since I left. . . ." **[/]** "I've been here by myself tonight as Eddie and Jim left this evening. They had a ride back in a plane lined up, but that fell through they had train reservations so they were all set." **[1 PARAGRAPH]** "It was nice that you had Agnes [Glenn] stay with you over the weekend—even if you didn't get anything done it was better than the monotony." **[3 PARAGRAPHS]** "All my love and kisses" **[/]** "Johnny" **[/]** "P.S. I convinced the guy I didn't steal any sheets."

**** To Mrs. J. H. Sproule, 348 Forest Ave., Dayton 5, Ohio ("Saturday night" [4/22/44], 10:54 PM, Postmarked 4/23/44, 4 PM, "Via Air Mail" with an 8¢ Air Mail stamp, Eglin Field BR., Fla.). Return Address: J. H. Sproule, % V. O. Q., Eglin Field, Fla. "Hello sweetheart" **[1 PARAGRAPH]** "Here it is Saturday night—I wish I were home—we could go dancing somewhere or to a show or visiting or even if we just stayed home, we'd be together darling and it would be wonderful!" **[/]**

"I went to the show this evening. It must have been an old one for I'd never heard of it. It was called 'The Young in Heart'—Roland Young, Janet Gaynor, Paulette Goddard, and Douglas Fairbanks Jr. were in it. It wasn't bad though—sort of a comedy about a fortune hunting family. . . ." **[1 PARAGRAPH]** "Tomorrow being Sunday I don't suppose I'll do a great deal—probably sleep a bit later than usual, go to mass, eat, do some reading or take a nap and then probably go to the show in the evening. . . ." **[/]** ". . . Now that I'm all by myself here I've inherited a down bunk so you won't have to worry about me getting up in a big rush and forgetting to step down first." **[3 PARAGRAPHS]** "All my love always" **[/]** "Johnny"

**** To Mrs. J. H. Sproule, 348 Forest Ave., Dayton 5, Ohio ("Sunday night" [4/23/44], 10:50 PM, Postmarked 4/24/44, 4 PM, "Via Air Mail" with an 8¢ Air Mail stamp, Eglin Field BR., Fla.). Return Address: J. H. Sproule, % V. O. Q., Eglin Field, Fla. "Hi darling" **[3 PARAGRAPHS]** "I mentioned above that it rained today, but the weather here has been so horrible this trip that it takes special emphasis. This place has completely disillusioned me toward 'sunny Florida' although I realize that there are much nicer parts of Florida than this." **[1 PARAGRAPH]**

"I'd forgotten all about that aviation cadet business too. Well by them sending that stuff back it will save me having to get another birth certificate which I was thinking I'd probably have to do some time." **[5 PARAGRAPHS]** "All my love and kisses" **[/]** "Johnny"

[JHS received a memorandum of March 27, 1943 from Col. F. C. Wolfe, Chief of the Armament Laboratory, Engineering Division informing him that "In your present assignment in the Bombing Branch, and your work on high priority projects, it is essential that you remain to continue your engineering work. It is therefore requested that you immediately submit the necessary forms in order that your application may be processed by the Officer Reviewing Board." Dad immediately prepared such an application, and a year and change later he received a letter dated April 13, 1944 from

Captain John A. Brown, Jr., Assistant Chief, Aviation Cadet Branch. Brown informed JHS that "Because of the recent curtailment of the Aviation Cadet Training Program . . . no further applications for aviation cadet ground duty training are being given consideration." Dad's birth certificate, college transcripts, and three letters of recommendation were returned. However this episode was not the end of Dad's adventures with the wartime Selective Service System for he received an "Order To Report Preinduction Physical Examination" dated June 4, 1945 instructing him to appear at 7:3 a.m. June 18. And on this same date JHS was "Rejected" for service, presumably as a consequence of blindness in one eye.]

**** To Mrs. J. H. Sproule, 348 Forest Ave., Dayton 5, Ohio ("Monday" [4/24/44], 9:25 PM, Postmarked 4/25/44, 4 PM, "Via Air Mail with an 8¢ Air Mail stamp, Eglin Field BR., Fla.). Return Address: J. H. Sproule, % V. O. Q., Eglin Field, Fla. "Darling" **[2 PARAGRAPHS]** "I was in the PX Saturday and seeing a nice eversharp pencil for a $1.05 I bought it The girl said they were going to have some fountain pens in Monday so th afternoon I stopped in thinking I'd take a look and see what they were like at least. When I asked about them, the clerk said yes, they had had some pens, 86 in fact, but they had all been sold. I didn't have any idea the shortage was quite that bad. Anyhow I didn't look at any fountain pens." **[/]**

"I thought I told you about the quote Sheet Incident unquote. Now when got down here I went over to this Capt. Smith's office and showed him th letter. I very patiently explained the circumstances to him and pointed o that: a: I had obviously not stolen the sheet—b: I knew nothing whatsoev about the alleged theft—c: I didn't intend to fork over $1.50—and d: I wa highly indignant at the implications of his letter." **[/]** "He replied that: a the letter had been written in his absence (this was possible since he was away when I first arrived and didn't return until the following Monday) b some sort of investigation into the whereabouts of such missing items ha to be made for the record or else he was personally liable for the financia loss. c: He was sure I had not taken the sheet in question, and that d: I should forget all about it. I have. How's that honey?" **[2 PARAGRAPHS]**

"The daily work that piles up at the office is handled somewhat like this—stuff that is rush is done by someone else and the rest is just delayed a while longer. When it finally gets done the lengthened period is just attributed to red tape and on down the line the people just give out with an extra curse or two for the incompetent way things are run, for the general inability of the responsible people to realize quote there's a war going on unquote and for general principles." **[2 PARAGRAPHS]** "All my love always" **[/]** "Johnny"

    **** To Mrs. J. H. Sproule, 348 Forest Ave., Dayton 5, Ohio ("Tuesday April 25" 11:05 PM, Postmarked 4/26/44, 8 AM, "Via Air Mail" with an 8¢ Air Mail stamp, Eglin Field BR., Fla.). Return Address: J. H. Sproule, % V. O. Q., Eglin Field, Fla. "Darling" **[1 PARAGRAPH]** ". . . It started to rain about 6 while I was helping a couple of G.E. fellows on a plane and we were just finishing up. They dropped me off at the cafeteria and after I'd eaten it was still raining so I came on back to the room and didn't go to the show." **[1 PARAGRAPH]** ". . . At any rate honey I'll drop you a wire when I expect to be home (unless it should chance that I can fly back and circumstances would be such that I'd beat the wire)." **[2 PARAGRAPHS]** [JHS draws a heart and X.] "Johnny"

    **** To Mrs. J. H. Sproule, 348 Forest Ave., Dayton 5, Ohio ("Wednesday" [4/26/44], 8:45 PM, Postmarked 4/27/44, 8 AM, "Via Air Mail" with an 8¢ Air Mail stamp, Eglin Field BR., Fla.). Return Address: J. H. Sproule, % V. O. Q., Eglin Field, Fla. "Kay darling" **[1 PARAGRAPH]** "The red flag flew over the operations tower most all of the day (signifying that the ceiling and visibility were so limited that that the field was closed for flying) so that pretty well stymied things. It didn't rain (except for a few sprinkles around 5 o'clock) but it was murky and overcast all day." **[/]** "I went to the six o'clock show, there being nothing else to do, and saw a show called 'Uncertain Glory' with Errol Flynn. A medium sort of show that was perhaps worth the price of admission of 15¢." **[4 PARAGRAPHS]** "Night now honey. Remember I love you." **[/]** "Always and forever" **[/]** "Johnny"

**** To Mrs. J. H. Sproule, 348 Forest Ave., Dayton 5, Ohio ("Thursday" [4/27/44], 10:10 PM, Postmarked 4/28/44, 4 PM, "Via Air Mail" with an 8¢ Air Mail stamp, Eglin Field BR., Fla.). Return Address: J. H. Sproule, % V. O. Q., Eglin Field, Fla. "Hello sweetheart" **[3 PARAGRAPHS]** "Last night three fellows from the [Wright] field came in. One from the Arm. Lab. whom I knew, the other two were from different offices and I hadn't met them before. Any rate all four bunks are now occupied, although now by virtue of seniority I'm occupying (sp?) a lower." **[1 PARAGRAPH]**

"We had one mission today and then the airplane was out of commission for of all things another gas leak. I'm hoping it will be fixed by tomorrow for I'm awfully anxious to depart from this place and be with you as soon as possible darling. I'm hoping I'll be able to leave by the first part of the week." **[2 PARAGRAPHS]** "All my love and kisses" **[/]** "Johnny"

**** To Mrs. J. H. Sproule, 348 Forest Ave., Dayton 5, Ohio ("Saturday" [4/29/44], 10:20 PM, Postmarked 4/30/44, 4 PM, "Via Air Mail" with an 8¢ Air Mail stamp, Eglin Field BR., Fla.). Return Address: J. H. Sproule, % V. O. Q., Eglin Field, Fla. "Hello sweetheart" **[2 PARAGRAPHS]** "Today was really a very satisfactory day. We got off three missions with fairly good results so I feel rather well pleased." **[/]** "Thanks for sending the folks' letter on down. I wrote to them just the other day, but I think I'll answer this one tonight and give them a big surprise with my promptness. **[/]**

"Went to the show tonight and saw a show, something of a bore it was, I don't remember the name—it had 5 or 6 different bands but no plot. Last night the show was something called 'Ladies Courageous'—all about how the women ferry pilots are helping to win the war—I'm sure that this is one picture which could never be noted for its verisimilitude." **[/]** "That tickled me hon your going over to the library for lunch! Now me when I go somewhere during my lunch hour it's some place where food is the main commodity." **[2 PARAGRAPHS]** "All my love and kisses" **[/]** "Johnny"

Chapter 10. Morocco, Maxwell AFB, England and the Continent, Merchant Marine—1956, 1958, 1962, 1963

MOROCCO (1956)—Sidi Slimane AFB, Camel seats and Casablanca. MAXWELL AFB (1958)—a 6-week summer course: readings, quizzes, side activities of ceramics, sunning and swimming amid the heat, visiting Florida friends, meals and the menu collection. Questions about the home front: Mike's stamps, social events at the Field and at the church, swimming lessons, Mike's school grades, Agnes Glenn's job hunt. Meanwhile, please send cigarettes and prospects for a 10% raise. ENGLAND (1962)—Air Ministry and Air bases, Naval facilities; hotel shuffle, sightseeing, strange food, visiting friends, dreams of Paris. GERMANY (1962)—special orders extension to Wiesbaden on the eve of the Cuban Missile Crisis. NEW YORK (1963)—Merchant Marine Academy classes and sightseeing in New York City.

**** To Mrs. J. H. Sproule, 406 Wilbur Ave., Dayton 5, Ohio (Sidi Slimane [Strategic Air Command base in Morocco], 7/10/56, Postmarked July ??, 1956, ARMY-AIR FORCE PO . . . .). Return Address: Officers' Open Mess 3906th Air Base Group, APO 117, New York, N.Y. "Hi sweetheart" **[/]** "This may be about the last letter that will get to you much before I get home. . . ." **[/]** "It looks to me now as though Col. Williams & I will leave Sidi about the end of the week—spend the weekend in Casablanca and start back on Monday. The schedule has some flexibility in it so I'll call you as soon as I can when we get to the States. **[THIS PARAGRAPH CONTINUES]**

If you have time would you buy 8 furniture caster things—the little cups that you put under furniture casters to keep them from pressing into the rugs—and mail them to Mrs. Andrew Anderson, 45th Day Fighter Squadron APO 117, New York, N.Y. She's a lady working in the PX here that I bought some things from and she said this is one thing she can't buy here so I said I'd send some to her. I've ordered a camel saddle for Berryman's and she will mail it to them for me when it comes in." **[1 PARAGRAPH]** "I'll sure be glad to get home to you & Mike cause I miss you." **[/]** "Bye sweetheart" **[/]** "All my love" **[/]** "Johnny"

**** To Mrs. J. H. Sproule, 406 Wilbur Ave., Dayton 5, Ohio ("Sunday," 5/12/58, Postmarked 5/13/58, 6:30 PM, "Via Air Mail" with two 3¢ stamps, Montgomery Ala.). Return Address: J. H. Sproule, Air Warfare Systems Employment Course, Air Command & Staff College, Maxwell AFB, Montgomery, Ala. "Hi sweetheart" **[/]** "We've arrived in good shape and are now checked in and at our school work. . . . We checked in at the school and spent half the morning and this afternoon in class. This is a series of lectures with outside reading." **[/]**

"We're staying in the BOQ on the base but had to wait till today at class to find out what address we'll have for mail—since they have a few thousand students here in various studies, it's important to have the right address—it is as follows J. H. Sproule, Air Warfare Systems Employment Course, Air Command and Staff College, Maxwell AFB, Montgomery, Alabama." **[/]** "It's not too clear to me just how hard we'll have to work on this school— quite a bit of outside reading to catch up on at the start but perhaps when this is done it will be possible to stay ahead of all of that." **[/]**

"These BOQ's and the classroom building and the mess hall and library are all quite new—(new since we were here in 55)—and laid out practically next to each other so it's all just a couple of minutes walk apart. The officers' club isn't too far away either." **[/]** "I've missed being with you!!!—But this is remarking on the obvious since I don't care much for short trips away from you—and long trips are just that much less desirable. One better note tho Honey is that I've learned that this course has been cut to six weeks instead of seven." **[5 PARAGRAPHS]** "All my love" **[/]** "Johnny" **[/]** "P.S. Tell A hello [Agnes Glenn has moved to Dayton from out west] and tell Mike that I'm sending him a hug and a reminder to be a good boy J."

**** To Mrs. J. H. Sproule, 406 Wilbur Ave., Dayton 5, Ohio ("Sunday," 5/18/58, Postmarked 5/19/58, 6 PM, "Via Air Mail" [stamp torn off], Montgomery Ala.). Return Address: J. H. Sproule, Air Warfare Systems

Employment Course, Air Command & Staff College, Maxwell Air Force Base, Ala. "Hi sweetheart" [/] "The first week of this operation is over and we start up again in the morning on the second week. After a week Rich [Richard M. Schulherr] & I have gotten to know our way around pretty well. It is a real benefit to have his car for although the BOQ where we're staying is only across the street from the mess hall and our school building there seem to be a lot of other errands & trips that come up like church & going to the officers' club and eating on the week end when the nearby mess ha. is closed—etc." [/]

"The weekend here is somewhat inactive but we haven't been reduced to going to the movies yet. ..." [/]

"One thing we haven't gotten around to yet is swimming—there are a couple pools available and it seems that either would be fairly convenient. I guess this will be more attractive when it gets a little warmer." [/] "There is quite a bit of outside reading required for this course so that takes up a fair amount of time on 'school nights.' We get a list at the end of the week . . . We had two quizzes the first week. I managed a 100% on the first as it wasn't too hard, but know that I didn't manage as well on the second—for one thing I should have hurried along a little faster. I'll find out what grade I did get this coming week—but I know it was passing at least." [1 PARAGRAPH]

"I expect we'll eat here at the officers' club tonight—they have a smorgasbord special every other Sunday and this is the night for it. We a in town last night. So far I've picked up a couple menus for the collection and probably will get a chance for a few more before this is over." [/] "We're looking into the possibilities of catching a ride home over Memor Day week end—I think we'll get back one way or another Honey—we'll write more about this as some of the details clarify." [/] "Bye for now and to A [Agnes Glenn] & Mike too!" [/] "All my love" [/] "Johnny"

  **** To Mrs. J. H. Sproule, 406 Wilbur Ave., Dayton 5, Ohio ("Tuesday noon," 5/20/58, Postmarked 5/21/58, 6:30 PM, one 3¢ stamp, Montgomery Ala.). Return Address: J. H. Sproule, Air Warfare Systems

Employment Course, Air Command & Staff College, Maxwell AFB, Montgomery, Ala. "Hi Honey," **[2 PARAGRAPHS]** "I hope that by now you've gotten over the press of activities on the Mother Daughter breakfast and that with den meetings at an end you can relax a bit." **[/]**

"What purpose does Father Railling have in mind for the Jubilee collection?—If it's to buy Father Steinkamp another Cadillac I'd say that about $5.00 was appropriate—if they're going to add it to the building fund or something like that $15.00 would be real fine." **[2 PARAGRAPHS]** "I'm glad Mike has escaped the measles—maybe he'll miss them all together. I have thought that I might find a package of stamps that I could send him but I haven't yet so I suggest you don't say anything about it. I plan to write him a note anyhow so he can feel he's getting in the letter business too." **[/]** "Bye for now" **[/]** "All my love" **[/]** "Johnny"

**** To Mr. Michael. Sproule, 406 Wilbur Ave., Dayton 5, Ohio (5/21/58, Postmarked 5/22/58, 6 PM, "Via Air Mail" [stamps torn off], Montgomery Ala.). Return Address: J. H. Sproule, Air Warfare Systems Employment Course, Air Command & Staff College, Maxwell AFB, Montgomery, Ala. "Dear Mike," **[/]** "I had been waiting to write to you until I could find some stamps to send you and also use this letter to tell you about them. I mailed them this afternoon so perhaps when you receive this letter you will already have the stamps. Since I am writing this letter in my room tonight it won't get mailed till tomorrow and the stamps will have a head start. As you can tell by looking at them they are mostly, if not all, foreign stamps. Since you don't have many of these I would like to suggest that you make a new set of pages for your stamp book with one page for each foreign country and then for example, put all the Canadian stamps on one page and all the stamps from the next country on another page and so on. This would be better than trying to sort them out according to value as you are doing for your United States stamps for two reasons—first you won't have too many from any one country and second since each country has a different money system it won't be easy to group them all according to value. If this isn't clear to you Mike, your mother can help explain it to you." **[/]**

"I don't want to write this whole letter about stamps since I miss you very much and I'd like to hear about what you have been doing! Have you finished up enough electives to get another arrow award at the pow wow coming up? I hope you have." **[/]** "I hope you are being a good boy and helping your Mother as much as you can. You know it's a big help to her if you just pay attention to her and mind her." **[/]** "Have you remembered to get your allowance from your mother? You remember we agreed that instead of my paying you in advance that you'd get it from her each week." **[/]**

"Another thing that I'm wondering about—have you or Kay remembered to keep the plants watered? And how about the castor beans we planted—are they up yet?" **[/]** "I hope you will write and tell me about all these things Mike. I miss you and your Mother and A [Agnes Glenn] very much. Give Kay a big kiss and A a hug for me—and write to me because I miss you and would sure like to hear from you." **[/]** "Bye for now" **[/]** "All my love" **[/]** "Johnny" [Note that this letter is written much more neatly, evenly, and carefully than any other in the whole collection.]

**** To Mrs. J. H. Sproule, 406 Wilbur Ave., Dayton 5, Ohio (5/23/58, Postmarked 5/24/58, 5 PM, "Via Air Mail" [stamps missing], Crestview Fla.). Return Address: J. H. Sproule, Air Warfare Systems Employment Course, Air Command & Staff College, Maxwell AFB, Montgomery, Ala. "Hi sweetheart," **[/]** "Here it is Friday so the second week is over and that is the first 1/3 of the course. We had been having rather full days of lectures and problem solving periods and today we had our third quiz. Incidentally I made 91 on the second one." **[/]** "With the weekend ahead we plan to drive down to see the [William W. and Dottie] Metz's tomorrow. I called Bill tonight and verified that they would be home. We will drive down in the morning. I don't think it will take over 2 or 3 hours." **[/]**

"Rich [Schulherr] & I have finished up the ceramic ashtrays we were working on. We picked them up at the shop this afternoon after class—where they had been for the final firing to put the glaze on. I think you'll like it—it's a modernistic shape and I finished it in black & white." **[/]**

"I'm glad your breakfast went well Honey . . . I hope you got the compliments you deserve on the program you made." **[/]** "Mike, I expect this letter won't arrive till the first of next week and you will already have played in your [piano] music concert at the Art Institute. I wish I had been there to see and hear you play. I know you'll do well. How about writing and telling me about it? And tell me about school too—I miss seeing you and knowing about these things you know!" **[/]**

"How was the IRE [Institute of Radio Engineers] luncheon and Wright Field museum tour Hon? Did any of your charges miss the bus? . . ." **[4 PARAGRAPHS]** "Bye for now" **[/]** "Give Kay a big kiss for me Mike" **[/]** "All my love" **[/]** "Johnny" **[/]** "Tell A [Agnes Glenn] hi & I hope all's well with her. Does air mail get these letters home any sooner?"

**** To Mrs. J. H. Sproule, 406 Wilbur Ave., Dayton 5, Ohio ("Sunday evening" [5/25/58], Postmarked 5/26/58, 8 PM, "Via Air Mail" with two 3¢ stamp, Montgomery Ala.). Return Address: J. H. Sproule, Air Warfare Systems Employment Course, Air Command & Staff College, Maxwell AFB, Montgomery, Ala. "Hi sweetheart," **[/]** "Rich & I were down to Ft Walton over the weekend to see the Metz's. We left Saturday morning & it takes about 3½ hours to drive down. As a matter of fact we arrived before Bill & Dottie got back. . . ." **[3 PARAGRAPHS]**

"Mike, Stevie & Donna [Metz children] said to tell you hello. Stevie is a cub scout too and he's also getting to be a real good swimmer. I hope you are all set to take swimming this summer so you can get to be a good swimmer too. Oh yes, Donna is starting to take piano lessons and she was real interested in how far along you've gotten. I told her how well you are doing and that you were playing at the Art Institute today." **[/]** ". . . The 5¢ air mail stamp on it would be good for Mike as it's been sometime since airmail was 5¢. You probably noticed that I supplemented it with a 1¢ stamp to bring it up to the required postage." **[4 PARAGRAPHS]** "Good night darling—" **[/]** "All my love" **[/]** "Johnny"

**** [To Mr. Michael Sproule; no envelope], "Monday, 26 May [1958]." "Dear Mike—" **[1 PARAGRAPH]** "I've enclosed a couple stamps that I acquired that look new to me. Also I've used those ½¢ stamps on this envelope so you can add them to your collection." **[/]** "You'll be happy to know that I got 100 on my last examination. . . ." **[/]** "Rich and I don't have any exact arrangements made yet, but we are still planning on getting home this coming weekend somehow even if we take the bus. I'm sure looking forward to being home even for just a little while." **[2 PARAGRAPHS]** "Goodnight darlings—see you soon." **[/]** "Always my love" **[/]** "Johnny"

**** To Mrs. J. H. Sproule, 406 Wilbur Ave., Dayton 5, Ohio ("Thursday evening" 5/29 [1958], Postmarked 5/30/58, 2:30 PM, "Via Air Mail" with two 3¢ stamp, Montgomery Ala.). Return Address: J. H. Sproule, Air Warfare Systems Employment Course, Air Command & Staff College, Maxwell AFB, Montgomery, Ala. "Hi darling," **[/]** "I'm not sure whether Mike thought the phone call was at an end or whether the operator pulled the plug when I told Mike goodbye—at any rate I was going to talk to you more but didn't seem to have any connection after Mike and I finished." **[3 PARAGRAPHS]**

"You know it's real hard to get used to some new newspaper. We have been picking up a Birmingham paper in the morning and scanning it out but it just doesn't offer much—even the comics are substandard—only saving feature, they have Peanuts & Lil Abner. So I've had a hard time figuring out this French trouble what with a poor newspaper and not catching news broadcasts as one does at home. I hope it doesn't get too bad over there." **[/]** "So far Rich and I haven't put in any time at the club pool—the only swimming was last weekend at the Metz's. . . ." **[2 PARAGRAPHS]** "Give Mike a kiss for me and tell A hi." **[/]** "Good night darling" **[/]** "All my love" **[/]** "Johnny"

**** To Mrs. J. H. Sproule, 406 Wilbur Ave., Dayton 5, Ohio (6/2/58, Postmarked 6/3/58, 7 PM, with two 3¢ stamp, Montgomery Ala.). Return Address: J. H. Sproule, Air Warfare Systems Employment Course, Air Command & Staff College, Maxwell AFB, Montgomery, Ala. "Hi darling," **[/]** ". . . Such fine newsy letters are a big lift to me. I know how you probably felt this past weekend Honey—it was a big let down to me because I was sure it would be possible to get home and I do miss you!" **[/]**

"We spent the [Memorial Day] weekend mostly puttering about. Friday morning we drove out to a little town about 15 miles away where there is a family owned commercial pottery. We had heard about it from a fellow down at the hobby shop and it was most interesting to see. The head man is an old fellow 84 years old who has been making and selling clay pots etc. for over 70 years. His son and a couple colored fellows seem to be all the help he had. They just use straight Alabama clay right out of the hillside but make some good looking pottery." **[/]** "I guess what with looking that place over and doing some work in the hobby shop and working a bit Sunday in the room you could say we spent practically a whole weekend puttering with ceramics. It was a slow period and I kept wishing I was home with you." **[1 PARAGRAPH]**

"I'm hoping all those various jobs you've fallen heir to won't be too much of a drag. I imagine it helps a lot with A [Agnes] there—like polishing the car & cutting the grass etc. How is her job hunting coming?" **[/]** "Whatever kind of tomatoes you planted will be real fine and I'm glad that you have the peppers in too—that ought to finish up the planting I'd think—except perhaps to have a recycle on radishes later. Have you had any of the first radish crop yet?" **[/]** "I probably won't get a letter written to the [Glenn and Elsie] Kelly's for a day or so but will try to write to them soon. As a matter of fact and except for one letter to Jerry & Hilda [Burtanger] I haven't written yet except to you and Mike." **[1 PARAGRAPH]**

"I hope you enjoyed opening day at the pool even though you didn't take in the barbecue. . . ." **[1 PARAGRAPH]** "Mike—Kay tells me your letter writing intentions only get strong at bed time—maybe that will get better after school is out. When is your last day of school? Are you going to get more good grades this time too? How much am I going to owe you for getting A's and B's?" **[/]** ". . . Have you written to tell Mom [Kiva Sproule] of this trip I'm on? I must write to her too right away—but not tonight as it's about bed time." **[/]**

"Could you wrap up 2 or 3 cartons of Wings [a cigarette brand] & send them to me? I'm going to run out of those I brought down before this course is over. It sure was swell to have two nice long letters from you today sweetheart and I'll be looking forward to the next. And I'll write again soon too." **[/]** "Good night to you and Mike and A." **[/]** "All my love" **[/]** "Johnny"

**** To Mrs. J. H. Sproule, 406 Wilbur Ave., Dayton 5, Ohio ("Sunday" 6/8/58, Postmarked 6/9/58, 6:30 PM, [stamps torn off], Montgomery Ala.). Return Address: J. H. Sproule, Air Warfare Systems Employment Course, Air Command & Staff College, Maxwell AFB, Montgomery, Ala. "Hi Darling," **[/]** "The Sunday evening quiet has set in here at the quarters and I can write to you without any interruptions. Many of the students seem to take off for somewhere over the weekend .." **[/]** "This ends the fourth week with only two more to go! 2/3 finished—...." **[2 PARAGRAPHS]**

"We have been getting a bit of sun the last few days. I bought a small piece of canvas at a surplus sale last Wed and we can use that to stretch out in the sun for a little while—being careful to not overdo it. Today for example I took about 20 minutes on each side and then called it quits. It shows up as a little bit of tan but I'm being careful to avoid a sunburn." **[/]**

"Well Mike how do you like school being out? I'm sure interested to know what grades you got on your last report card. Kay mentioned once before that you seem to remember about writing only at bedtime—maybe now that school is out and you won't have any homework you could remember in time to write me about your grades and the various other things you'v been doing. You know I miss you and it helps to get a letter now and then **[/]**

"Last night we had dinner in town. We ate at a place called Dale's Penthouse which is up on top of an apartment house about 10 stories high which provides a good view of town. I have their menu for the menu collection—as a matter of fact I've gotten 6 or 7 since we've been down here. Tonight we ate at the club—it was smorgasbord night and they hav a very good one—all you can eat for $1.75 and a choice of 50 or 75 different things. Wish you had been here darling—you could pass up the desert and concentrate on the roast beef and turkey." **[2 PARAGRAPHS]** "All my love" **[/]** "Johnny"

   **** To Mrs. J. H. Sproule, 406 Wilbur Ave., Dayton 5, Ohio (6/9/58 "bedtime," Postmarked 6/10[?]/58, 8 PM, [stamps torn off], Montgomery Ala.). Return Address: J. H. Sproule, Air Warfare Systems Employment Course, Air Command & Staff College, Maxwell AFB, Montgomery, Ala. "Hi Darling," **[2 PARAGRAPHS]** "Spent rather an uneventful week end but did putter along with some more ceramics work. I don't know if the level of interest will be maintained or not—I know my interest in all these sidelines will go down when I get home with you darling! One thing I thought was that with your abundant natural talent for decorating that you might like to finish up a couple of these things—we'll see about that later and you can judge for yourself." **[/]**

"I sure agree with you about A not taking a job that will involve awkward traveling or other disadvantages. Tell her to be patient and this will all work out in due time." **[/]** "Has anything come of your idea to get Mike started taking swimming lessons?" **[2 PARAGRAPHS]** "All my love" **[/]** "Johnny"

   **** [To Mrs. J. H. Sproule; no envelope], "Maxwell AFB Tue 10 June" [1958]. "Hi Darling," **[/]** "Thanks a million for my Father's Day present of cigarettes which arrived today. It is a great convenience to have cigarettes on hand and not have to remember to buy them or find a cigarette machine." **[1 PARAGRAPH]** "I guess that you can tell that I'm out of the writing paper you gave me to bring down. Fortunately I have this tablet so it will be no problem except that I'll have to fold the letters differently—and I still have envelopes." **[/]**

"I wrote to Mom tonight also so perhaps I'll get somewhat caught up on some of the other letters I did intend to write. I had a letter from Jerry and Hilda 2-3 days ago—about Friday I think. I haven't answered it yet and it might turn out like they were doing when it looked like we'd get back Memorial day weekend—namely wait till I get home. . . ." **[/]**

"We had another hot day today but tonight there is a nice cool breeze. Our rooms are on the third floor and have a couple good sized windows so it hasn't been too hot to sleep well at least so far. There are large fans built in at each end of the hall so that gives circulation even if there isn't a breeze." **[1 PARAGRAPH]** "Goodnight sweetheart—tell A hi and give Mike a kiss for me and tell him I said for him to be a good boy." **[/]** "All my love" **[/]** "Johnny"

**** [To Mrs. J. H. Sproule; no envelope], "Thursday night Maxwell AFB" [6/14/58]. "Hi Sweetheart," **[/]** "I thought I'd dash off a short message tonight even though there isn't much news to write. Tomorrow will end the next to last week of this course and then we'll be in the final stretch." **[3 PARAGRAPHS]** "I saw an encouraging note in tonight's paper indicating that the Senate & House joint committee had agreed upon a 10% pay raise so hopefully if the Senate & House both pass it and the President signs it a 10% raise will result. Also an unusual feature is the retroactivity to Jan 1 feature so this might take care of some of the expenses we've made or planned. I guess time will tell about this." **[2 PARAGRAPHS]** "All my love" **[/]** "Johnny"

**** [To Mrs. J. H. Sproule; no envelope], "Maxwell Sunday night" [6/17/58]. "Hello Darling," **[/]** "Tomorrow starts the last week of this operation—I guess you could say we are in the home stretch. I will be most glad when this is finished and I'm home with you. I think I wrote in the last letter that I expect to be home this coming Saturday. Since we'll be able to get away sometime in the middle of the afternoon Friday I would think we will get home about supper time Saturday." **[2 PARAGRAPHS]** "Mike I was glad to hear that you got at least one A. We'll talk more about that when get home. I miss talking to you, you know!" **[4 PARAGRAPHS]** "All my love" **[/]** "Johnny"

**** [To Mrs. J. H. Sproule; no envelope], "Maxwell Monday night [6/18/58]. "Hi Darling—" **[/]** "I had a real good day today 'cause I received two letters from you—written Thurs. & Fri. You do write such good letters!" **[2 PARAGRAPHS]** "I'm glad A is squared away on a job and I hope it will suit her. She ought to be able to manage even riding the bus for a little while—since I'll get back Saturday next week won't be any riding problem for her." **[1 PARAGRAPH]** "Thanks in advance for the sport shirt sweetheart—I thought the cigarettes were to commemorate Fathers Day!" **[1 PARAGRAPH]** "Mike, your mother tells me you have been pretty good. I'm glad to hear that. Keep it up and it won't be long till I'll be seeing you." **[1 PARAGRAPH]** "All my love" **[/]** "Johnny"

**** To Mrs. J. H. Sproule, 3713 Briar Place, Dayton 5 Ohio U.S.A. ("Sunday 7 Oct" [1962], Postmarked 10/8/62, 9 AM[?], with a 1 pound 3 schilling stamp and a "BY AIR Mail" sticker, London [the cancellation stamp reads "CIVIL DEFENCE JOIN NOW"]). Return address: Cumberland Hotel, Marble Arch, London W. 1., England. "Hi Darling" **[/]** "It was so good to talk to you & Mike last night even though it was so brief. We all arrived safely and I'm feeling fine though it is a problem to adjust to the clock time here which is 5 hours ahead of 'stomach' time—. . . ." **[1 PARAGRAPH]**

"Also decided to change hotels today—that is decided today to change hotels so by the time you get this my address will be % Stratford Court Hotel / 350 Oxford Street / London, West 1, England" **[/]** ". . . We'll move day after tomorrow (Tuesday) and we'll have a better and more convenient place." **[4 PARAGRAPHS]** "I guess this about sums up things so far except that a. I miss you / b. I love you / c. I wish we were together" **[/]** "All my love always" **[/]** "John"

**** To Mrs. J. H. Sproule, 3713 Briar Place, Dayton 5 Ohio U.S.A. ("London Wed. 10 Oct 1962," Postmarked 10/10/62, 7:15 PM, with a 1 pound 3 schilling stamp and JHS's handwritten "Via Air Mail," Paddington W.2. [the cancellation stamp reads "CIVIL DEFENCE IS COMMON SENSE"]). Return address: JH Sproule % Park Court Hotel, 75 Lancaster Gate, London, W.2., England. "Dear Kay Mike & A" **[1 PARAGRAPH]** ". . . In the process of moving from the Cumberland Hotel, it turned out that before we went to the Stratford Court Hotel we found another place more convenient to which we did move yesterday—its address: Park Court Hotel, 75 Lancaster

Gate, London W.2. England. In the event that you or the office have sent my mail to me at the Stratford Court Hotel let me know as I can see if I can pick them up. . . ." **[/]**

"However starting tomorrow we will be taking some side trips from London to visit nearby military installations but we'll be returning to London each night except for one of the trips that will require an overnight stay." **[/]** ". . . One highlight would certainly be the meals. For breakfast for instance they have such things as herring and broiled tomatoes—they have eggs but they aren't the same. They slice the bread very thin but the toast ends up tough. Well that's just an example." **[/]** "Another startling thing is the way they drive on the left hand side of the road. I knew they did of course but knowing about it and seeing it are two completely different things." **[/]**

"They don't really have any skyscrapers but the whole area is full of 4, 6, or 8 story bldgs—ie they're built up but not like New York or Chicago and at the same time one doesn't see any 1 or 2 story buildings. . . ." **[/]** "It has been good to find that it's not at all difficult to travel on the tube system which is necessary to get from one place to another and it's not too expensive to travel this way. Also it's possible to get used to a different money system but still you always have to stop and think about it. The pound = $2.80 20 schillings per pound & 12 pennies per schilling." **[1 PARAGRAPH]** "Love," **[/]** "John"

**** To MRS. JOHN SPROULE, 3713 BRIAR PLACE, DAYTON (OHIO), WESTERN UNION TELEGRAM OCT 10 62 313 P EST . . . PD, INTL FR CD LONDON VIA RCA 10 1826. [hand stamped "DUPLICATE OF TELEPHONED TELEGRAM"] "HI DOLL THOUGHT I WOULD SEND LOVE IN DIFFERENT MESSAGE FORM STOP CURRENT ADDRESS NOW PARK COURT HOTEL 75 LANCASTER GATE LONDON W2 IF MAIL WAS SENT TO PREVIOUS HOTEL ADDRESSES ADVISE WHERE AND WHAT LOVE / JOHN."

**** [To Mrs. J. H. Sproule; no envelope], "London 12 Oct 1962." "Dear Kay Mike & A" **[/]** ". . . In fact you can hardly tell us from natives the way we bustle or dash around on the underground as they call it here.

It's been necessary to learn this as we go from place to place for meetings. The first three days this week we met in London at the Air Ministry building and the last two have had to travel out of London about 75 miles to a Naval facility on the southern coast. Next week we will have three days of travel and then meetings back in London on Thur & Friday to finish up this UK visit. **[THIS PARAGRAPH CONTINUES]**

It turns out that Whiting and [Overton] Caperton and I need to visit the Hq. United States Air force in Europe at or near Wiesbaden West Germany for 2 or 3 days after finishing up here in London on the 19th so it will then be the middle of week after next before we finish up our business and start back. We'll be able to forecast a more precise return date when we work out a few details early next week." **[/]**

"We have this weekend free so I expect to do a bit of sight seeing—hope to take in at least a few of the outstanding sights. One can't take in too many because they are spread around and this is a pretty good sized town. Also some of the places like the Tower of London, I understand, are fairly extensive and one shouldn't just zip past—like you can at the Grand Canyon for example." **[/]** "I don't have anything specific worked out yet to get in a short visit to Paris but I'm still thinking of it. . . . " **[/]**

"Yesterday and today our trips let us see something of the English country side, small towns and seacoast so gradually our experience is broadening." **[1 PARAGRAPH]** "I've just about adjusted to the 5 hour time differential now. For the first two or three days it was difficult to get used to eating and sleeping on a time schedule 5 hours ahead of 'stomach' time." **[/]** "Hope everything is going fine at home and that it isn't taking too long for letters and cards to reach you. I sent cards to the address list you made out for me and I also wrote to Mom tonight so she'll know something of what I'm doing." **[/]** "Good night now   All my love   John"

**** To Mrs. J. H. Sproule, 3713 Briar Place, Dayton 5 Ohio U.S.A. ("London Sunday. 14 Oct 62," Postmarked 10/? /62, ? time, with five 3 schilling stamps and pre-printed "Via Air Mail," Paddington). Return address: JH Sproule % Park Court Hotel, 75 Lancaster Gate, London, W.2.,

England. "Dear Kay Mike & A" **[/]** "Just a few lines to let you know that everything is going along well. Our London visit is half over now and we've made suitable progress although it is evident that our work is seriously interfering with our sightseeing." **[1 PARAGRAPH]** ". . . I gave some thought to flying over to Paris this morning to go to church and view Paris briefly but gave it up due to a number of reasons—time etc. Still hope to get there however." **[/]**

"I mentioned in my last letter I think, that Whiting, Caperton & I expect to visit the HQ USAFE at their request after we finish here in London so this should put us home sometime around the 24th or 25." **[1 PARAGRAPH]** "All my love" **[/]** "John"

    **** To Mrs. J. H. Sproule, 3713 Briar Place, Dayton 5 Ohio U.S.A. ("London. 15 Oct 1962," Postmarked 10/16/62, 6:45 PM, with one 3 schilling stamp, two 6 pence stamps, and pre-printed "VIA AIR MAIL," Paddington W.2., London). Return address: JH Sproule % Park Court Hotel 75 Lancaster Gate, London, W.2., England. "Dear Kay Mike & A" **[/]**

"Hello again from London. I was very happy to have your letter this evening darling when I got back to the room after the day's business. I spent last night at the Howletts and he [Bob] took me over to Faraborough this morning where I joined our group and then spent the day in meetings and equipment demonstrations. I hadn't been able to find Howletts listed in the phone book so earlier last week I dropped them a post card and when they got the card they telephoned me their phone number and that how we got together. They have been transferred from the London assignment that Bob had to Bascombe Down which is about 75 mi from London. It is approx the equivalent of Eglin Field and/or Edwards AFB in Calif. where operational & flight evaluations take place. Bob has a good job there and he likes it there as does [his wife] Freddie. They are fine—seem just the same as when they left Dayton—and both send their regards." **[**

"I also had a letter (a note really) from Eviston inclosing copies of orders amendment authorizing my leave—if I take it." [Dad had planned to visit Paris and other areas but came home more quickly because the Cuban missile crisis, October 16-29, 1962, interfered and he didn't want to be stuck in Europe if some kind of war broke out.] **[/]**

"Would you please call Bill or Madeline and let them know I received the order amendment. You might also tell him of the request we have from Hq USAFE at Wiesbaden to visit there and discuss QRC & electronic warfare that I mentioned in my last letter. Our plan now is to go to Wiesbaden (ie fly to Frankfurt from London) Sat the 20th and be there 2 or 3 days. When I say our I am referring to Caperton Whiting & myself." **[4 PARAGRAPHS]** "All my love" **[/]** "John"

**** [To Mrs. J. H. Sproule; no envelope], "Oct 20 1962 Aboard Lufthansa Flight 121." "Dear Kay Mike & A" **[/]** "Just a few lines while we're enroute from London to Frankfurt (which is the nearest airport to our business destination). I'd expected to drop you a card from the London airport but the connection (just ran out of ink) [a shift from a black fountain pen to a blue ball point] between the Airport bus and the flight was somewhat short. The flight time is just over an hour and we'll be taking off shortly as we're just taxiing out now. The scheduled arrival in Frankfurt is just after noon and then we'll go to Wiesbaden by staff car and we'll probably be there till Wed—at least that is our present expectation. I'll mail this from Frankfurt when we arrive so you should have this before we leave Frankfurt. While I have the amendment to my travel orders authorizing leave I'm not sure at the moment just what I'll do about it. I would like to see Paris but will wait till I see how our business goes at Wiesbaden before deciding on any side trip." **[/]**

"We're airborne now and at our 30,000 ft cruising altitude. Lufthansa (on this flight at least) is using a Boeing 707 jet and the flying conditions are very smooth. It's interesting to hear the flight announcements because they are given in German and then repeated in English." **[2 PARAGRAPHS]** "We'll be landing shortly now—we had a sandwich & coffee served a little bit ago and now they're cleaning up the trays and our aircraft is descending having just crossed over the Rhine." **[1 PARAGRAPH]** "Bye for now" **[/]** "John"

**** [To Mrs. J. H. Sproule; no envelope], "Oct 21 [1962] Wiesbaden." "Hi Again" **[1 PARAGRAPH]** "We arrived in good shape and got checked into the General Von Steuben which is really a visiting officers quarters but in actual practice is just like a down town hotel." **[2 PARAGRAPHS]** "All my love" **[/]** "John"

**** [To Mrs. J. H. Sproule; no envelope], [Executive Seminar Center U.S. Merchant Marine Academy] "Kings Point NY Monday morning Oct 14 [1963]." "Dearest Kay and Mike" **[/]** "Just a few lines to let you know that all is going well in this course and that I've become a bit more accustomed to living in a military academy branch with the bugle calls and announcements coming over the loudspeaker systems at all hours of the day and night and all meals in one giant mess hall." **[/]** "Today starts the second and last week and the time is more than half over because the week end is over and we'll be leaving here Friday afternoon. The course has been interesting and is giving an insight into the operation of the higher levels of the government." **[/]**

"We had a class Saturday morning so that helped speed the weekend along. Ray Nordlund and I went into NY City Saturday afternoon, visited the UN building, Radio City Music Hall and had dinner. Yesterday except for church and meals I spent the day playing bridge. Well I did do one other thing—I went through the Sunday issue of the N. Y. Times newspaper—all 489 pages of it though obviously I didn't read it all. Of course a tremendous amount of it is ads." **[2 PARAGRAPHS]** "All my love" **[/]** "John"

Epilogue

This epistolary record of Dad's early career adventures comes to a close in 1963. JHS continued at Wright Patterson Air Force Base, with his final position as Chief, Test/Simulation Branch in the Electronic Warfare Avionics Division (ASD ENADD). Here he concluded his career in 1980 with work on the F-16 and F-17 airplanes, having begun with the B-29 bomber in 1942. After 1963, Dad's work-related travels included participating in an air-penetration briefing at the Pentagon on the eve of President Richard Nixon's B-52 bombing campaign against North Vietnam.

Dad never talked about his work in anything other than the most general terms—even later in his life. Probably the most detailed story I ever heard was his remarking on having once ridden in a cramped experimental machine-gunner's capsule affixed to the outer-most portion of a B-29's wing—this for a mid-1940s test of new vantage points for a bomber's defensive armaments. And this brings to mind Dad's oblique comments one day about a study of defensive gunnery showing that the fewest ammunition jams occurred when members of the bombing crew personally loaded their guns.

Then too, there was Dad's related story of when, shortly before the Korean War, the Armament Lab advised Air Force headquarters of test results showing reliability problems with the gunnery turrets of the B-50. Notwithstanding what I took to have been an imperative phraseology emanating from Wright-Patterson, no response from the Air Force higher ups was forthcoming. Some time later, the armament group received a message of alarm from Air Force operations alerting them to the recent discovery by bomber crews that the turrets of the B-50s, now actively engaged in Korean War combat, were subject to failures.

Dad was an early member of the Institute of Radio Engineers [later a unit of the Institute of Electrical and Electronics Engineers] as well as a charter member in 1964 of the Association of Old Crows, this a group of specialists in electronic warfare. Son Mike and daughter-in-law Betty joined a crowd of 200 or so at Dad's July 25, 1980 retirement luncheon in a large room at the Imperial House North, Dayton. A font of affection emanated not only from long-term colleagues but also from the young engineers whom Dad always made a special point to mentor and champion. The festivities included a moment when 50 or so participants came forward to present Dad with a book in commemoration of his longstanding practice of gifting his associates with apt bibliographic fruits gathered from many an estate sale in the Dayton area.

After his retirement, Dad merged two of his avocations—buying interesting stuff at estate auctions, things that might be repaired or repurposed, and his passion for all sorts of crafts. Among other things, Dad collected metals to melt down and refashion as rings and other jewelry; he re-bound old books, including making his own marbleized paper; he assembled a store of old colored glass to refashion as lead-rimmed glass boxes and decorations; and he collected old wood to repurpose as plaques and ornaments. Dad and Mom collaborated at points, with Mom painting pictures and Dad supplying picture frames either by rehabilitating old frames or fashioning new ones.

Given the scale of Dad's buying and building, he and Mom opened "John's Artiques" in 1978 as an outlet not only for Dad's creations but also as a way of moving along a growing trove of stuff. So great was the extent of Dad's collecting (and nearly all the family accumulation owed to Dad), that at the time they moved from Ohio to Reno, Nevada in October 1986, four of the largest moving vans available were required to haul away the bounty from 105 West Main, Tipp City, Ohio. Out came the boxes, hour after hour, from the giant attic (piled 6-feet high with only a few walking corridors among the stacks), from two apartments on the second floor long repurposed as storage areas, from the first-floor living quarters and small antique shop, from the full basement loaded top to bottom, and from an ample garage. One van went directly to Saint Vincent De Paul and other charities; two vans-worth were disposed of at a two-day auction (October 14-15, 1986); and one van headed to Reno where Dad spent the next 11 years gradually working down the not-inconsiderable residue through consignment auctions.

Dad and Mom, who loved the West, enjoyed their years in Reno—attending National Association of Retired Federal Employees' events, taking in casino dining, shows, and nickel slots, browsing auctions and sales. They also enjoyed their grandkids, John and Kevin, once buying Betty and Mike a new set of luggage in hopes that we would take more and longer trips during which time they could keep the kids. Yet Reno was the closest location to Palo Alto, California, to which I their son could induce them to move. Still the Palo Alto and Reno Sproules visited back and forth regularly, even during the winter when I-80 might at any time become impassable.

The story of John Harper Sproule, Jr. is that of a son of Depression and War persisting against adversity and making good in the postwar boom and its aftermath. He was and is greatly missed.

Appendix: Family of John Harper Sproule, Jr.

Father: John Harper Sproule, Sr.: born April 13, 1887, Raton, New Mexico; died November 24, 1964, Los Angeles, California; buried Forest Lawn Cemetery, Los Angeles, California

Uncle (father's brother): Luther Sproule: born March 27, 1885, Raton, New Mexico; died September 3, 1952, Albuquerque, New Mexico

Aunt (by marriage): Elizabeth Boeke [Sproule]: died sometime aft 1955; married Luther Sproule, October 1, 1917, Riverton, Wyoming

Aunt: Grace Edith [Sproule] Wells: born January 15, 1882, Raton, New Mexico; died March 19, 1943; married Chester Mitchell Wells, April 20, 1906, Raton, New Mexico; C. M. Wells lived September 16, 1881- December 20, 1940

Aunt: Mary Alice [Sproule] Anspach: born April 14, 1889, Raton, New Mexico; died ca. 1977, California; married Orland Leroy Anspach, November 24, 1913 at home of Lowther and Mary Sproule, Riverton; O. L Anspach lived ca. 1887-September 23, 1974

Cousin: Rodney Chester Anspach: born March 29, 1920, Alhambr California to Mary Alice and Orland Anspach

Cousin: Malcolm Lowther Anspach: born February 7, 1923, Alhambra, California to Mary Alice and Orland Anspach

Aunt: Amy Viola [Sproule] Wilkening: born March 15, 1895, Delta Colorado; died March 13, 1981, California; married Charles Wilkening October 24, 1925, Wilmar, California; C. Wilkening lived February 2, 1885 May 16, 1954

Mother: Kiva Leota Seaman [Sproule]: born April 9, 1889, O'Neill, Holt County, Nebraska; died February 7, 1966, Riverton, Wyoming; burie Mountain View Cemetery, Riverton; married John Harper Sproule, Sr., November 20, 1917, Emmett, Gem County, Idaho

Brother: Walter Eugene Sproule: born October 11, 1920, Riverton, Wyoming; married Alice Irma Dierks [Sproule], July 14, 1945, Evanston, Wyoming; died: February 23, 2002, Greenbank, Washington

Son: James Michael Sproule, born February 8, 1949, Dayton, Ohio; married Betty Ann Mathis [Sproule], March 3, 1973, Columbus Ohio

Grandson: John Harold Sproule: born February 18, 1981, Louisville, Kentucky to J. Michael and Betty Ann Sproule

Grandson: Kevin William Sproule: born December 7, 1982, Louisville, Kentucky to J. Michael and Betty Ann Sproule; married Mary Ann Latoreno [Sproule], December 6, 2014, Monterey, California

Great-grandson: Luke Michael Sproule: born November 14, 2015, Hong Kong, China to Kevin William Sproule and Mary Ann Latoreno Sproule

Great-grandson: Nathan Edward Sproule: born September 9, 2019, Cebu, Philippines to Kevin William Sproule and Mary Ann Latoreno Sproule

Wife: Katherine Veronica Glenn [Sproule]: born February 24, 1915, Fullerton, Nebraska; died July 5, 2000, Los Altos, California; buried Our Mother of Sorrows Cemetery, Reno, Nevada; married John Harper Sproule, Jr., Dayton, Ohio, February 15, 1943

KVS' Father: John Lawrence Glenn: born December 25, 1866, Nebraska; died June 15, 1928, vicinity of Arapahoe and Riverton, Wyoming

KVS' Mother: Emma Pauline Carrington [Bowe] Glenn: born May 21, 1876, Kentucky; died November 29, 1938, Riverton, Wyoming

KVS's Siblings: (1) Harold Bowe (1901-1963): son of Emma Pauline Carrington [Bowe] Glenn and James Edward Bowe; J. E. Bowe lived November 7, 1880-ca. 1906; [hereafter born to Emma Glenn and John Lawrence Glenn]; (2) Joseph Patrick Glenn (1913-1980); (3) Agnes Elizabeth Glenn (1917-2007); (4) John Bernard Glenn (1919-1982); (5) Anna Belle Glenn [Begg] (1922-1986)

Grandfather (paternal): Lowther Sproule: born May 26, 1845, County Tyrone, Ireland; died August 28, 1931 at 2315 Isabel St., Wilmar, California

Grandfather Lowther Sproule's Siblings (among eight or so) including (1) brother Samuel Corbett Sproule: born December 25, 1848, Petersville, Queens County, New Brunswick, Canada; died 1909; as adult, lived in Raton, New Mexico, one son of whom was Samuel Corbett Sproule II (12-29-1888 to 5-4-1960), also of Raton; (2) sister: Ann Sproule, born ca. 1835 in Ireland, lived in the western U.S.

Grandmother (paternal): Mary Norris Remsberg [Sproule]: born November 13, 1861, Lamar, Barton County, Missouri; died August 17, 1936 2130 Del Mar Ave., Wilmar, California; buried Memorial Forest Lawn Park, Los Angeles, California; married Lowther Sproule November 11, 1880, Raton, New Mexico

Grandfather (maternal): Sam Seaman

Grandmother (maternal): Mae (or May) Lakey [Seaman]

Great-aunt: Sister of Mae Lakey: Clyda Lakey [Martin] Burns: born March 18, 1877, Des Moines, Iowa; died March 6, 1962, Riverton, Wyoming; buried Mountain View Cemetery, Riverton; married M. J. Martin (? to at least 1918); 2nd marriage to Charley Leroy Burns, September 14, 1932, Billings, Yellowstone County, Montana; C. L. Burns born August 22, 1886, Defiance County, Ohio.

Great-grandparents (paternal): Harper and Eliza Sproule emigrated from County Tyrone, Ireland to New Brunswick, Canada in 1847-1848 with seven children, the youngest at the time being Lowther Sproule

Great-grandfather Harper Sproule of County Tyrone, Ireland; born ? ; died November 15, 1848 in area of Petersville, Queens County, New Brunswick, Canada

Great-grandmother Eliza Sproule of County Tyrone, Ireland: born ?; died ?; second marriage to family friend, Samuel Corbett of New Brunswick, Canada 1848-1849

Great-grandparents (maternal): William and Permelia Lakey lived in O'Neill, Nebraska with granddaughter Kiva Leota Seaman [Sproule] in 1900 as established by the Census of 1900

Great-grandfather: William W. Lakey

Great-grandmother: Permelia Jane Rhone [Lakey]: born January 12, 1855; died November 9, 1926, Riverton, Wyoming; buried Mountain View Cemetery, Riverton; moved to Riverton from Arpan [?], South Dakota with her daughter, Clyda Lakey [Martin] Burns, and her granddaughter Kiva Leota Seaman [Sproule] sometime around 1909

Made in the USA
Las Vegas, NV
20 August 2023

76325178R00138